Studies in Childhood and Youth

Series Editors: Allison James, University of Sheffield, UK, and Adrian James, University of Sheffield, UK.

Titles include:

Hanne Warming (*editor*)
PARTICIPATION, CITIZENSHIP AND TRUST IN CHILDREN'S LIVES

Karen Wells, Erica Burman, Heather Montgomery and Alison Watson (*editors*)
CHILDHOOD, YOUTH AND VIOLENCE IN GLOBAL CONTEXTS
Research and Practice in Dialogue

Rebekah Willett, Chris Richards, Jackie Marsh, Andrew Burn, Julia C Bishop (*editors*)
CHILDREN, MEDIA AND PLAYGROUND CULTURES
Ethnographic Studies of School Playtimes

Karen M. Smith
THE GOVERNMENT OF CHILDHOOD
Discourse, Power and Subjectivity

Spyros Spyrou and Miranda Christou
CHILDREN AND BORDERS

Leena Alanen, Liz Brooker and Berry Mayall (*editors*)
CHILDHOOD WITH BOURDIEU

Studies in Childhood and Youth
Series Standing Order ISBN 978–0–230–21686–0   hardback
(*outside North America only*)

You can receive future titles in this series as they are published by placing a standing order. Please contact your bookseller or, in case of difficulty, write to us at the address below with your name and address, the title of the series and the ISBN quoted above.

Customer Services Department, Macmillan Distribution Ltd, Houndmills, Basingstoke, Hampshire RG21 6XS, England

Childhood with Bourdieu

Edited by

Leena Alanen
Department of Education, University of Jyväskylä, Finland

Liz Brooker
Institute of Education, University of London, UK

Berry Mayall
Institute of Education, University of London, UK

First published 2015 by
PALGRAVE MACMILLAN

Palgrave Macmillan in the UK is an imprint of Macmillan Publishers Limited,
registered in England, company number 785998, of Houndmills, Basingstoke,
Hampshire RG21 6XS.

Palgrave Macmillan in the US is a division of St Martin's Press LLC,
175 Fifth Avenue, New York, NY 10010.

Palgrave Macmillan is the global academic imprint of the above companies
and has companies and representatives throughout the world.

Palgrave® and Macmillan® are registered trademarks in the United States,
the United Kingdom, Europe and other countries

ISBN: 978–1–137–38473–7

This book is printed on paper suitable for recycling and made from fully
managed and sustained forest sources. Logging, pulping and manufacturing
processes are expected to conform to the environmental regulations of the
country of origin.

A catalogue record for this book is available from the British Library.

A catalog record for this book is available from the Library of Congress.

Contents

Notes on Contributors

Leena Alanen is a sociologist and Professor (Emerita) in Early Childhood Education and Docent in the Sociology of Childhood, at the University of Jyväskylä, Finland. She has been active in promoting Childhood Studies since the 1980s, through her own research and in international research projects and networks, such as the International Sociological Association (ISA) and the European Sociological Association (ESA). She is currently co-editor for *Childhood: A journal of global child research* (Sage). Her research interests include children and childhood in social theory, intergenerational relations, and the intersection of gender and generation.

Géraldine André is a Postdoctoral Researcher for the National Fund for Scientific Research in Belgium. She is currently visiting fellow at LSE, and in Belgium, she is affiliated to Pôle Sud and the Lasc at the University of Liège. Her PhD on working class youth and vocational education with a Bourdieusian perspective was published by Les Presses Universitaires de France (2012). Her postdoctoral research focuses on the case of African child workers in small-scale artisanal mining. With this focus, she aims at analysing the effects on the legislation of children's rights on the evolution of processes of socialisation in sub-Saharan Africa.

Liz Brooker is a Reader in Early Childhood at the Institute of Education in London. As a former early years teacher, she developed a research interest in the cultural transitions of young children from ethnic minority communities into English mainstream schools and preschools. Since returning to teach in universities, her interest in transition has extended to the experiences of infants and toddlers, and the contrasting beliefs of parents, practitioners and childcare providers about children's best interests. Her most recent studies are of young children's play experiences, and of childminders. She is an editor of *Early Years: An International Research Journal*.

Pascale Garnier is a sociologist and Professor of educational sciences at Paris 13 University (France). She studied sociology in Ecole des

Hautes Etudes en Sciences Sociales (EHESS, Paris), with Boltanski, a close colleague of Bourdieu. Her PhD, published in 1995, was about an historical sociology of childhood in France. Her main points of interest and research are the theoretical analysis of childhood and children, early childhood education (politic, partnership, practices), body, physical activities and material culture. She belongs to the networks of sociology of childhood and children of the European Sociological Association (ESA) and the International Association of French Speaking Sociologists (AISLF).

Mathieu Hilgers is Associate Professor of Anthropology at Université Libre de Bruxelles, visiting fellow at University of London (Goldsmiths) and associate researcher at the Department of African and African American studies at Harvard University. He has worked extensively in Africa and has published several papers on Bourdieu, notably on his theory of dispositions and his theory of social field. Together with Eric Mangez, he edited *Bourdieu's Theory of Social Fields. Concepts and Applications* (Routledge, 2014) which gathers the world best specialists to provide the first complete in-depth introduction to Bourdieu's theory of field together with a range of case studies that test the theory, and critical discussions emphasising its potentiality and limitations.

Johanna Kiili is currently working as a post-doctoral researcher at the University of Jyväskylä, Finland. She is off duty from her standing post as a senior officer in the Office of Ombudsman for Children in Finland. She has a PhD in Social Sciences (Social Work) and has previously worked as a lecturer in social work, as a project coordinator and as a researcher. Her research interests include children's participation, child welfare and intergenerational relations.

Abigail Knight is a researcher at the Thomas Coram Research Unit, Institute of Education, University of London, where she carries out research with and about children, young people and their families. With a background in history and the social sciences, her research interests include the lives of disabled children, food and family life, notions of 'home' and 'belonging' for children, and using historical sources in sociological enquiry. Her doctoral study concerned the experiences of teenagers travelling long distances to school each day and the implications of these journeys for their social lives and connectedness with their local areas.

Berry Mayall is Professor of Childhood Studies at the Institute of Education, University of London. She has worked on sociological approaches to childhood since the 1980s, ran the first UK seminar group on childhood in the early 1990s, started one of the first MAs in the sociology of childhood (with Priscilla Alderson) and has written many journal papers and books. Most recently she has written *A History of the Sociology of Childhood*, in order to highlight its antecedents and current directions (2013, Institute of Education Press).

Johanna Moilanen is an MSc and doctoral student in social work at the Department of Social Sciences and Philosophy, University of Jyväskylä, Finland. She also holds the position of Senior Lecturer at the JAMK University of Applied Sciences, School of Health and Social Studies. Her research interests include child welfare history, the history of social work and historical sociology.

Virginia Morrow is Associate Professor in the Department of International Development, University of Oxford and Deputy Director of Young Lives. Her research focuses on children's work in developed and developing countries, sociological approaches to the study of childhood and children's rights, the ethics of social research with children, children's understandings of family, and children and 'social capital'. She has been co-editor of *Childhood: A journal of global child research* since 2006.

Uma Vennam is Professor of Social work at Sri Padmavati Mahila Visvavidyalam, Tirupati, Andra Pradesh, India. Uma is Lead Qualitative Researcher for Young Lives. She has an MA in Social Work, specialising in Urban and Rural Community Development, from Tata Institute of Social Sciences, Bombay and a PhD from the University of East Anglia. She has been involved in various research projects dealing with poverty alleviation, rural livelihoods, SLMF, poverty and HIV/AIDS, trafficking of women and children, child labour and Aids Prevention Education Programme (APEP) for school children, working with international agencies, including the World Bank, DFID and UNICEF.

Mari Vuorisalo is currently working as a university teacher at the Department of Education, University of Jyväskylä, Finland. She has a PhD in Education (Early Childhood Education). Her research concerns children's everyday life and participation in a preschool setting. In her recent PhD studies she utilised Pierre Bourdieu's theory of practice, especially the concepts of field and capital. Her post-doctoral research focuses on the interplay between children's habitus and preschool practices, and the consequences from this to inequalities in the preschool.

Karen Winter is a Lecturer in Social Work at Queen's University Belfast. Her research, which is mainly qualitative, is focused on understanding the lives of young children in care. One research project concerned their involvement in decision making and used Bourdieu's concepts of habitus, field and capital to explore the micro-dynamics within review meetings that lead to ongoing experiences of marginalisation and exclusion for both children and their parents. More recent work has involved the publication of a book regarding professional communication and relationships with young children in care and she is engaged in other related research projects (including the education of young children in care and the experience of disabled children in the care system).

1
Introduction

Leena Alanen, Liz Brooker and Berry Mayall

Our aims

In compiling this book, our principal aim has been to offer a contribution to work on the sociology of childhood. For us this means considering the social status of childhood in relation to the large-scale influences, sedimented in history, that condition childhood's social status in any given society or setting. Carrying out this work can be understood as requiring analyses of societal institutions and agencies, over time; thus, to refer to an important instance, Jens Qvortrup (1985) considered the social status of childhood in minority world societies nowadays, through consideration of the history of children's contributions to the division of labour in those societies. In this work at macro-level, Qvortrup was pointing out that childhood is a structural component in society; and that the social grouping represented by the term childhood has to be considered in interrelations with adulthood. This set of propositions can be contrasted (to some extent) with a strand of work that starts from the lived experiences of children, as recounted by children; and that seeks to foreground children's agency. What we see as especially exciting and challenging is to put together these two sorts of work, with the aim of reaching better understanding of why and how childhoods on-the-ground are as they are, through interrelating private troubles with public issues. Like many others we have become enthused by the work of Pierre Bourdieu, whose life-long passionate concern was to investigate these interconnections, and whose inspirational work has led to many investigations – mainly focused on adult lives. Our book brings together contributions from some of the researchers who have sought to work with Bourdieu's concepts, in order to work towards understanding childhoods.

In setting out thus briefly our aims, we do not wish to discount the valuable work that has been carried out using a range of disciplines under the heading of childhood studies, especially over the last 30 years or so. People, especially in the UK, have become accustomed to thinking in terms of social constructionism: differences between childhoods, as they are understood and operationalised by adults, across time and space. We now know much more than we did about how children experience childhoods, and about the varieties of children's experiences. Many studies have sought to work with and for children, by placing children's experiential knowledge of childhood at the forefront of their observations. Here one important strand has been consideration of whether and how far children's rights (as set out in the UN Convention on the Rights of the Child 1989) are respected, again with a focus on how children themselves experience such respect or disrespect. Examination of possibilities for and hindrances against respect for children's human rights, with accompanying consideration of what changes in conceptualisations of children and of childhood are required in order to respect their rights, has been hugely important, both in leading to new thinking and in practical terms. Work carried out in the 'majority' or 'developing' world,[1] notably on children's work and the emerging clash now that global forces promote schooling, has not only been valuable in itself, for those societies, but has forced rethinking of the division of labour in children's developed world lives, between work and schooling.

Underpinning these important developments has been the work of both scholars and activists, working in a range of disciplines. Anthropology has been important in alerting us to variation in childhoods across time and place; historical research has not only uncovered such variations, but has shown how the social is rooted in the historical; geographers have explored the significance of people's understanding of the meanings of the place they know or live in; economists have taught us to think harder about the economic contributions children make to family and societal welfare. Activists working for the welfare of children have analysed the practical applications of state policies – in education, health, welfare – in order to uncover how children themselves fare in their relations with such services and with the adults who control them.

However, in this book, we want to align ourselves with those who take a sociological approach to childhood. And by this we mean that we try to understand how a society conceptualises childhood, which requires studying the policies and practices – and their historical bases – that construct or modify how childhood is lived. Using that understanding we can move to better appreciate how children themselves live their lives; and what their knowledge about their experiences depends on and relates to. Central to consideration of childhood are childhood's relations with adulthood; for generational relations, operating at every level of society and intersecting across the macro and micro, serve to define childhoods.

Whilst Bourdieu has attracted many scholars, who have investigated a range of topics in the light of analysis of his famous concepts (field, habitus, capital), most of the work has focussed on adults. However, important work on childhood has included for instance: in the UK, Paul Connolly's work on sexual and racial identities among primary school children (1998), and Diane Reay's on the intersections of social class and gender in primary schools (1998); in the US, Joseph Agbenyega and Sunanta Klibthong's study of inclusion in preschools (2012); and in continental Europe, the work of Charlotte Palludan (2007) and, much earlier, of Chamboredon and Prévot (1975). We wanted to include chapters dealing with a range of topics concerning children in society; and the contributors in the end were those who had some experience of working with Bourdieu in relation to childhood and who had the time to commit to our enterprise. This book aims, through consideration of a range of examples, to provide perspectives on how Bourdieu can help us to understand childhood. We say more about the chapters below.

We aimed to be as collaborative as possible, given that all our contributors are busy people. So we held an initial meeting to discuss the prospects for the project, and two subsequent meetings to consider drafts. Each of the contributors also took on the task of commenting on two of the draft chapters. We hope that these processes helped to make the book into a whole, where we share similar concerns, where each chapter follows much the same ordering, and where we address a range of issues that affect children's experiences. Finally we note here that since each of the book's editors have contributed what they can to the work, we list ourselves, as editors, in alphabetical order to make that point clear!

Bourdieu's concepts

We have found that Bourdieu provides a convincing and useful way of linking up societal concerns, ideas and institutions with the detailed examination of everyday negotiations. And since a crucial component of how children negotiate childhood is through inter-generational negotiations, where their social status is consolidated or challenged, Bourdieu provides a toolkit that helps us to understand these negotiations.

Here we give a brief introduction to his key concepts: field, habitus and capital. Our authors each take account of these and consider in detail how the particular case they have studied is illuminated by investigation of these concepts.

Field

The chapters in this book each focus on an arena, an environment, or a space in which childhood is under question. This may be 'the family' or a preschool, for instance. In his work Bourdieu uses the term 'space' in two interconnected senses. The first meaning is literal: activities occur and actors act in physical spaces that also have both practical and symbolical significance in relation to each other. The second Bourdieusian meaning of space is metaphorical, as he speaks of space as also *social*. In this latter sense, actors are conceived of as occupants of multiple places within multiple relatively autonomous domains – *fields* – that together constitute the total social space. These multiple fields in turn constitute the status, class and social positions of the actors, their place in society. Thus, a person, an actor is always placed, or located, which means that Bourdieu's social topology is also always an embodied sociology, and this means forefronting *habitus* as another key concept in the Bourdieusian frame.

Especially in his later works, Bourdieu repeatedly underlined the centrality of thinking of society and social life in terms of *fields*:

> The notion of field reminds us that the true object of social science is not the individual, even though one cannot construct a field if not through individuals... *It is the field that is primary and must be*

the focus of the research operations. This does not imply that individuals are mere 'illusions', that they do not exist: they exist as agents – and not as biological individuals, actors, or subjects – who are socially constituted as active and acting in the field under consideration by the fact that they possess the necessary properties to be effective, to produce effects, in this field. And it is knowledge of the field itself in which they evolve that allows us best to grasp the roots of their singularity, their point of view or position (in a field) from which their particular vision of the world (and of the field itself) is constructed. (Bourdieu and Wacquant 1992: 107; our emphasis)

The notion of *field* gained this analytical weight and methodological significance for Bourdieu's sociological thinking when he moved towards analysing contemporary French society and its structuredness into fields and as fields (Swartz 1997: 117). He argues from his 1960s study of Algeria (Kabylia) that in an 'archaic' society there is only one field, whereas in modern differentiated societies their number grows: fields exist in parallel to each other, they intersect and subfields may emerge within larger fields.

> In analytical terms, a field may be defined as a network, or a configuration, of objective relations between positions. ... In highly differentiated societies, the social cosmos is made up of a number of such relatively autonomous social microcosms, that is, spaces of objective relations that are the site of a logic and a necessity that are specific and irreducible to those that regulate other fields. For instance, the artistic field, or the religious field, or the economic field all follow specific logics: while the artistic field has constituted itself by rejecting or reversing the law of material profit, ... the economic field has emerged, historically, through the creation of a universe within which, as we commonly say, 'business is business', where the enchanted relations of friendship and love are in principle excluded. (Bourdieu and Wacquant 1992: 97–8)

In Bourdieu's conceptualisation, modern societies are composed of multiple domains of action – *fields* – that are distinct from each other. A field is a relational historical formation, 'a network, or a configuration, of objective relations between positions'. Accordingly, action (practice) taking place in a field is understood and explained only by locating the agents – individuals and institutions – in their current social fields, the structure of relations that differentiate (and connect) the agents, and the 'game' that is taking place among them, the 'game' in the field being struggles over the control of the species of *capital* that is valued and held as legitimate in the field.

Moreover, each field has its own rules, or logic, so the game and the rules of one field are different from the games and the rules in other fields. What the fields do share is a homologous structure: all fields are structured by relations of dominance. Finally, fields are dynamic formations: they have their birth (genesis) and developmental history so the 'game' played in a field may remain even after the field disappears (Bourdieu and Wacquant 1992: 94–115).

Habitus

Bourdieu developed his concept of habitus from his ethnographic studies in Algeria (see Goodman and Silverstein 2009) and in his natal province of Béarn, in the 1950s and 1960s. The concept is part of Bourdieu's comprehensive theoretical effort to overcome the mechanical opposition between objectivism and subjectivism and to develop his solution to the problem of social change.

> I developed the concept of 'habitus' to incorporate the objective structures of society and the subjective role of agents within it. Habitus is a set of dispositions, reflexes and forms of behaviour that people acquire through acting in society. It reflects the differing positions people have in society, for example, whether they are brought up in a middle class environment or in a working class suburb. It is part of how society reproduces itself. (Bourdieu 2000: 19)

Habitus is produced when people 'internalise' the material, cultural and intellectual structures that constitute a particular type of environment. Bourdieu (1977: 72) describes habitus as a 'system of durable, transposable dispositions, structured structures predisposed to function as structuring structures'. For him, the 'primary' habitus, created in early childhood, is the basis for the development of the 'secondary' habitus by various agents of secondary socialisation (schools, peer groups, the media and so on) which people meet as, in their social trajectory during their lifetime, they traverse a number of social fields and get involved with the *practice* specific to each field. Thus 'the habitus – embodied history, internalized as a second nature and so forgotten – is the active presence of the whole past of which it is the product' (Bourdieu 1990; 56). The nature of various habituses can thus be detected and tested in the practices people engage in, in distinct social fields.

Capital

The concept of capital derives from Bourdieu's analyses of the educational system of France in the early 1970s. Usually in social science (and in everyday discourse) the term 'capital' is associated with the economic sphere and monetary exchange. Bourdieu's use of the term however is broader and conceptually distinctive (Moore 2008).

Capital, in Bourdieu's thinking, exists in three main forms: economic, cultural and social (Bourdieu 1986).

The main idea of *economic capital* comes from Marx, but in a Bourdieusian frame the concept covers all types of economic ownerships that can be capitalised in any distinct field.

Cultural capital in turn can exist in three forms: in the *embodied* state, that is, in the form of long-lasting dispositions of the mind and body; in the *objectified* state, in the forms of cultural goods; and in the *institutionalised* state, guaranteed by institutional recognition, such as academic qualifications and exam titles (Bourdieu 1986: 243). *Social capital* is

> the aggregate of the actual or potential resources which are linked to possession of a durable network of more or less institutionalized relationships of mutual acquaintance and recognition … which provides each of its members with the backing of the collectively-owned capital, a 'credential' which entitles them to credit, in the various senses of the term. (op. cit. 248–9)

The three forms of capital are made meaningful through *symbolic capital*, which for its part is connected with symbolic power and symbolic struggles over the value of various kinds of capitals. Through symbolic struggles and processes the values of various agents' capital possessions are constantly valued and revalued in their target fields. Therefore, also minor activities and efforts to change the balance of social fields matter.

Introduction to our chapters

The nine chapters that follow apply Bourdieu's concepts as tools for analysing a wide range of different phases of childhood, as well as a range of 'fields', in terms both of geographical location and institutional domain. Our contributors use a range of research methods to tackle their research questions. All of them have been working for some years in their chosen field of childhood, and all have chosen at some point to employ Bourdieu's concepts to support their analysis of that field. All our contributors, whatever their national origin (Belgium, Finland, France, India, UK) have had experience of a European education at some time in their own background and have shared in the growing awareness of Bourdieu's work over the last two decades. Their work has prompted a number of shared questions: what do we mean by the education field, or the family field? how does consideration of relational processes help us understand childhood experience? how can we understand the importance for children of child-adult relations? what characterises children's sense of responsibility through the generations?

As editors, we originally arranged the chapters to reflect the chronological phases of childhood, but have since decided that it would be more helpful for readers to group them into the broad domains they discuss. The first group focuses on young children's socialisation and education – in the family, in preschool, primary school and secondary school – and on the lives children live in societies where schooling is seen as the principal purpose of childhood. The next group offers discussions of childhoods in majority or developing world countries, where schooling may be a much less salient aspect of many children's lives. And the third group focuses on the social welfare and support systems which run alongside the school system in most societies.

In Chapter 2, Berry Mayall frames her discussion by focusing on Bourdieu's treatment of two constant aspects of children's experience of childhood: time and embodiment. Illustrating her arguments using research conversations carried out over several studies in England, Mayall teases out the ways in which the passing of time changes the dynamics of childhood relations and, by means of Bourdieu's concept of *hysteresis*, allows changes in the structures of society and of individual lives to be accommodated. The changing role of children's bodies in adults' relations with children as they grow is seen to intersect with time and with the different fields of home and school to pattern children's lives.

In Chapter 3, Liz Brooker looks at the lives of very young children and their families through the lens of recent UK government policy, which appears to attempt to bestow much-needed cultural capital on families who are deemed to lack it. By referring to policy documents, Brooker describes the rationale for the kinds of parenting schemes, enrichment programmes and interventions which have been introduced over several decades, and explains the poor outcomes from current schemes with reference to Bourdieu's account of how cultural capital is acquired. Bourdieu's own project of understanding the persistence of social inequalities is foregrounded here, along with evidence of the value of ethnographic research with families in revealing the sources of such inequalities.

Chapter 4, by Pascale Garnier, applies Bourdieu's concept of the logic of practice to a particular field: the contribution of parents to the educational progress of their preschool children in the French *école maternelle*. Drawing on two sets of interviews carried out two years apart, Garnier explains how Bourdieu's own concepts of 'practical logic' and 'theoretical logic' derive from his study of Merleau-Ponty, and shows how these concepts are enacted in parents' decisions about whether to purchase, and encourage their children's use of, the commercially published preschool workbooks, which are widely available in France.

Chapter 5, by Mari Vuorisalo and Leena Alanen, considers the preschool field in Finland, or rather the co-existing fields which are found in a single classroom in the year before children start formal schooling. Vuorisalo's detailed ethnographic case-study identifies the different kinds of capital which are available to different children, and the ways in which children can construct and exploit inequalities in their peer group, despite the teacher's efforts to pursue an inclusive agenda, while simultaneously reinforcing differences in the children's social and cultural capital.

In Chapter 6, Abigail Knight moves the educational story forward to the transition from primary to secondary school in England, and to the impacts on children's social belonging of travelling to a school a long way from their own home and neighbourhood. Knight's open-ended interviews with such children and their parents trace the educational policies and private sources of parental decisions, and the social networks which result, which are experienced both positively and negatively by children as they negotiate relationships with adults and children in their familiar and less familiar fields.

Chapter 7 is the first of two chapters applying Bourdieu's ideas to the daily lives, and longer-term prospects, of children in the developing world. Géraldine André and Mathieu Hilgers draw on anthropological methods, including observations and interviews, to examine varying forms of domination experienced by children working in the mining industry in two societies in sub-Saharan Africa. Their broader project draws on Bourdieu in order to analyse the impact of the globalisation of childhood on children's individual dispositions, and on the dynamics of domination in the neoliberal moment that currently shapes sub-Saharan Africa.

In Chapter 8 Virginia Morrow and Uma Vennam use case-studies taken from a longitudinal empirical research study, to report on the social support networks of children in two villages of Andhra Pradesh, India. Morrow and Vennam examine how forms of social capital are accessed and exploited by two case-study children in each of these villages, revealing the complex intersections of economic and social factors at the level of state and village with children's personal histories and trajectories, and the ways in which they attempt to exercise their own agency.

The final two chapters are concerned with aspects of the social welfare system in two countries. In Chapter 9,[2] Johanna Moilanen, Johanna Kiili and Leena Alanen offer a historical account, using archival material, of the development of the volunteer 'support person' system in Finland, including its radical rethinking of children's needs and wishes based on changes in legislation during the 1960s and 1970s. The field of struggle here includes many competing perspectives: a policy of control, and a policy of support; professional social workers and volunteers; municipal agencies and NGOs.

In Chapter 10, Karen Winter uses interview data to describe how the views of children (and their parents) may be marginalised by the decision-making process, including case review meetings, in the social support system of Northern Ireland. Winter identifies the specific kinds of capital (knowledge) which inform the decisions made about the custody and care of children, and the symbolic violence which shapes the outcomes.

The chapters have been written partly in response to wide-ranging changes in policy towards and about children, over the last 15 years or so. By using Bourdieu's concepts (field, habitus and capital, and others, see for instance Grenfell 2008), our contributors have been able to investigate how large-scale policies and socio-economic changes relate to the character of intergenerational interactions at individual and societal levels. Through the use of Bourdieu's toolkit, our contributors have provided convincing accounts of the power of policies devised by adults, and of individual adults, to shape children's lives. We point to the effectiveness of children's agency, through intergenerational relational processes, to contribute to the shaping of their experiences, but also to situations where their knowledge is sidelined or rejected. Of particular interest is the agency of parents acting to mediate public policies through their ongoing responsive and respectful interrelations with their children, in contrast to the more formulaic and inflexible operation by child welfare staff of large-scale policies affecting children's lives.

Finally we note the importance of taking account of time passing, in these chapters. Both by collecting information across time, and by considering the passage of time, our authors contribute to an understanding of how change is accounted for in Bourdieu's concepts. Thus, for instance, Moilanen, Kiili and Alanen show how concepts have changed in the Finnish welfare field, Mayall considers how time passing in the lives of children, leads to changes in habitus and capital, Morrow and Vennam show how changes in family circumstances over time affect children's relations with the education field and also shape the capitals they bring to bear in managing their lives.

Notes

1. Several terms are used to differentiate the so-called 'developed' and 'less developed' worlds: minority, northern, developed versus majority, southern, developing. In this book, we have retained the preferred use of individual contributors, rather than aiming for consistency.
2. The editors would like to point out that the format of this chapter, and its references, are in accordance with the Finnish requirements for doctoral theses, and have not been re-formatted for the purpose of inclusion in this volume.

References

Agbenyega, J. and Klibthong, S. 2012. Transforming selves for inclusive practice: Experiences of early childhood preservice teachers, *Australian Journal of Teacher Education*, 37 (5), article 2 [online].

Bourdieu, P. 1977. *Outline of a theory of practice*. Cambridge: Cambridge University Press.

Bourdieu, P. 1986. The forms of capital. In J. G. Richardson (ed.) *Handbook of theory and research for the sociology of education*. New York: Greenwood Press, pp. 241–58.

Bourdieu, P. 1990. *The logic of practice*. Stanford, Ca: Stanford University Press.

Bourdieu, P. 2000. The politics of protest: An interview with K. Ovenden, *Socialist Review*, 242: 18–20.

Bourdieu, P. and Wacquant, L. 1992. *An invitation to reflexive sociology*. Chicago: Chicago University Press.

Chamboredon, J.C. and Prévot, J. 1975. Changes in the social definition of early childhood and the new forms of symbolic violence, *Theory and Society*, 2 (3): 331–50.

Connolly, P. 1998. *Racism, gender identities and young children: Social relations in a multi-ethnic inner-city primary school*. London: Routledge.

Goodman, J.E. and Silverstein, P.A. (eds) 2009. *Bourdieu in Algeria. Colonial politics, ethnographic practices, theoretical developments*. Lincoln and London: University of Nebraska Press.

Grenfell, M. (ed.) 2008. *Pierre Bourdieu: Key concepts*. Stocksfield: Acumen.

Grenfell, M. 2010. Working with habitus and field: The logic of Bourdieu's practice. In E. Silva and A. Warde (eds) *Cultural analysis and Bourdieu's legacy*. London and New York: Routledge, pp. 14–30.

Moore, R. 2008. Capital. In M. Grenfell (ed.) *Pierre Bourdieu: Key concepts*. Stocksfield: Acumen, pp. 101–17.

Palludan, C. 2007. Two tones: The core of inequality in kindergarten?, *International Journal of Early Childhood*, 39 (1): 75–91.

Qvortrup, J. 1985. Placing children in the division of labour. In P. Close and R. Collins (eds) *Family and economy in modern society*. London: Macmillan, pp. 129–145.

Reay, D. 1998. *Class work: Mothers' involvement with their children's primary schools*. London: UCL Press.

Swartz, D. 1997. *Culture and power: The sociology of Pierre Bourdieu*. Chicago: Chicago University Press.

2
Intergenerational Relations: Embodiment over Time

Berry Mayall

Introduction

In this chapter, I reconsider the usefulness of Bourdieu for under-standing how childhoods are shaped and the contributions made by both children and adults and by childhood and adulthood to re-establishing, shaping and modifying powerful structures.

To start with I note some assumptions on which this chapter rests. First of all, I work on the sociological basis that institutional and ideological structures shape childhoods and child-adult relations. Long-established traditions, policies and beliefs structure how child-hoods are understood and how they are lived in specific societies. Thus, on the one hand, I will want to argue that childhoods will differ according to time and space; on the other hand, I insist that childhood is a permanent structural form in society and that any account of how society works must take account of what children contribute to social relations both within and across generations and what childhood contributes to the division of labour. (As compared to the state of play 30 years ago, there is now a proliferation of papers and books that argue this case and that provide empirical data in support of it, for instance Qvortrup et al. 1994; Jenks 1996; Hutchby and Moran-Ellis 1998; Mayall 2002; Qvortrup 2009; James 2009; Alanen 2011.)

We can usefully follow Bourdieu in considering how these tradi-tions, policies and beliefs are absorbed into people's understanding of the characteristics and status of differing social groups in society (habitus) and how people also bring to bear their acquired social, cultural and economic capital to the field where negotiations take place. As Bourdieu says (*Distinction* 1986: 483), his concept of habitus has been so constructed that we do not have to choose between 'objectivist' theories (as presented, for instance, by Durkheim) and 'subjectivist' theories (for instance in ethnomethodology); ontology and epistemology are interfused in his theory.

> What we have to do is to bring into the science of scarcity, and of competition for scarce goods, the practical knowledge which the agents obtain for themselves by producing – on the basis of their experience of the distributions, itself dependent on their position in the distributions – divisions and classifications which are no less objective than those of the balance sheets of social physics.

Secondly, I assume that intergenerational processes take place at both institutional and personal levels; and that the two kinds of processes are essentially interrelated. Under consideration here is how these processes shape and reshape children's and adults' experience, and how they seek to reassert the ascribed characteristics of each social group, but are challenged, especially by the less powerful negotiators in a relational exchange.

In this chapter, I consider the usefulness of taking account of both embodiment and time as interrelated factors helping to explain generational relations at both institutional or structural levels and at interpersonal levels. Whilst Bourdieu did not work on exploring childhood in active relation to adulthood, we can perhaps explore the mileage for including childhood as social status – which will provide an important focus for what Bourdieu calls game-playing, where concepts inherent or ascribed to childhood and adulthood are in negotiation and perhaps struggle over concepts of childhood. What I am proposing is further exploration of these struggles in the light of the interlinked concepts of embodiment and time.

How Bourdieu can help: field, hysteresis and habitus

Bourdieu's concept of field (*le champ*) where negotiations take place is central to his approach (Bourdieu and Wacquant 1992: 94–115). For a start, it recognises that homes (for instance) are not necessarily environments where harmony in loving relationships prevails. Instead the home is where negotiations and even battles are fought about power and about how far ascribed characteristics and status are accepted by the players. And what we have to study is how agents, struggling for scarce goods, produce, reproduce and challenge their social status. Bourdieu argues that people bring with them habitus and varying forms of capital; these concepts too are useful, since they help us deal with intersections of agency and structure.

In his book, *Outline of a Theory of Practice* (1977/72) Bourdieu draws on his work in Kabylia in Algeria, and discusses his key concepts: structures, habitus and practices, in the light of his findings there (1977: 78–87). As Cheryl Hardy (2012) points out, Bourdieu's interlinked concepts of field and habitus include the understanding that both may change in character and that, as interlinked, interrelated concepts, change in the one will lead to responsive change in the other. However, she notes, this idea about change is so fundamental to Bourdieu's conceptualisation that it is not forefronted at all points in his writing. For us, thinking about children and childhood, their habitus and its interrelatedness with fields, the fact that children grow, in both bodily and competency terms, is an important topic. Furthermore, the fact that the political and social world of education undergoes frequent changes in ethos and practice must lead us to think about the negotiations between children and parents with an eye to the impacts of changes in the children and changes in the field on their negotiations. And we have to include consideration of the point that the field of education has changed since the parents of these children absorbed their understandings of what an education system and the practices of a school might most suitably be. These points will be taken up in a later discussion of the negotiations between children and parents, in the education field.

But first we must refer to the rather daunting word 'hysteresis' (see Hardy 2012 for discussion), used by Bourdieu as if we all know what it means. Recourse to the Shorter Oxford English Dictionary (OED) gives us its definition of the term: it comes from a Greek word meaning 'coming late' and was first used in the UK (1881) to describe 'the lagging behind of magnetic effects behind their causes' (thus, iron filings take a bit of time to respond to the pull of a magnet).

What is under consideration is a disjunction between people's dispositions, their understandings of their place in the world, and the field in which they are acting and negotiating. Because there is or may be a 'structural lag' between the opportunities on offer in a field and the dispositions that people bring to the field, they may fail to grasp opportunities available to them (Bourdieu 1977: 83) Both the field and the habitus are subject to change; for field conditions change over time, and an individual's history is ongoing. Thus, for example, a change in the socio-political trends in society away from courtly and knightly ideals can be held to account for the fact that Don Quixote's behaviour seems out of synchrony with the social worlds he encounters, an example given by Marx and quoted by Bourdieu (1990: 62). The knight has not responded to these social changes. The field has changed but he has not; he brings outmoded assumptions and practices to social situations and challenges. Similarly, in England in the late twentieth century and continuing in the first years of the twenty-first century, governments' concepts of education, and education policies reflecting them, have changed, leaving teachers and parents uncomfortable with the new regime of testing and norms; for they themselves had grown up with other understandings of education, including relatively 'progressive' ideas. But it may also be that a person's habitus changes; for though Bourdieu emphasises at many points how beliefs, assumptions and practices are absorbed and retained from early childhood, he also leaves open the possibility that people may acquire forms of capital (social, economic or cultural) that allow them to profit from the opportunities offered in a field, and from the changing character of the field. Thus, for instance, expanded educational opportunities may allow or even encourage someone to move into work not usually associated with the social class they inhabited initially; and in so doing they may lose connections with the social worlds they grew up in; thus a working-class person may rise to a university job. Indeed Bourdieu himself moved from humble beginnings as the son of a postman in rural south-west France to the pinnacles of the French academic world in Paris (Grenfell 2012); the French education system allowed him to acquire the cultural capital to make this journey. Hardy points to this kind of disjunction in her reference to an example of how a working-class person who achieves success in the world of boxing may lose his earlier established position in his community (example given in *The Weight of the World* 1999: 158–67).

The English home-school education field?

Fields where negotiations and struggles take place have to be understood as arenas or spaces (in time) where certain ideas hold sway. Defining the borders is tricky, but in the case of education, it seems arguable that homes as well as institutions are currently – and increasingly – implicated (e.g. James and James 2001). For I think we can consider English education (at all levels) as a field, where not just teachers, but parents too are involved in the education of children, and children themselves are deeply involved in negotiations about their status in intergenerational relations, in part because they experience objectification as objects of adult socialisation. I would like to consider, with particular reference to the English context, the nexus of home-school, where we have interpenetration of home agendas and education agendas, with homes expected to contribute to school agendas, as well as to endorse or conform to them, and parents involved in ongoing discussions with school staff about their children's schooling. Thus we have currently a situation where the home-school field is a field in which, at policy and ideological levels, childhood is seen as a time for socialisation in the interests of state agendas, and parents are seen essentially as agents in ensuring the conformity of childhood to these state agendas (I develop this point below). At personal levels, children are faced with the double supervision and control of adults – both parents and teachers, acting in concert; and while 'the home' has traditionally been for children a place of relative freedom – often described by children as where they have their 'free time' (Mayall 2002: chapter 7), that free time is now increasingly sucked into the educational/socialisation policy ideological arena. It is indeed notable that children themselves put high value on their 'free time', as is instanced in this snippet from a conversation where I had asked 8-year-olds to discuss the value of play. According to them play's central characteristic is the freedom it affords from direct adult control:

> It's our free time, from school, teaching, reading and homework.... It's our time when we do what we like, more or less. (Mayall 2002: 134)

Habitus – an on-going learning experience?

Further, in the arena of child-adult relations, we may explore in more detail the concept of habitus. Habitus for parents may include ideologies learned long ago (Bourdieu and Wacquant 1992: 115–22), for we adults have absorbed our society's ideas about what childhood is and should be. But in other respects habitus – as far as doing parenthood goes – is not something well established and fixed (or acquired in childhood). For though ideas about childcare and about parenting are handed down the generations (and consolidated through policies and childcare books), yet parents learn how to parent, while doing the job of parenting and they learn in negotiations with their children. This means that we have to take account of time – time during which both adults and children learn what it means to do childhood ('childing'?) and what it means to do parenting; also what it means to negotiate childhood and parenthood with each other. These considerations allow us to take on board the ideas in the term hysteresis – which recognise that both field and habitus may change over time.

In the light of the points made above about change, it would seem that the concept of dispositions, what we bring with us to negotiations, has to take account of learning processes. Dispositions cannot be regarded as fixed. For whilst the case of child-parent relations may at first glance seem to challenge some of Bourdieu's arguments about reproduction, he does take account of challenges to the status quo. Thus he argues that we must recognise 'the structuring activity of agents' (*Distinction* 1986: 467). People shift power within a field through their negotiations. And in particular, he notes that young people may challenge adult authority in their attempts to redefine their status. These attempts, he notes, include young people's efforts to improve their own status, including their own power in society, by attempts to diminish the power of older people, relegating them to the relatively low status of old age.

Thus, I would like to argue, at the intersections of institutionally endorsed ideas and interpersonal negotiations, can be interposed the idea that people learn, along the way, and notably through experience and through those interpersonal negotiations. We have to include in our explorations how knowledge, including theoretical and experiential knowledge, is modified by learning across time, and through interaction.

Embodiment as a critical component of child-adult relations

English sociologists working within medical sociology have explained that we must take account of two major ideas on the body (Turner 1992; Shilling 1993, 2005). Thus: foundationalism tells us that the body is something physical, it is a real bodily reality, both identified and experienced as physical (for a fuller discussion, see Chapter 4). On the other hand interpretivists tell us that, yes, we have a physical body, but that we understand our bodies and those of others solely via our interpretations. So there are foundationalists and interpretivists. But one may add that there is a wider point on ontology, for traditional sociology itself has been interested only in adulthood (and only in masculine adulthood); it has analysed society as if it consisted solely of adults. We can say that sociology has been adult-centred. Indeed, this point allows us to suggest that mainstream sociology can be seen as regarding adults as ontologies, as complete; whereas children are deemed as incomplete projects in the course of socialisation, they are epistemologies!

These ideas are important when we think about children. The relations between small children and their parents are based, in part, on the value parents give to the child's body. We can readily agree that the care required by the child is indeed physical, at the same time as emotional and social. Feeding and cleaning the child involve direct attention based on parents' physical action and responsiveness to the physical character and activity of the child. Yet at the same time children learn that parents value interacting with them; so they find they are valued for their social relations with their parents, where parents initiate interactions through smiles and words and hugs; and where children too initiate interactions, expressed through smiles and cries. That is, children learn, from birth, that they are valued in a double way, and inextricably, as body and as person, in relations with parents.

But the plot thickens. The body of the child as ontology has to relate to the body of the child as epistemology. Because social life even in their early days demands that children's bodies make way, or accommodate to the social world they live in. For instance the very young child has to learn to sleep when adults sleep, and to eat the kinds of food the family provides. And above all, when children first leave the home and go, for instance to the nursery, they will find that they have to submit their bodies to the demands of that social institution, its assumptions and practices (for detailed discussion of some of these, see Chapter 5). And the demands made by educational institutions become more and more stringent and exigent, across the years – at primary (or first) school, and later at secondary school and beyond. These processes whereby children's lives are moulded from the start by adult expectations, norms and practices have been explored by Judith Ennew (1994: 126), who notes that 'modern childhood constructs children out of society, mutes their voices, denies their personhood, limits their potential'. One example, but one which may loom large in young children's anxieties during the primary school day, concerns toileting and getting a drink of water.

> Berry: And what about if you want to go to the lavatory?
> Sandra: Well, you have to ask Miss X (class teacher).
> Berry: And does she let you go?
> Sandra: Sometimes.
> Berry: Why does she sometimes not?
> Mother: Do you think sometimes if you've just come back from play, or if you're just going to be going to play in a couple of minutes?
> Sandra: No, if you've just come back from play and you want to get a drink or you need to go to the toilet, she says no, because you had all that time to get it in the playground. (Mayall 1994: 62–3)

As the conversation continues, Sandra (aged five) explains that the teacher tends to cast doubt on the children's moral probity, for she suggests that they may be avoiding their work, by prolonging their absence from the classroom. This example comes from my exploration of how children in one primary school, aged five and nine years, look after their bodies and their health, at home and at school. This study (*The Greenstreet Study*) indicated, through discussions with children and their mothers, that children had more control over what they required in order to stay healthy, at home than at school. I think that results partly from the fact that their parents continued to evaluate their children as bodies as well as actors within social relations; whereas teachers had other priorities (Mayall 1994). When I discussed their work with the teachers, they made it clear that they aimed to care for 'the whole child' but that they thought they should socialise the children into the social norms of the school; and they also had a job to do, in delivering the curriculum. I thought that this balancing act sometimes operated against the interests of the children.

The experiences of carrying out this small-scale study led me on to a larger-scale study of the status of children's health at primary school. This was the *Children's Health in Primary School Study (CHIPS)*. We included a questionnaire survey of 1 in 20 primary schools in England and Wales (620 schools replied, a response rate of 60%) followed by case-studies of six varying primary schools (Mayall et al. 1996), where we collected data with children, teachers, school nurses and play-ground assistants. Whilst most studies in schools concern social and academic processes and progress, this one tried to take account of the point that children, each day, have to manage their bodily selves in an environment that may not be favourable. Again, this study led me on: I had learned that children gave full and important accounts of their experiences. So I decided on a further study (*The Childhood Study*) which built on these two earlier ones, and explored children's ideas about childhood and parenthood, with children aged 9–10 and 12–13. I was then able to use data from these three studies to discuss theoretical implications, in two books (Mayall 1996; Mayall 2002); the main focus was on the status of childhood in society. The three studies are described more fully in the Appendix to my 2002 book. This chapter draws on some of the data from these studies.

Embodiment is systematically studied in Bourdieu's book *Distinction* (1986). He points to ways in which people's bodily dispositions are acquired; what he calls primary habitus is acquired in early childhood. This argument is based on the ideas inherent in the concept of 'socialisation' – viewed as training given by adults to children. Secondary habitus is acquired through interactions in arenas of socialisation such as the school, or the employment agency. His analysis shows that people, through their gestures and movements, display their social status and their understandings of their social status. What he shows to pervade French society resonates with UK society, where social status is represented in bodily movements, stance, carriage, speech patterns and habits. Thus Bourdieu points to forces that make for continuity and stability. But he also allows for change, through the negotiations and conflicts that take place in interaction. Social agency is therefore important. More generally, he sees the social structure as embodied (1986: 467). Bourdieu's discussion is mainly about how social class is embodied, but we may wish to widen the application of his ideas to consider how childhoods are embodied, not only by social class, but by age (to be considered in the next section).

A useful primer on this topic – as regards the UK scene – is a set of papers edited by Alan Prout (2000). He sets out a social constructionist argument in his introduction and the book includes valuable empirical studies, focusing on children's experience of embodied childhoods (e.g. James 2000). As noted above, I too did some studies in the 1990s on how children manage their bodily persons at home and then at school (1994, 1996). Allied work on the sociology of the emotions is important here – since emotional state is closely linked to physical well-being (Hochschild 1979, 1983; Bendelow and Williams 1998).

We may point here to increasing public concern about government policies that aim to alter the English state education system (e.g. Alexander 2010; Ball 2013; Mortimore 2013). The changes to the education system which favour testing children and assigning children into categories according to their performance on tests, have met with dismay among adults who grew up with other ideas. Critics argue, for instance, that children should be conceptualised as active creative participants in learning; that children will learn well only if they are happy; and that policies that promote their happiness are in short supply in schools; indeed proponents of private schools argue that one of the merits of these schools is that they emphasise the promotion self-esteem (including happiness) among the children, partly for its own sake, but partly as a basis for children's learning and success in later life (e.g. Mortimore 2013: 15).

The relative status of the mind and body in English education policies and practices

A key topic here is the understandings that permeate education policies at all levels. These understandings include consideration of the relative status of the mind and body. Thus in England – at structural levels – policies, curricula and hence practices at nursery level (ages two to five) have become increasingly focused on the cognitive. Whilst the nursery tradition in England, dating from the mid-nineteenth century, traditionally encompassed children's physical, emotional and mental activity and exploration (valued for itself and for its learning potential), nowadays we have trends towards cognitive readiness for school (including learning numbers, colours and words). The downward pressure from 'real' school is increasingly felt in nurseries (Yelland 2010; Penn 2011). This development has also been traced for France, in Pascale Garnier's (2011) discussion of policy and practice changes in the *écoles maternelles* (and see Chapter 4 for her study of work books for pre-schoolers).

At school level (5 to 18 years) nowadays, physical activity takes a very lowly place, compared to academic work; and again, this trend towards hugely prioritising the mind over the body gathered pace in the 1990s, when many – largely political – factors conspired. These included international league tables and Conservative concern that state schools 'failed' the children (as compared to private schools). Symbolic was the selling off of school playing fields.

However, if we then move from the important structuring forces in the education system towards intergenerational relations at individual levels and at levels of practice, we find that the embodied character of the child maintains a place and a status within child-adult negotiations, both at home and in nurseries and schools. Parents, at home, take into account the embodiment of the child, as well as the child's cognitive and emotional characteristics and wishes; their experience over time has taught them the value of a multifaceted engagement with their children. Children themselves advance their bodily feelings, wishes and troubles in their negotiations for parental response (e.g. Mayall 1986; 1994). These demands echo feminist work on how women's bodies are understood in various social settings and how women negotiate their embodied selves (e.g. Martin 1987). At nursery, staff have educational agendas, passed down from national policies, and their work is controlled both by long-established traditions and by more recent policy pronouncements. But as childcare staff, they too – in their daily work – are also expected to take account of child embodiment; and will be asked by the child to do so (e.g. Holligan 2000). As to schools, I suggested above that primary school teachers think they have to balance attention to the 'whole child', to the social order of the school and to the curriculum. But the concept of an equal balance between physical and mental education (traditionally part of the private school ethos) was never fully endorsed for state-educated children; and in the last 20 years, concern about academic attainment has narrowed the space and time for school attention to children's bodies and emotional well-being. Thus a teacher in my CHIPS study pointed to the double problem he faced, in the mid-1990s. The school had been built in the 1970s in response to national policy dictating small class sizes – but now, educational policy had changed (towards larger classes) and as housing provision in the area grew, more children were crammed into the space and the national curriculum demanded that children spend most of their time in the classroom.

> A lot of them, particularly the older boys, you know, feel that they are being kept in, they are being so tightly controlled – you've got to control them tightly because if you don't your classroom discipline – and in effect the way every child in the classroom learns is affected. So it is a balance. I mean, I would think some children find it quite a strain, because they want to be, again particularly boys, older boys, they want to be out doing all these boyish things, they want to be running and climbing and jumping and they're not, they're kept down in the classroom – their natural spirits are thwarted. (Mayall 2002: 73)

It is important to take account here of the extent to which generational processes, whereby adults and children interrelate, are sensitive not only to national policies but to children's embodied selves. I have long argued that parents at home are – and can be – more sensitive to the demands of children's bodies than schools are or can be (Mayall 1994). But the ideas promoted by the education system pervade parent-child negotiations. School takes priority. Thus in the morning a parent has to get a tired child to school on time; and at the end of the day a tired child still has to do the homework set by the school.

Time in relational processes

The classification struggle: concepts of childhood

I have suggested along the way that things change across time, in relations between children and adults, at structural and institutional and at practice and individual levels. These relational processes are summed up by Bourdieu within the concept of 'the classification struggle': at stake in negotiations in a field is 'power over the classificatory schemes and systems which are the basis of the representations of the groups, and therefore of their mobilisation and demobilisation' (*Distinction* 1986: 479). Furthermore there may be a time-lag (or hysteresis) in the responsiveness of each negotiating agent to changes in one or both sides. In England, as I have mentioned, we have seen radical shifts in national policies on education, over the last 25 years or so. At the macro-level, concepts of childhood – what it should consist of, and how childhood's relations with adulthood should be structured, have altered. It is not surprising that whilst children's rights have been grudgingly (and gradually) recognised since 1991 at the level of lip-service among English policy-makers, nevertheless policies and practices that deny children's rights have been formalised and reinforced. Thus one kind of temporal influence is changes over time in ideas about childhood – what its function is – and in corresponding policies and practices. These concepts of childhood are crucially important in structuring the education system – across schools and homes. If children are to be valued mainly for their later economic contributions to society, then the education system will reflect this opinion.

The field of child-parent negotiations

At interpersonal levels – and here we take child-parent negotiations as a topic for discussion – an important defining feature of these negotiations is that both children and parents change over the period of childhood, in what knowledge and assumptions they bring to the negotiating table. They acquire knowledge and assumptions experientially, but also in response to large-scale changes. For instance, it has been noted that children nowadays have access to a much wider range of knowledge (via computers, for instance), and to interactive social relations (via technologies such as Facebook), compared to earlier generations. The content of school curricula has widened, as compared to the curriculum 30 or more years before; so children know more. Some of children's strength to resist their identification in national policies as socialisation projects, as not yet people, may result from their knowledge, their creative intelligence and their changing social relations. Children's ability to challenge how they (as children) are classified is limited; but we see their challenges in a refusal to conform, in taking a leave of absence from school and in denying the legitimacy of school agendas. So some children and young people are engaged in challenges to their defined characteristics. This point resonates with the argument put forward by Margaret Mead, that perhaps it is not so much or not only, nowadays, that children learn from the earlier generation, as that adults are now being asked to learn from children (for discussion see Qvortrup 2009: 29). But of course some adults are resistant to this proposition.

So time brings in changes; obviously, as children get older – and so their demands and what they bring to the negotiating table change. Furthermore, as they get older they become more sophisticated, more competent in their negotiations with adults, and more challenging.

Also important is that parents themselves change over time. As time passes, parents bring to bear their acquired experiential knowledge of their child's capabilities and character. Parents hand over more and more of bodily self-care to children at home – and children assert their self-care abilities. But parents also have to continue to balance the multifaceted components of their child (physical, emotional, mental) depending on the urgency/demands of the specific situation. They put an ill child to bed, rather than insisting on teeth cleaning. Parents bring increasing competence and experience to the negotiating table. They may become more easy-going. Their experiential knowledge of the conformity proposed by the education system may lead them to concede decision-making to their children, especially to children in their teenage years. On the other hand, parental concern with their children's futures (both academic and social) may also harden their approach to child-adult negotiations, as I go on to discuss.

Educational institutions, child-parent negotiations and puberty

As time passes children move out from home into nurseries, schools and public spaces. These movements raise at least two questions: How does embodiment work in these places? And how far do adults – parents and institutional staff – take account of how over time bodies change and children's demands change? We may take the example of puberty – as dealt with by schools and homes (Prendergast 2000); for puberty coincides with ever more restrictive institutional requirements on children both at school and at home; and with increasingly assertive demands by children. The embodiment of, in particular, boys at secondary school has been investigated by Prendergast and

Forrest (1998). An allied topic has been explored: adult perception of young people as threats when they congregate in public spaces (Matthews et al. 2000). In so doing, they appear to some adults to challenge public space as the legitimate province of adults only; and indeed it may be that they deliberately do this in some cases (see also Holloway and Valentine 2000).

As I noted earlier, it may be mainly or most dramatically in the teenage years that young people may challenge their assignment to childhood. When they do so, their challenge in effect serves to reposition older people as having lower status, by asserting their own important positioning in society (*Distinction* 1986: 478–80). Through these challenges, they are shifting boundaries and barriers. However, both parents and schools also have responsibilities for ensuring that young people toe the educational line. A clash of agendas ensues when both parents and schools seek to reject the sexualised, embodied character of young people in favour of academic work. Young people may accept description or conceptualisation of their social status defined as lacking responsibility, in return for the licence young people are allowed. 'Having one's fling' goes with irresponsibility. On the other hand, they may reject classification as irresponsible and yet insist on 'having their fling' – having it both ways. This kind of account of young people's dilemmas and choices allows for the function of social forces in defining the status of young people; it contrasts with what Bourdieu calls the 'psycho-babble' of those who seek biological determinants of young people's behaviour and demands.

In my Childhood Study, an interesting case here was presented to me by Muslim girls, a younger pair aged 10 and an older pair aged 12, concerning the degree of fit between what was expected of them at home and how they experienced these expectations. The younger girls reported enthusiastically on their home lives.

Berry: And has life changed at all recently?

Rumena: Yes, since I've turned 10, I've got more responsibility. I've got to learn to do things that my Mum does. You have to learn more things.

Sidra: My Mum does the cooking. But I clean the house, put the washing in the machine and learn a lot of stuff for the future. (Mayall 2002: 52)

Rumena and Sidra said they were enjoying their new domestic responsibilities, and looking forward to their future lives running a household. According to their accounts, their mothers' expectations and their conformity matched. And at their age, the demands of the education system allowed them time for traditional home life. In the telling phrase of Bourdieu and Wacquant (1992: 127), it seems they felt like 'fish in water'; they did not feel the weight of the water. The older girls, at secondary school, presented a more complex picture (Mayall 2002: 82–3). Cultural and religious practices required that as girls got older and approached puberty, they should take a fuller part in household life – socialising with the extended family, as well as carrying out more household duties. But their mothers (and to some extent their fathers) also valued highly the girls' school achievements. Negotiations between the girls and their mothers brought into play the girls' superior knowledge of what the school demanded – the precise character and importance of homework assignments, the standards required, deadlines for delivery. So daughters, while recognising their domestic obligations, somewhat challenged their mothers' authority about the appropriate use of time at home; they needed to spend time away from family interactions, doing their school work. Looking to the future, the girls told me that they also saw value in pursuing their studies to A levels and even to university degrees; and they also knew (from older girls' narratives and experiences) that they might thereby be able to delay marriage; and that these qualifications would lead to advantage in the marriage market, and thence to the higher status of the family. Similar topics and ideas are explored by Katie Gavron (1997) in her study of Bangladeshi young people in an area of East London. So here we have a case where educational opportunities and traditional gendered practices required careful child-parent negotiation, compromise and learning. Family habitus was being modified by the state education provision and requirements, and it seems that important mediators in effecting this modification were girls, in consultation with their mothers.

Longer schooling, longer childhoods – a recipe for alienation?

Finally on this topic, we may note a further – obvious – change that has implications for child-adult relations: the increasing length of compulsory school attendance in minority world societies. This policy change has in turn implications for societal understandings of children as agents. If children are to be schooled to 16 or 18, then sexual activity, and in particular pregnancy and child-birth have to be demoted as legitimate concerns for young people and even classed as abnormal or deviant. This leads on to the point that, if we look at children's embodiment from children's own points of view, I think we have to consider the concept of the alienated body. The complex relations between embodiment and social experience are complicated by ambiguity in how children experience adult responses to their bodies. So for instance a young child finds her body is loved and respected by parents, but her experience outside the home may be of a body not respected, rejected from the social. For at school, bodies are managed, and later mostly rejected and alienated. Children at school have to learn to subdue their bodies. There is also a social class element in recognition of bodies; at private schools, recognition integral to what is deemed valuable about children's achievements (at ideological levels) includes sporting achievement. For children in state schools, provision for sporting activities may be poorer and achievement less highly valued, as compared to academic achievement.

In this section of the paper, therefore, I have suggested (briefly) that time plays an important part in structuring child-adult relations at both institutional and policy levels, and at individual levels; and that interactions at individual levels will reflect changes at institutional and policy levels. Not only do policies change over time, but children become subject – or object – to differing institutions as they grow older. And at personal levels, both children and adults – especially parents – learn to change their demands in accordance with changing bodies and with consequent changes in understandings of what childhood consists of and most crucially of the social status of childhood – and of teenagerhood – in relation to adulthood.

Discussion

This chapter has drawn on Bourdieu to discuss how the status of childhood is defined, negotiated and challenged. It can be said that the ideas discussed by Bourdieu resonate with the explorations into the civilising process elaborated by Norbert Elias (1978). He documented how social conventions and social behaviours changed over time and became more elaborate. In turn, the socialisation of children into social norms took longer, as European societies developed;

childhood itself lasted over longer periods of time. Similarly, in the field of education, what it is thought necessary for children to know has increased over time; and correspondingly, the time children spend being schooled has increased; but, importantly, lengthening the period of adult social control over children is a central adult value here (Hendrick 2003: chapter 6). These trends give scope for considerable resistance by children, whose bodily demands and interests, as well as their claims to personhood, may clash with policy agendas, especially as they get older.

As Bourdieu notes, conservation of the social order rests on people's acceptance of their social position, their social status, vis-à-vis the social status of that social group with which they are negotiating (1986: 471). Modifications to the social order result when people successfully challenge their ascribed social status. When we are considering children and childhood, Bourdieu implicitly makes a very useful contribution through focusing on the struggles that take place over the classifying of children as a social group. And many of the relational difficulties parents and children face as they negotiate can be well understood using this framework. His argument builds on earlier thinkers' work. Thus he notes (1986: 483, note 24) that he endorses Goffman's argument: we don't just accept labels; by accepting the label, we constitute the labels and embed or reinforce them. By requiring children to remain in 'education' or 'training' until they are 18, we reinforce the notion that they are not fit to join the adult world.

Interrelations between work and working conditions on the one hand and people's embodiment on the other are a topic insufficiently considered in respect of children and childhood. As regards adults, bodies and embodiment are somewhat brushed aside in, for instance, workplaces. And though it is true that hours of work, and conditions of work are negotiated using embodied arguments, yet adults are expected to do their work despite their bodies. However, predominant theoretical conceptions of childhood in minority world societies insist on the concept of socialisation (the journey children make towards adulthood) and its corollary, the higher status of adulthood compared to childhood. Thus the time present of childhood is devalued. This is particularly so in English schools (and increasingly in nurseries). One of the contributions of recent childhood studies is to insist on the experiences of childhood, as presented by children;

and these statements derived from experiential knowledge clearly indicate that children value the time-present of childhood.

Children's physical competence and their embodied wishes change over time, and require careful consideration in child-adult negotiations. These have to take place at individual levels and are an ongoing component of childhood's experiences. Important, but relatively neglected as theoretical and policy-related topics, are the implications of children's physical (and linked emotional) abilities and wishes for wider policy levels; compulsory schooling at ever increasing ages; planning for playing fields, playspaces; but also more broadly for recognition of children's right to use public space and to be respected rather than vilified and/or rejected. In the English context, at least, the value of the time-present of childhood is in urgent need of upgrading. And the notion that the 'education' that takes place in people's early years is what matters most in the life-span also needs reconsideration.

Finally, I have pointed to some aspects of how structural change impacts on child-adult negotiations. Bourdieu again helps us here, by pointing to the impacts of deeply held beliefs on practices and how modifications of habitus can take place within family negotiations, where the new generation can act as agents of change. I have suggested that the new structural conditions – where young people learn from new technologies, and, in particular, where girls respond to educational opportunities, perhaps offer these young people better bargaining power, and above all agency in child-adult negotiations.

References

Alanen, L. 2011. Moving towards a relational sociology of childhood. In R. Braches-Chyrek et al. (eds), *Kindheiten, Gesellschaften: Interdisziplinäre Zugänge sur Kinderheitsforschung*. Opladen: Barbara Budrich Verlag, pp. 21–44.

Alexander, R. (ed.) 2010. *Children, their world, their education*. London: Routledge.

Ball, S. 2013. *The education debate*. Second edition. Bristol: Policy Press.

Bendelow, G. and Williams, S. (eds) 1998. *Emotions in social life*. London: Routledge.

Bourdieu, P. 1977. *Outline of a theory of practice*. First published in French 1972. Cambridge: Cambridge University Press.

Bourdieu, P. 1986. *Distinction*. London: Routledge and Kegan Paul.

Bourdieu, P. 1990. *The logic of practice*. Cambridge: Polity Press.

Bourdieu, P. 1999. *The weight of the world: social suffering in contemporary society.* Translated into English by P. Parkhurst Ferguson, S.Emanuel. J.Johnson and S.T.Waryn, Cambridge: Polity Press. Originally ublished as *La Misere du Monde* Paris-Seuil 1993.

Bourdieu, P. and Wacquant, L. 1992. *Invitation to reflexive sociology.* Cambridge: Polity Press.

Elias, N. 1978. *The civilising process.* Translated into English by Edmund Jephcott. Oxford: Blackwell.

Ennew, J. 1994. Time for children or time for adults? In J. Qvortrup et al. (eds), *Childhood matters: Social theory, practice and politics.* Aldershot, Avebury Press, pp. 125–44.

Garnier, P. 2011. The scholarisation of the French école maternelle: Institutional transformations since the 1970s, *European Early Childhood Education Research Journal*, 19 (4): 553–63.

Gavron, K. 1997. Migrants to citizens: Changing orientations among Bangladeshis of Tower Hamlets, London. Unpublished PhD thesis, University of London.

Grenfell, M. 2012. Biography. In M. Grenfell (ed.) *Pierre Bourdieu: Key concepts.* Durham: Acumen, pp. 11–25.

Hardy, C. 2012. Hysteresis. In M. Grenfell (ed.) *Pierre Bourdieu: Key concepts.* Durham: Acumen, pp. 126–48.

Hendrick, H. 2003. *Child welfare: Historical dimensions, contemporary debate.* Bristol: Policy Press.

Hochschild, A. 1979. Emotion work, feeling rules and social structure, *American Journal of Sociology*, 85: 551–75.

Hochschild, A. 1983 *The Managed Heart: The commercialisation of human feeling.* Berkeley CA: University of California Press

Holligan, C. 2000. Discipline and normalisation in the nursery: The Foucaultian gaze. In H. Penn (ed.) *Early Childhood services: Theory, policy and practice.* Buckingham: Open University Press, pp. 134–46.

Holloway, S. and Valentine, G. (eds) 2000. *Children's geographies: Playing, living, learning.* London: Routledge.

Hutchby, I. and Moran-Ellis, J. (eds) 1998. *Children and social competence.* London: Falmer Press.

James, A. 2000. Embodied beings: Understanding the self and the body in childhood. In A. Prout (ed.), *The body, childhood and society.* London: Routledge, pp. 19–37.

James, A. 2009. Agency. In J. Qvortrup, W. A. Corsaro and M.-S. Honig (eds), *Palgrave handbook of childhood studies.* London: Palgrave Macmillan, pp. 34–45.

James, A.L. and James, A. 2001. Tightening the net: Children, community and control. *British Journal of Sociology*, 52 (2): 211–28.

Jenks, C. 1996. *Childhood.* London: Routledge.

Martin, E. 1987. *The Woman in the Body.* Buckingham: Open University Press.

Matthews, H. et al. 2000. The unacceptable *flaneur*: The shopping mall as teenage hangout. *Childhood*, 7 (3): 279–94.

Mayall, B. 1986. *Keeping children healthy*. London: Allen and Unwin.

Mayall, B. 1994. *Negotiating health: Children at home and primary school*. London: Cassell.

Mayall, B. 1996. *Children, health and the social order*. Buckingham: Open University Press.

Mayall, B. 2002. *Towards a sociology for childhood*. Buckingham: Open University Press.

Mayall, B., Bendelow, G., Barker, S., Storey, P. and Veltman, M. 1996. *Children's health in primary schools*. London: Falmer Press.

Mortimore, P. 2013. *Education under siege: Why there is a better alternative*. Bristol: Policy Press.

Penn, H. 2011. *Quality in early childhood services: An international perspective*. Maidenhead: Open University Press.

Prendergast, S. 2000. 'To become dizzy in our turning': Girls, body maps and gender as childhood ends. In A. Prout (ed.) *The body, childhood and society*. London: Palgrave Macmillan, pp. 101–24.

Prendergast, S. and Forrest, S. 1998. Shorties, low-lifers, hardnuts and kings: Boys, emotions and embodiment in school. In G. Bendelow and S. Williams (eds) *Emotions in social life: Critical themes and contemporary issues*. London: Routledge, pp. 155–72.

Prout, A. (ed.) 2000. *The body, childhood and society*. London: Palgrave Macmillan.

Qvortrup, J. 2009 Childhood as a structural form. In J. Qvortrup, W. A. Corsaro and M.-S. Honig (eds) *The Palgrave handbook of childhood studies*. London: Palgrave Macmillan, pp. 21–33.

Qvortrup, J., Bardy, M., Sgrittta, G. and Wintersberger, H. (eds) 1994. *Childhood matters: Social theory, practice and politics*. Aldershot, Avebury Press.

Shilling, C. 1993. *The body and social theory*. London: Sage.

Shilling, C. 2005. *The body in culture, technology and society*. London: Sage.

Turner, B. S. 1992. *Regulating bodies: Essays in medical sociology*. London: Routledge.

Yelland, N. (ed.) 2010. *Contemporary perspectives on early childhood education*. Maidenhead: Open University Press.

3

Cultural Capital in the Preschool Years: Can the State 'Compensate' for the Family?

Liz Brooker

Introduction

The question posed in the title to this chapter is prompted by the current English government's apparent thinking in devising policies for young children and their families. Asking this question while thinking about Bourdieu immediately evokes the assertion made by his contemporary, the sociologist Basil Bernstein. Bernstein's article, 'Education cannot compensate for society' (1970) challenged the contemporary belief that schooling could reverse the early disadvantage experienced by children from lower social classes. The inequalities that Bernstein describes, which he saw as unevenly distributed across social groups, were very similar to those that Bourdieu was simultaneously identifying as 'forms of capital' (1997 [1986]), the most important of which in relation to school success was cultural capital. Bernstein's rationale for his assertion lay in an account of how inequalities constructed during early childhood are entrenched during the school years, and persist through the life-course. Bourdieu, by alternative routes, was tackling very similar questions: in particular, how the acquisition of life's advantages – leading in the end to knowledge and power – begins in the earliest relationships within the family, and how these advantages are legitimised by the education system. This chapter considers contemporary UK policy-making on inequality in the light of Bourdieu's explanations, and concludes that politicians' efforts to 'compensate' for family inequalities reveal a misunderstanding of how advantages are acquired.

The chapter first takes up Bourdieu's rationale for the study of everyday lives in families and institutions: to explain how social inequalities are reproduced within modern societies. In particular it focuses on Bourdieu's account of the ways in which cultural capital is acquired in the home, becomes incorporated into the child's habitus and is subsequently transposed into the field of schooling. The patterns of inequality that Bourdieu, with his colleague Passeron, described in French society as early as 1977 [1970] are equally evident in English society more than 40 years later, although the similarities may be masked by the demographic and socioeconomic changes which have occurred over this period. Secondly, I examine the policy initiatives that have been developed over recent decades, and particularly under the last two English governments, which have aimed to reduce social inequality and exclusion by bestowing various forms of educational capital on children and families deemed to lack it. I suggest that this policy approach can have only limited success, as it is based on a superficial understanding of the nature of cultural capital, and of the ways in which the cultural goods that matter in the early years are acquired. At the same time I argue for greater reliance on evidence from ethnographic research for understanding those social, economic and educational processes which construct families and children as deficient and needy before they start school.

Although Bourdieu's own projects and theorising focused on school-age children and adults, his concepts and explanations lend themselves very readily to the study of the lives of infants, toddlers and preschool children, as well as those just entering school. Self-evidently, children's construction of identities (a complex individual habitus) and advantages (in the form of social and cultural capital) deriving from the resources of the family and community are most visible in the earliest years, when their experiences are largely confined to the private sphere of the home, and the semi-private sphere of the childcare or preschool setting. What is also self-evident however is that this private sphere may be difficult for researchers to access, and that different methodologies and methods may be needed to explore individual lives within families rather than more publicly accessible aspects of life. Bourdieu's own work, after his early ethnographic studies in Algeria, was mostly large scale, using survey methods to draw findings from nationally representative samples. He did not venture into homes or scrutinise early socialisation processes.

Similarly, when formulating public policy for early childhood, governments and advisors normally rely on large-scale statistical data for evidence, and may misrecognise some of the less obvious processes in young children's experiences which qualitative work may reveal.

Identifying the sources of inequality

From the 1960s and 1970s, sociologists have sought explanations for the persistent social and economic inequalities which are associated with children's academic progress from the start of their school careers. Once it was acknowledged that IQ was malleable, and fairly evenly distributed across social groups, the question became: what is it about being brought up in a poor family which makes it more difficult for a child to succeed academically? Early debates considered both material circumstances (such as living in overcrowded accommodation, lacking books and a quiet place to study) and the cultural climate of both homes and schools (Douglas 1964; Douglas et al. 1968; Sharp and Green 1975). Bernstein (1971, 1975) was prescient in arguing that the quality of the child's home experiences and family relationships – including the forms of language used within the family, and the activities children observed or participated in – could determine, by the age of five, whether a child would be *more* or *less* prepared for school success. While some working-class children succeeded against the odds, they were the exception to a tacitly acknowledged rule that children who began school at a disadvantage were unlikely to flourish academically. Thus the logic seemed clear: children's early socialisation experiences, and the parenting practices they were offered, were responsible for their school progress, both initially, in terms of their 'school readiness', and over a longer period, in terms of their parents' 'involvement' or support for schooling. The English class system, in short, provided the blue-print for educational achievement in English schools (Douglas 1964, Douglas et al. 1968).

More recently, analysis of the British Birth Cohort studies of 1958, 1970 and 2000 (Feinstein 1998, 2003; Dearden et al. 2011) has revealed just how early in their lives children may be assigned to low-performing or high-achieving groups. Feinstein's (2003) analysis showed two crucial trends: first, that children's educational assessments are highly correlated with their social class status by the age of 22 months; second, that children from higher socioeconomic groups assessed as low-performing at 22 months are able to catch up and overtake their low-SES peers by the age of five, while high-performing children from lower social groups slowly drop behind their better-off peers. At the same time, the effects of minority ethnic status, bilingualism and gender intersect in ways which further confound the poor chances of poor children (Gillborn and Gipps 1996; Gillborn and Mirza 2000). In every case, the contrast between children's home experiences and the expectations of a resolutely middle-class school culture was seen to predict below-average academic progress.

Policymakers, recognising these statistical patterns, have consistently directed their efforts towards overturning the trends. The potential success of their efforts, however, depends on a proper understanding of the processes involved in producing the 'pupil' by the start of school, and this is where Bourdieu's account is enlightening.

'The domestic transmission of cultural capital'

In the field of education, cultural capital is the most potent form of symbolic capital, both in terms of its effectiveness (in producing good educational outcomes at the end of schooling) and of its legitimacy (it appears to have been earned rather than purchased). Bourdieu's essay, 'The Forms of Capital' (1997 [1986]) offers a concise summary of its characteristics and the sources of its power. The concept evolved, he explains

> in the course of research, as a theoretical hypothesis which made it possible to explain the unequal scholastic achievement of children originating from the different social classes by relating academic success.... to the distribution of cultural capital between the classes and class fractions. (1997: 47)

By looking at 'the specific profits which children from the different classes and class fractions can obtain in the academic market' as a return on their parents' investment, he was able to break with 'the commonsense view, which sees academic success or failure as an effect of natural aptitudes' (1997: 47). While economists had tended to explain this relationship in monetary terms (costs of tuition, purchase of books, length of schooling as opposed to earning), Bourdieu's research had revealed a more potent factor: 'the best hidden and socially most determinant educational investment, namely, the domestic transmission of cultural capital' (1997: 48). What economics, and other 'commonsense' explanations have failed to recognise, he adds, is that 'ability or talent is itself the product of an investment of time and cultural capital' so that 'the scholastic yield from educational action depends on the cultural capital previously invested by the family'(1997: 48).

So cultural capital, like all other forms of capital, is the product of labour, in this case of the time and effort invested (in traditional western societies) by mothers, or other early caregivers. It assumes different forms as the child develops. The capital acquired in the home during the early years is in an 'embodied' state: the knowledge, skills and attitudes which inform the family environment are internalised by the child, and taken with her/him to school, where they may be put into play. For the power of capital is only realised in use, and Bourdieu points out that forms of capital take effect, 'like aces in a game of cards', depending on how they are played (1987: 3–4). These advantages may subsequently be 'objectified' (as books, musical instruments and so on) and are eventually 'institutionalised' (as recognised qualifications, certificates and diplomas).

However, symbolic capital takes effect through its complex enmeshment with economic capital: while cultural capital is produced from the efforts, choices and investments of individual family members, these choices and investments may themselves be the result of inherited privileges. Those mothers (it is usually mothers) with sufficient economic capital to stay at home with their children, or to buy in early tutoring, and possessed of sufficient cultural capital of their own to pass on, can endow their children with the knowledge, skills and attitudes which will give them an advantage when they start school. As Bourdieu explains, the education system, while believing itself to be meritocratic, sanctions and legitimates this transmission of hereditary capital in the form of cultural capital, because cultural capital acquired in the home is always seen as *earned*, through the efforts of the individuals and the investment of time – 'Like the acquisition of a muscular physique or a sun tan, it cannot be done at second hand' (1997: 48). It thereby 'manages to combine the prestige of innate property with the merits of acquisition' (1997: 49).

For this reason, the early disadvantages experienced by children from homes low in cultural capital may persist through their school career. Not only will the nature of their home culture be identifiable throughout their schooling, but Bourdieu suggests it is unlikely that they will ever catch up with the children who were given a head start at home. For the real potency of cultural capital lies in its scarcity:

> any given cultural competence (e.g. being able to read in a world of illiterates) derives a scarcity value from its position in the distribution of cultural capital and yields profits of distinction for its owner. (1997: 49)

This is an important observation. Children from dominant groups, on the whole, make an early start to becoming literate: early literacy is a rare and valued commodity. By the time that children from less advantaged groups become literate, the skill they have acquired is relatively commonplace, and valued less. Thus, as overall levels of educational attainment rise, the attainments of disadvantaged groups will almost always continue to be unimpressive.

The enormous power of family cultural capital in shaping a child's future lies in the fact that, among more privileged classes, the acquisition of cultural capital begins from birth.

> The initial accumulation of cultural capital, the precondition for the fast, easy accumulation of every kind of useful cultural capital, starts at the outset, without delay, without wasted time, only for the offspring of families endowed with strong cultural capital; in this case, the accumulation period covers the whole period of socialization. (Bourdieu 1997: 49)

To compound the disadvantage of children from non-dominant groups, Bourdieu also declares that the 'negative capital' they may have acquired through their early learning in the family will need to be un-learned when they enter the education system: they have not only wasted time, but have accumulated additional obstacles to academic progress.

In summary, Bourdieu argued that French middle-class children's acquisition of cultural capital derived its effect from 'the amount of time devoted to acquiring it', which in turn depended on the family's financial ability to invest in their children's socialisation. Families from lower social groups were seen as less able to give their children a head start in these crucial years, although they might succeed in identifying some characteristics of the preferred capital of the dominant culture, and trying to emulate them. But Bourdieu emphasises that cultural capital requires the longest possible time of acquisition, and it may be too late to catch up when children begin statutory schooling.

The characteristics of cultural capital: early schooling in the UK

What is it that young children need to 'catch up on' in order to be seen as ready for school learning? As Bourdieu and Passeron (1977 [1970]) explain, the 'cultural arbitrary' ensures that knowledge and skills which are valued in some contexts may have no value in others; this is also true of early childhood education (ECE) provision. All ECE systems reflect the values circulating in their particular society: European countries, including the Nordic nations, are recognised as holding different priorities for childhood, and different goals for early education, from many English-speaking nations (Bennett 2008; Wagner and Einarsdottir 2006). In England, the early years are currently viewed as a time to become 'school-ready' in specific ways, by acquiring certain items of knowledge and skills, and certain specified social behaviours. By the time they are five years old, children have moved from preschool to primary school, and have been assessed against the 'specific areas of learning' (DfE 2012) of the Early Years Foundation Stage. These include emergent literacy skills (such as naming letters of the alphabet and the sounds they typically make); early mathematical skills (such as counting and adding small numbers); and early science and humanities knowledge such as understanding aspects of the natural and social worlds. An itemised list of 'early learning goals' or ELGs enables children to be assessed and labelled as high-performing or low-performing at the start of school. A similar list of skills identifies the social behaviours which are required of children starting school: the ability to sit quietly and listen, respect others, take turns and share. Within this framework, a child who scores low on the checklist (the Foundation Stage Profile [DfE 2012]) may legitimately be described as unready for school.

Ethnographic research, including Rist's (1970) classic study of US teachers' impressions in the first week of school, and Waterhouse's similar UK study (1991), has demonstrated the impact of such early judgements on children's careers. There is evidence that children only rarely overturn an adverse early impression, whether this is gained subjectively (on the basis of the child's appearance and behaviour, or the family's reputation) or 'objectively' through the administration of standardised tests, or preschool profiles. Since these baseline assessments rely on culturally specific knowledge such as the names of colours and shapes, or the identification of vocabulary items such as violins, windmills and turtles, they may be testing for items which lie outside the experience of children from certain groups.

It could be argued that one positive aspect of a prescriptive early curriculum is that all families, in principle, can choose to access the statutory content and 'teach' it to their children. It makes sense, similarly, for public policy to aim to supply the requisite forms of knowledge and skills to young children in order to ensure they are all 'school-ready'. This strategy of compensating for early inequalities can be implemented either directly, by providing curriculum-informed ECE for children at earlier and earlier ages, or indirectly, by teaching parents to provide more 'school-like' homes for their children (Epstein 1990). Both courses of action can be understood as attempting to supply cultural capital to young children whose homes do not naturally provide it; both seek to compensate for the assumed inadequacies of families; and both have led recent English child/family policies on inequality and social exclusion. Clearly, both also assume a deficit view of families based on a uniform set of criteria (an instance of the 'cultural arbitrary') and would be described by Bourdieu as imposing symbolic violence on the individuals who are so judged.

Cultural capital in the preschool years: alternative versions

Since the publication of the first curriculum guidance for children aged from three to five years (QCA 2000), and then of a framework for children from birth to five (DCSF 2008; DfE 2012) the preschool years have in effect constituted the start of the English National Curriculum. Children's attainment in the 'specific areas of learning' constructs a baseline for future academic performance throughout their school careers, thus fuelling teacher expectations. Children

who begin preschool demonstrating some mastery of these requirements, and can transpose this cultural capital into the field of formal
schooling, have already gained the 'head start' which Bourdieu
describes.

This 'national' curriculum, however, may be completely at vari-
ance with the 'natural' curriculum offered in families. My own ethnographic study of 16 families as their children started school (Brooker
2002) revealed a range of different parental beliefs about children's
development and learning, and their own role in supporting this.
The variation in parenting practices was cultural, informed by the
intersection of parents' socioeconomic status (which ranged from
poor to very poor) with their nationality and ethnicity (including
UK, African-Caribbean and South Asian heritages) and the individual
habitus which reflected each parent's personal experience of being
parented, and of education, employment and migration. In consequence, the 'curriculum' each had in mind for their child combined
aspects of their inherited knowledge and their current awareness; and
it frequently differed slightly for each of their children, as their expectations for a particular child were informed by that child's position
in the family, their sex, and the child's perceived individual tempera-
ment and potential.

Fundamentally, the study showed that each parent's goals and
expectations for each child reflected their understanding of the role
and status of young children in general: what was the purpose of early
childhood? For parents recently migrated from South Asian villages,
the 'natural' curriculum for their four-year-old girl might involve
teaching her to perform household chores, including caring for babies
and toddlers. At the same time, such parents exhorted their little girls
to 'sit still, listen and study hard' when they started school. A similar
family's curriculum for their young son might involve accompanying
male relatives to the mosque and sometimes to their work in shops
and restaurants, learning the early books which precede the Qur'an,
and establishing appropriate social relationships with adults in the
community. Like their sisters, boys were also strictly instructed to sit
still and listen when they got to school – to 'learn from the teacher'.
The notion that parents were responsible for imparting the content
of the official curriculum to their preschool children was quite
unfamiliar to them, unless they had previously seen older children
through primary school (Brooker 2003).

In other families the reverse was true: some parents believed that the preschool years were a chance for children to 'get ahead', and that the parents' role was to put their child in the way of gaining as much advancement as possible. These, mostly English-heritage, families, had an idea of the curriculum which was relatively similar to that of the national framework. As one mother said, 'I taught them to say their colours, I always said, "a blue car, a red bus", saying the colour first, so they learned it'. A Bangladeshi mother, by contrast, expressed her surprise at being asked if she had taught her daughter the names of colours: 'Why would I do that? No, we don't do that. If I ask her "Do you want to wear your pink dress?" she knows which one I mean, she says "yes"'.

While Bourdieu emphasises the power of the cultural arbitrary in any society, which is imposed from above, he recognises that culture itself is arbitrary: that there is no objectively right or wrong way to bring up young children. Instead every culture, and every type of cultural capital, derives from the field of practice in which it develops. However, the role of the state includes preserving and reproducing the culture of dominant groups in society. In this sense all cultures are *not* equal: in the English education system, knowledge of the Qur'an is *not* as valuable as knowledge of English nursery rhymes, because power resides with those brought up on nursery rhymes. Families seeking access to power for their children must get their feet on the ladder when they are very young, if they are not to be marginalised by the education system. Hence there is a kind of logic in the argument for increasing social justice and equality in a society by offering the cultural capital which is acquired naturally in dominant groups to those who may otherwise miss out on it.

Interventions: the state compensating for the family

The history of direct intervention in children's family experiences goes back a long way, but its most famous landmark was the introduction of Head Start in the USA in the 1960s (Vinovskis 2005), as part of Lyndon Johnson's 'Great Society' programme. Research on the effectiveness of Head Start, in which poor Black children were brought into day care and enrichment projects, also highlighted a strong programme of support for parents and parenting which inspired a series of subsequent initiatives. Globally, parenting interventions were evaluated as an effective means to reverse the life-chances of disadvantaged children through involving their parents (almost always mothers) in some of the lengthy investments of time and skills which were understood to promote school-readiness (Evans 2006). Among the many variants were programmes which sought to improve parents' own educational attainments, and those which instructed mothers in how to instruct their children in curriculum areas, such as the Turkish Early Enrichment Project (Kagitcibasi et al. 2001). In the UK, burgeoning support for 'parent involvement' (Bastiani 1993, Epstein 1990) focused most strongly on the primary school years, until increasingly it was recognised that many of children's key opportunities and advantages had been established before they were five. From this point on, research-informed interventions have been directed at ever younger age groups.

Describing and promoting the Home Learning Environment (HLE)

A key contribution to English government thinking on children's early learning was made by a large-scale longitudinal study, the Effective Provision of Preschool Education (EPPE) project (Sylva et al. 2004). In addition to describing, from an analysis of 3000 children's experiences, what kind of preschool education was most effective, the EPPE study identified a set of factors in the Home Learning Environment (HLE) (Melhuish et al. 2001, 2008), which were associated with children's good development and school-readiness – in other words, with their acquisition of cultural capital in a form which could be transposed from home into the field of schooling. These elements, only slightly reconfigured, have been adopted in analyses of the Millennium Cohort Study data (Dearden et al. 2011, De la Rochebrouchard 2012) and are taken as a proxy for good parenting and hence as a framework for intervening in children's lives from the age of two. The original HLE indicators included two separate scales – social factors, such as playing with friends, eating meals together and having a regular bedtime, and educational factors, such as visiting the library and reading with adults. Further analysis suggested that the seven items in the educational scale were the most significant for predicting children's school- or preschool-readiness, and so these are the indicators now used. They are: being read to; visiting the library; playing with numbers; painting and drawing; being taught the names of letters; being taught the names of numbers; learning songs, rhymes and poems (Dearden et al. 2011).

New Labour policies 1997–2010

In the years following the election of 1997, government policy on inequality and exclusion took a largely benevolent approach to parents, who were seen as doing their best in difficult circumstances. Universal support for young families was provided first through Sure Start Local Programmes and then through the ambitious Sure Start Children's Centre programme, whose National Evaluation (Belsky et al. 2007) helped to identify the most effective means to support families. The current Children's Centre programme was intended to build on these strengths by offering a supportive and inclusive resource for all families (Goff et al. 2013).

Typical of the stance taken by the Labour government was an evaluation of services (Evangelou et al. 2008) which took a relatively liberal approach to supporting parents in creating school-like cultural capital. Unlike traditional approaches which viewed the teaching of letters and numbers as essential to boost children's chances, this evaluation worked from the assumption that for young children, learning to play or 'learning through play' was the best preparation for formal learning; hence, teaching parents to play with their children could have long-term benefits (Evangelou and Wild 2014). The evaluation of initiatives included a long-standing project called PEEP (Peers Early Education Partnership) which brought together mothers and their young children in supported play sessions so that mothers could learn (from participating in activities and observing the practice modelled by play-workers) how to play with their children in ways which might have useful educational outcomes (Evangelou and Wild 2014).

These initiatives formed part of the Ten-Year Strategy for Childcare (HM Treasury 2004), which in turn was informed by evidence from large-scale studies; these studies, while benefitting from representative national samples, were restricted in scope by their reliance on survey and assessment data, which gave no insights into children's individual home experiences. Even more seriously, such studies tended to create a universal model of 'best practice in parenting', aligned to dominant ideas of cultural development, which was insensitive to many of the parenting practices of minority groups (Brooker 2003). Once such a normative model was in place, families could be judged by their ability to conform to it.

Coalition policies 2010–14

Under the Coalition government of 2010–15, a harsher economic climate has helped to reinforce a more negative stance towards parents and young children, whose 'best interests' it seems are served by policies to bring more parents into line with normative mainstream practices. The universal services of Children's Centres, which fostered social integration, have been replaced by 'targeted' services for the '120,000 most troubled families' identified by the government's statisticians as in need of remediation (Mathers et al. 2014). The characteristics of the HLE have been reduced to minimum requirements for parenting, and checks on children at the age of 24 months now identify those families who are already failing, and require intervention in the form of state-provided day care or parenting classes.[1]

By reducing 'good parenting' and a good home environment to a handful of ticks on a tick-list, such policies tend to ignore the wealth of different but arguably adequate parenting styles revealed by research (for instance Göncü et al. 2000), and to impose a cultural arbitrary on the nation's diverse families. The possession of a library ticket offers a prime example of the rather tokenistic indicators which have become proxy predictors for future academic success: the child who visits a library is assumed to possess important cultural capital, which is lacked by the child who does not. The many possible variants on this simple equation are ignored (the child who owns a ticket but rarely visits the library; the child with no ticket but a collection of favourite books at home; the child who looks at older siblings' school books; the child who is bought a comic every week; the child whose grandparent shows him or her their hobby magazines). As countless studies have shown (Heath 1983; Gregory et al. 2004) there are many routes to early literacy, and possessing a library ticket does not guarantee access to this scarce resource.[2]

After identifying the nation's troubled families, the Coalition (while closing hundreds of children's centres and nursery schools: *Guardian* 22 February 2014) launched a major initiative to rectify them, by creating up to 260,000 free nursery places for the two-year-old children growing up in the poorest families (Mathers et al. 2014). The evaluation of an earlier pilot involving 13,500 children had however shown that the gains in terms of children's cognitive and social development, as well as the improvements to their HLE, were vanishingly small in comparison with the money invested (Smith et al. 2009). Smith et al.'s analysis produced only one positive outcome: that children in the highest quality childcare settings had eight more words in their vocabulary (of the 100 test items) than children who either had no intervention or were in lower-quality settings. A re-evaluation when the pilot children started school (Maisey et al. 2013) found that: 'There was no evidence of an improvement in the EYFS profile scores of the pilot group at age five when compared with children in the matched comparison group' (Maisey et al. 2013: 7).

Mathers et al.'s (2014) analysis of these developments concludes that the poor outcomes to date are due to the poor quality of available nursery provision.[3] A more challenging conclusion might be that one year of part-time nursery attendance is insignificant in comparison with the long-term investment which more privileged parents can make in their children. In Bourdieu's terms: how can a short-term intervention 'compensate' for low levels of cultural capital acquired in the family?

Alternative approaches to cultural capital: learning from ethnographic methods

As the above allusion to ethnographies of life in families has suggested, ethnographic approaches are arguably the optimal route to understanding children's early experiences in the private sphere of the home – the sphere in which cultural capital is first constructed. Meaningful findings from traditional ethnographies are however hard to achieve, requiring a lengthy investment of time, effort and economic capital: Heath's (1983) ground-breaking study of Appalachian families, for instance, derives its power from the researcher's many years of physical presence in the locality. Hence the traditional ethnographic strategies of looking and listening – observing and interviewing – may need to take new forms, overturning the once strict paradigm boundary between quantitative and qualitative studies.

Data from the 'All Saints' study' of 16 families described above (Brooker 2002, 2003) derived from a year spent attempting to gain insights into the families' lives from the perspectives of the children and parents, while simultaneously studying the children's much more visible lives in the classroom. The inquiry called on the traditional techniques of ethnography, including lengthy semi-structured interviews, which were partly inspired by the methods of the large-scale longitudinal study of the Newsons (1963, 1968). These authors' insights into the minutiae of parenting practices, and their subtle shaping of children's development, revealed in detail how small individual differences can have large and long-term effects, including on the construction of school-readiness and positive dispositions.

An additional challenge in the All Saints' study was that 8 of the 16 families spoke little or no English in the home, so that some parents' views had to be accessed through an interpreter, and required lengthy reflection and discussion before a culturally meaningful account could be achieved (Brooker 2003). It was for this reason that, in addition to the individual interviews with parents, the more structured tool of a 'daily diary' was developed, as a means to gain a fuller picture of each individual child's life at home at the age of four.

Accessing the cultural capital of homes: daily diaries

I introduced the 'diary' itself (a sheet of A4 paper, initially marked with times from 6:00 a.m. to 9 p.m.) to the parent during a home visit, if necessary through an interpreter, and I described it as a way for me to get a better idea of how the child spent her or his time at home. Trust and familiarity had already been established through frequent contacts in the classroom, and friendly support for the child, over a period of two to three months. With the tape recorder running, the parent and I (and possibly an interpreter) sat side by side and worked through the list of times as prompts to describe the events of the previous day:

> Parent: (pointing to first time) Still asleep then...
> Researcher: So when did she...?
> Parent(pointing):   A bit before 7 o'clock... she hears her brother...
> Researcher: What does she hear?
> Parent: Sometimes he puts his Play Station on loud, sometimes he comes in and tells her Wake Up!

Parents soon warmed to this discussion and evidently enjoyed talking about their child's 'day'. These informal narratives were pinned down both by the times on the sheet and by my own occasional prompts: *You dropped in to see his auntie on the way back – do you do that most days?* The transcripts and scribbled records revealed much that proved of interest in the analysis of children's social, cultural and developmental experiences: where children slept and with whom; whether they washed and dressed themselves, watched TV before breakfast, helped with younger children or household chores; if they accompanied siblings to school and into their classrooms; what they generally talked about on their trips; who visited the house during the day, who watched television or looked at books with the child; how they occupied themselves during the day; what happened after older siblings returned from school; when they ate and slept.

While each of the diaries recorded the day's experiences of an individual child, many of the themes identified by the Newsons (1968) emerged as inter-family or intra-group practices. One clear example was responsibility. Both the interview and the diary discussion, for instance, revealed the extent to which children took responsibility for themselves (self-care), for others such as younger siblings, or for small household tasks which were theirs alone (clearing the breakfast table, or bringing in the milk bottles from the front step). These small details not only confirmed broad cultural patterns, but mapped on to the recognised developmental indicators discussed for instance by Melhuish et al. (2008) in evaluating Sure Start outcomes.

An interview question about children's participation in family literacy activities was equally revealing. A mother who had invested in a collection of children's books from a mail order firm, and whose child would score high on a 'books in the home' rating, revealed that *'he's not allowed to touch them until he's older, we don't want them scribbled on so we'll let him look at them after he's learned to read'*. Another mother, in a home superficially devoid of books except for the Qur'an, indicated a heap of old comics under an armchair, and reported that her child constantly enjoyed them, and also liked to sit on her lap while she read 'romances from the library'. These potentially significant variations in the form, quantity and quality of cultural capital available to the child were unlikely to emerge except through extended discussion of this kind, and would not be accessed through a questionnaire survey. Instead the home which included a collection of children's books, despite the fact that they were unread, might be ranked highly on a rating of the home learning environment, while the other home, though rich in interest and stimulation, would score very poorly on the HLE indicators.

While data analysis inevitably requires some reduction and simplification of the information acquired through ethnographic methods, it remains important to hold on to the detailed content from which these broader themes emerge, to avoid the kind of oversimplification which leads to the production of crude indicators – library tickets, number of books in the home, or even the mother's possession of a university degree. Children's acquisition of school-like cultural capital is far more subtle than this.

Early learning in the home: how might it mediate entry to education?

To understand how some of the early experiences described here take effect in the longer term, we need to return again to Bourdieu's account. Cultural capital acquired in the home is a complex phenomenon, which means that using it as a predictor for future success is a risky enterprise. Some of the reasons for this are addressed here.

Cultural capital in young children has numerous aspects

When identifying 'advantage' in children under five, we have to consider all aspects of development. Physical growth, including gross and fine motor skills, are closely entwined with other culturally valued skills as well as with nutrition, exercise and housing conditions: playing the violin or piano at an early age are examples of valued skills in some societies, while in others the emphasis may be on calligraphy or origami. Even in young children, preferences for body shape or movement, as well as for skin colour and hair quality, are similarly inflected by culture and by gender. Bourdieu's account of early cultural capital as embodied is true in this physical sense as much as in the sense that a child's learning of all kinds is internalised and goes with them everywhere.

Cultural capital is only valuable in relation to particular fields of practice

Since culture is arbitrary, the valued qualities acquired in one field of practice, such as the home, may lose their value in another, such as the school. A child who is highly esteemed within the home and community field for their ability to sit still and silent during religious worship, or to memorise Qur'anic verses, or to take care of a crying infant, may not demonstrate any of the qualities which are valued in the field of education, such as showing initiative and outgoing behaviours in the classroom. Bourdieu, who described capital as being transposable across the boundaries between fields, rarely took account of the increasing plurality of values in many societies.

Cultural capital is invested, by the child and family, in accordance with the child's habitus

Bourdieu's many references to the nature of the habitus can leave this as a somewhat slippery concept, and one which is hard to pin down in research data. But essentially this 'system of dispositions' (1990 [1980]) is a tendency in the child to approach daily experience in certain ways: with determination and resilience or uncertainty and a faint heart; with confidence and self-esteem or fear of failure; with ambition to compete and succeed, or with a preference for holding back and watching. These dispositions, described in traditional developmental psychology as innate or inherited traits (Katz 1995), are learned through early experiences with adults, and reflect those adults' own individual and collective habitus, which may include their own history of education or employment, of migration or subjection, or of successfully partaking of a dominant status in society. The habitus is what may dispose a child to invest actively in their own success, ensuring that a teacher acknowledges their achievements (and their parents') or to stay quiet and accept a lesser place in the field of power that exists in the classroom. While the habitus is transformed, little by little, over time and through experience, early impressions and assessments of children by teachers may leave permanent marks on their educational trajectory.

The consequence of these and other factors is that entry to the field of schooling, governed as it is by the cultural arbitrary of the dominant group, may be the moment in which children's and families' deficits are first constructed. Failure to complete the two-year-old check-list, failure to conform to social behaviours in preschool, delay in learning the English ABCs, all tend to constitute a failing child where no failure was previously apparent. Meanwhile those strengths of families and children which are absent from the checklist remain invisible: rather than 'compensating' for the family, early interventions may label the family and child in ways which disadvantage them.

Can the state compensate for the family? Alternative approaches

As this chapter has argued, intervention policies designed to make up identified deficits in the parenting practices of poor families are for a number of reasons unlikely to meet their targets. Attempts by the state to first, define good parenting in the form of a seven-item tick-list, second, assess diverse families by these criteria, identifying many as deficient, third, impose top-down short term measures such as day care or parenting courses on such families, and four, assess children on a prescriptive list of knowledge and skills at the start of their school career, do not come close to reflecting Bourdieu's account of how cultural capital is acquired from birth, absorbed into the primary habitus, and invested into institutions outside the home. Instead they promote the labelling of non-traditional families as dysfunctional, and of children from marginalised groups as low achievers.

An alternative approach to combating inequality would be to recognise the damaging effect of the cultural arbitrary on families outside the dominant group, and the symbolic violence which is employed in enforcing it. Assessing children and families against narrow criteria has no place in creating inclusion and equality. Instead (following practice in New Zealand: Carr 2014), families themselves could contribute to the assessment of their child's development, in an equal partnership with educators, while the preschool curriculum could attempt to incorporate the 'funds of knowledge' (Moll et al. 1992; Hedges 2010) – values, knowledge and skills – of families and communities.

In the longer term, as Bourdieu recognised, the reproduction of social and educational inequality can only be ameliorated by the reduction of economic inequality: by redistributive fiscal policies. In the short term, it seems clear that current policies are based on a misunderstanding of the nature of cultural capital, which risks exacerbating, rather than compensating for, the diminished life-chances of children from poor families.

Notes

1. Among the more surreal of the Coalition's initiatives (CentreForum 2011) was the notion of a 'Five a day' parenting code (resembling an ongoing 'Five a day' fruit and vegetable campaign). Completing this check-list ('read to your child for 15 minutes; play with your child on the floor for 10 minutes; talk to your child for 20 minutes with the TV switched off' etc.) was intended to meet all children's developmental requirements.
2. Equally the indicator 'child has a regular bedtime' is one which, though derived from the national sample of the EPPE study, exemplifies a cultural arbitrary which ignores the culturally diverse routines of families. While statistically such an indicator is seen to act as a proxy for 'organised' as opposed to dysfunctional or 'troubled' families, in individual cases it may simply reflect the cultural organisation of family life and child develop-ment within a particular community, where children's sleep patterns have been accommodated to family and employment needs (Brooker 2003).
3. This conclusion opens up yet another contentious field for exploration: Mathers and her colleagues judge 'quality' by the use of standardised scales (ECERS, ITERS) which describe yet another monocultural and normative model which has been heavily critiqued (Dahlberg and Moss 2005). These issues are too large for further exploration here, but they muddy the waters of any statistical analysis, and risk undermining any claims made for the intervention

References

Bastiani, J. 1993. Parents as partners. In P. Munn (ed.) *Parents and schools*. London: Routledge.

Belsky, J., Barnes, J. and Melhuish, E.C. (eds) 2007. *The National Evaluation of Sure Start: does area-based early intervention work?* Bristol: The Policy Press.

Bennett, J. 2008. Early childhood services in the OECD countries: Review of the literature and current policy in the early childhood field. Innocenti Working Papers. 2008–01. Florence: UNICEF

Bernstein, B. 1970. Education cannot compensate for society, *New Society*, 26th February.

Bernstein, B. 1971. *Class, codes and control*: (volume 1) *Theoretical studies towards a sociology of language*. London: Routledge and Kegan Paul

Bernstein, B. 1975. *Class, codes and control*: (volume 3) *Towards a theory of educational transmissions*. London: Routledge and Kegan Paul.

Bourdieu, P. 1990 [1987]. *In other words: Essays toward a reflexive sociology*. Cambridge: Polity.

Bourdieu, P. 1990 [1980]. *The logic of practice*. Cambridge: Polity.

Bourdieu, P. 1997 [1986]. The forms of capital. Reprinted in Halsey et al. (eds), *Education, culture, economy, and society*. Oxford: Oxford University Press.

Bourdieu, P. and Passeron, J-C. 1977[1970]. *Reproduction in education, culture and society*. London: Sage.

Brooker, L. 2002. *Starting school: young children learning cultures*. Maidenhead: Open University Press.

Brooker, L. 2003. Learning how to learn: parental ethnotheories and young children's preparation for school, *International Journal of Early Years Education*, 11 (2): 117–28.

Carr, M. 2014. Assessment of play. In L. Brooker, M. Blaise and S. Edwards (eds), *The Sage handbook of play and learning in early childhood*. London: Sage.

CentreForum. 2011. http://www.centreforum.org/index.php/14-news/releases/229-5-a-day-positive-response.

Dahlberg, G. And Moss, P. 2005. *Ethics and Politics in Early Childhood Education*. Abingdon: RoutledgeFalmer.

Department for Children, Schools and Families (DCSF) 2008. *Early years foundation stage*. Nottingham: DCSF Publications.

Dearden, L., Sibieta, L. and Sylva, K. 2011. The socio-economic gradient in early child outcomes: evidence from the Millennium Cohort Study, *Longitudinal and Life Course Studies*, 2 (1): 19–40.

De la Rochebrochard, E. 2012. The home learning environment as measured at age 3, Millennium Cohort Study Data Note 1. London: Economic and Social Research Council.

Department for Education 2012. *The early years foundation stage*. https://www.gov.uk/early-years-foundation-stage.

Department for Education 2012. *The early years foundation stage profile*. https://www.gov.uk/early-years-foundation-stage.

Douglas, J. 1964. *The home and the school*. London: McGibbon and Kee.

Douglas, J, Ross, J. and Simpson, R. 1968. *All our future*. London: Peter Davies.

Epstein, J. 1990. School and family connections, *Marriage and Family Review*, 15 (2): 99–126.

Evans, J. 2006. *Parenting programmes: an important ECD intervention strategy*. Paper commissioned for the EFA Global Monitoring Report 2007, Strong foundations. (efareport@unesco.org).

Evangelou, M., Sylva, K., Edwards, A. and Smith, T. 2008. *Supporting parents in promoting early learning: the evaluation of the early learning partnership project*. London: DCSF.

Evangelou, M. and Wild, M. 2014. Promoting social inclusion: connecting home and educational play. In L. Brooker, M. Blaise and S. Edwards (eds), *Handbook of play and learning in early childhood*. London: Sage, pp. 378–90.

Feinstein, L. 1998. Which children succeed and why? What are the keys to success for British schoolchildren? *New Economy*, 5 (2): 99–103.

Feinstein, L. 2003. Inequality in the early cognitive development of British children in the 1970 Cohort, *Economica*, 70: 73–97.

Gillborn, D. and Gipps, C. 1996. *Recent research on the achievement of ethnic minority pupils*. London: HMSO.

Gillborn, D. and Mirza, H. 2000. *Educational inequality. Mapping race, class and gender*. London: Ofsted.

Goff, J., Hall, J., Sylva, K., Smith, T., Smith, G., Eisenstadt, N. and Sammons, P. 2013. *Evaluation of children's centres in England, Strand 3: Delivery of family services*. London: Department for Education.

Göncü, A., Mistry, J. & Mosier, C. 2000, Cultural variations in the play of toddlers. *International journal of behavioural development.* 24 (3): 321–9.

Gregory, E., Long, S. and Volk, D. 2004. *Many pathways to literacy.* London: Routledge Falmer.

Guardian newspaper, 22.04.2014. Letter to the editor from ECE experts.

Heath, S.B. 1983. *Ways with words: Language, life and work in communities and classrooms.* Cambridge: Cambridge University Press.

Hedges, H. 2010. Whose goals and interests? The interface of children's play and teachers' pedagogical perspectives. In L. Brooker and S. Edwards (eds), *Engaging play.* Maidenhead: Open University Press, pp. 25–38.

HM Treasury. 2004. *Choice for parents, the best start for children: a ten year strategy for childcare.* HMSO: Norwich.

Kagitcibasi, C., Sunar, D., Bekman, S., Baydar, N. and Cemalcilar, Z. 2009. Continuing effects of early enrichment in adult life: the Turkish Early Enrichment Project 22 years later, *Journal of Applied Developmental Psychology,* 30: 764–79.

Katz, L. 1995. Dispositions: definitions and implications for early childhood practice, *Talks with Teachers,* Norwood, NJ: Ablex, pp. 47–69.

Maisey, R., Speight, S. and Marsh, V. with Philo, D. 2013. *The early education pilot for two year old children: Age five follow-up research report.* London: NatCen Social Research, Department for Education.

Mathers, S., Eisenstadt, N., Sylva, K., Soukakou, E. and Ereky-Stevens, K. 2014. *Sound foundations: A literature review.* London: The Sutton Trust.

Melhuish, E., Sylva, K., Sammons, P., Siraj-Blatchford, I. and Taggart, B. 2001. *The Effective Provision of Pre-school Education Project, Technical Paper 7: Social/behavioural and cognitive development at 3–4 years in relation to family background.* London: Institute of Education /Department for Education and Science.

Melhuish, E., Sylva, K., Sammons, P., Siraj-Blatchford, I., Taggart, B. and Phan, M. 2008. Effect of home learning environment and preschool centre experience upon literacy and numeracy development in early primary school, *Journal of Social Issues,* 64 (1):157–88.

Moll, L., Amanti, C., Neff, D., and Gonzalez, N. 1992, Funds of knowledge for teaching: using a qualitative approach to connect homes and classrooms. *Theory into practice.32 (2) 132–41.*

Newson, E. and Newson, J. 1963. *Infant care in an urban community,* London: Allen and Unwin.

Newson, E. and Newson, J. 1968. *Four years old in an urban community,* London: Allen and Unwin.

Qualifications and Curriculum Authority (QCA). 2000. *Curriculum guidance for the foundation stage.*

Rist, R. 1970. Student social class and teacher expectation: The self-fulfilling prophecy in ghetto education, *Harvard Educational Review,* 40 (3): 411–51.

Sharp, R. and Green, A. 1975. *Education and social control. A study in progressive primary education.* London: Routledge and Kegan Paul.

Smith, R., Purdon, S., Schneider, V., La Valle, I., Wollny, I., Owen, R., Bryson, C., Mathers, S., Sylva, K. and Lloyd, E. 2009. *Early education pilot for two year old children evaluation.* DCSF research report.

Sylva, K., Melhuish, E.C, Sammons, P., Siraj-Blatchford, I. and Taggart, B. 2004. *The effective provision of preschool education (EPPE) project, Technical paper 12: The final report.* London DFES/Institute of Education.

Vinovskis, M. 2005. *The birth of Head Start.* Chicago, IL: University of Chicago Press.

Wagner, J. and Einarsdottir, J. (eds). 2006. *Nordic childhoods and early education.* Greenwich, Ct: Information Age Publishing.

Waterhouse, S. 1991. *First episodes: Pupil careers in the early years of school,* London: Falmer.

4

Between Young Children and Adults: Practical Logic in Families' Lives

Pascale Garnier

Introduction

Bourdieu devotes little attention to childhood in his empirical studies, and inscribes it in a theoretical conception of socialisation.[1] It seems that for him, the younger the child, the more strongly the structure of the social world is internalised, shaping the future social trajectory of the adult (Bourdieu 1977). This is evident in *Distinction* (1984), where Bourdieu highlights the importance of early childhood in the constitution of dispositions in relation to the position of the family in the social space. I would like to show that this conception of social-isation can be developed, through considering my empirical work concerning family practices in the field of early childhood education and using Bourdieu's *theory of practice*. His large and consistent theo-retical concern contrasts a *practical logic* engaged in by individuals acting in the midst of a situation with a *theoretical logic* that considers social practices from a distance as objects of thought. Articulating the empirical research study and the theoretical thinking is a necessity in Bourdieu's idea of sociological research. In contrast to the divi-sion of labour, which is also a division of power, between 'theori-cism' and 'methodologism', between the 'great theorists' who are not concerned about facts and avoid fieldwork, and the empiricists who lean toward the illusion that the facts speak by and for themselves, Bourdieu argues that research must be at the same time empirically and theoretically grounded, including an explanation of the philo-sophical anthropology that it involves. His approach pays great attention to the epistemological, social and political gaps between individuals engaged in action, and the sociologist's work.

The first part of this chapter highlights the differences between practical logic and theoretical logic, focusing on the roots of these concepts in the phenomenological philosophy of Merleau-Ponty, and the theoretical implications of using these notions in considering the time of practices. In the second part of the chapter, I present an empirical case study concerning the use of home workbooks by young children in France. Though there is not space here for a complete analysis of the field of production of these kinds of goods, it is possible to show how they must be understood in the light of relationships between families, institutions and markets, and what kind of social definitions of childhood these workbooks involve. After an account of the methods used, I give an analysis of families' practices, focused on the importance of tensions or conflicts between children and parents, and demonstrate how the use of home workbooks is far from a simple pedagogical transmission, as if young children were a kind of blank slate. I also use the example of the use (or not) of home workbooks to show how parents' practices take into account both the present and the future of their child. Finally I point to parents' reflexivity toward their practices and, in doing so, to the tension between practical logic and theoretical logic in family life itself.

From theoretical logic to practical logic (and back again)

The ambition of establishing a theory of practice is a permanent object of thought in Bourdieu's work from the 1970s, from *Outline of a Theory of Practice* (1977 [1972]), to his last publications, such as *Science of Science and Reflexivity* (2004 [2001]), and included in *The Logic of Practice* (1990 [1980a]), *An Invitation to Reflexive Sociology* with Loïc Wacquant (1992), and *Pascalian Meditations* (2000 [1997]), among other publications. Bourdieu's work evolves and changes, but the theoretical difference between a practical logic and a theoretical logic can be considered as a permanent touchstone of his social theory. It is certainly grounded on his ethnological studies in Algeria and in the South of France at the beginning of his career and is deeply rooted in his own 'split habitus', described in his self-analysis by his own social trajectory (Bourdieu, 2004).[2] He tends to prioritise practical reason and to consider human activities as practices.

The critical challenge of embodiment: the phenomenological stake

When Bourdieu explains the specificity of the logic of practice, he often refers directly or implicitly to the phenomenology of Merleau-Ponty, as many have noted: Wacquant (1992), Butler (1999), Frère (2011), among others. To explain a pre-reflexive and infra-conscious mastering of the social world as the fundamental conception of the 'practical sense', Wacquant (1992: 20) refers to Merleau-Ponty's idea of an 'antepredicative unity of the world and our life'. This means that the phenomenologist gives the ontological priority to our embodied beings in the present and in the cultural world. He describes an existence without any distance or representation: 'my body has its world, or understands its world without having to pass through representations, without submitting itself to an objectivising function' (Merleau-Ponty, quoted in Frère 2011: 164). The phenomenologist deals with an immediate understanding of the cultural world, in action, before a conscious and reflexive representation of the object and the body. In situated action, the experience of one's own embodied being is opposed to the reflective movement that disentangles the object from the subject and the subject from the object. 'Things and my body are made from the same stuff', writes Merleau-Ponty (1968), underlining an ontological complicity with the world where subject and object are confused, or more exactly, wrap around and encroach themselves upon each other.

For the phenomenologist there will always be a gap between our ontological complicity with the world and its representation and objectification, as well as a gap between the time of action itself, and the time after or before, when action can be considered as a thing, can be a matter of representation, of thinking, of language. The attempts to take into account our immediate familiarity with the world need operations of reconstitution that are always secondary: 'the reflection recuperates everything except itself as an effort of recuperation, it clarifies everything except its own role' (Merleau-Ponty 1968: 33). The representation of our being-in-the-world cannot reach immediacy: 'A lost immediacy, arduous to restore, will, if we do restore it, bear within itself the sediment of the critical procedures through which we have found it anew; it will therefore not be the immediate' (Merleau-Ponty 1968: 122). For Merleau-Ponty, the relationships between adults and children are also immediately practical and living relations, owing to their shared existence of being-in-the-world. Their production as objects of knowledge requires a critical reflexivity aware of the weight of our conception of childhood upon the life of the child: 'We must progressively disentangle what comes from us from what is his own being... With sufficient critique, we can hope to constitute a real knowledge' (Merleau-Ponty 1988: 90).

From phenomenology to social sciences: a translation

Similarly to Merleau-Ponty's emphasis on our entanglement with the world, Bourdieu writes of our ontological complicity with the social world, grounded in our embodied and situated existence: 'The actor engaged in practice knows the world, but with a knowledge, as Merleau-Ponty has shown, that is not based on an external relation of a knowing conscience' (Bourdieu 2000: 170). Bourdieu also refers to Merleau-Ponty in his consideration of this symbolical mastering as an action upon an action: 'produced by an "operation of the second power" which, as Merleau-Ponty observes, "presupposes the structures it analyses" and more or less rigorously accounts for them' (Bourdieu 1977: 20). But there is a distance between the philosophical approach of our embodied being-in-the-world and sociology as a scientific knowledge of social facts, as Wacquant has underlined: 'The peculiar difficulty of sociology, then, is to produce a precise science of an imprecise, fuzzy, woolly reality' (Wacquant 1992: 23). Distinguishing sociology from philosophy as a science grounded on empirical data, the problem of the gap between our embodied existence and representation becomes for Bourdieu the question of how individuals acquire a symbolical mastering of their practices and how the sociologist himself works with their representations.

For the sociologist, the problem lies in translating practices into representations, choosing a language for describing the practices he wants to analyse. The concept of *habitus*, related to the individual, and the concept of *field*, related to the situation, represent together the translation of our being-in-the-world for Bourdieu's sociological thinking, even though he is aware of the difficulty of this translation:

This is the most complicated problem that we can think of, because it requires that we think with what we are thinking and this is determined, at least partially, by what we want to think: so I have good reasons, I say it sincerely, not to speak about it as it should be spoken about. (Bourdieu 1980: 88)[3]

The question becomes that of the social conditions in which we can take into account the world and our lives as objects of representation: 'What has to be objectified is not the lived experience of the knowing subject, but the social conditions of possibility, and therefore the effects and limits, of this experience, and, among other things, of the act of objectification' (Bourdieu 2004: 93). At the same time, the question is how the practice of the sociologist himself is a specific case of translation, an objectification of people's practices, including their own translation from a practical mastery to a symbolic mastery of their practices. For Bourdieu, this necessarily involves an objectification of the operations of objectification, a critical reflexivity, which goes hand-in-hand with a permanent fight against intellectualism, for 'a scientific practice which does not question itself does not really know what it is doing' (Bourdieu and Wacquant 1992: 208).

The scholastic illusion

Against intellectualism, Bourdieu refers to the *scholastic illusion,* the temptation to apply a theoretical logic to analysing social practices, instead of taking into account the specificity of a practical logic:

Misunderstanding or forgetting the relationship of immanence to a world which is not perceived as a world, as an object placed in front of a perceptive subject, conscious of himself as a spectacle or representation that is able to be seen with a simple glance, is without doubt the elementary and original form of the scholastic illusion. (Bourdieu 2000: 170)

He refers also to a *scholastic disposition,* a bias based on an intellectual attitude toward the world, which reasons as if agents were rational actors, and also denies their own situated conditions.

The knowledge of practice is always local and can be considered as incoherent from the position of theoretical logic:

Practice has a logic which is not that of the logician. This has to be acknowledged in order to avoid asking of it more logic than it can give, thereby condemning oneself either to wring incoherences out of it or to thrust a forced coherence upon it. (Bourdieu 1990: 86)

Scholastic illusion leads to a miscomprehension of action and the specific time of action; it goes along with retrospective illusion and teleological illusion (Bourdieu 1980). Practices are completely in the present but at the same time they are filled with a practical intentionality that is completely different from conscious reason, calculation, planning for the future. Bourdieu describes practical intention as an 'attention to the world, as that of the athlete who is about to jump, a corporeal tension, active and constructed toward an imminent future' (Bourdieu 2000: 172). It can be understood as a 'posture' in the sense given by Wallon (1970), a plastic corporeal attitude of the body that gives birth to action, inscribing in advance the situation in the gesture itself without other representation.

This is why the time of action is a present oriented toward the future and filled with past. It has nothing in common with a conscious project of action that can be planned before and it is also completely different from a perspective *a posteriori*, giving the result of the action, from an external point of view, as if it were the goal. To forget the temporality of action in the practical logic of action itself is to theorise social life as mechanistic, and to substitute the social production of time with a collection of heterogeneous moments. Instead of a linear, continuous and homogeneous conception of time often produced by theorisation, Bourdieu urges for the importance of uncertainty: 'To reintroduce uncertainty is to reintroduce time, with its rhythm, its orientation, its irreversibility, substituting the dialectic of strategies for the mechanics of the model, but without falling into the imaginary anthropology of "rational actor" theories' (Bourdieu 1990: 99). The idea of *strategy* must not be confused with a rational action, deliberate will or conscious choice toward the future. It is rather the 'feel for the game', making the good choice without choosing, which fits the situation without calculation. Bourdieu often illustrates the idea of strategy by the examples of sports, music and dance, which involve an embodied practical knowledge in the present of action. The sense of time in action is also completely different from an external and logical point of view, in which practices are reified and time is put in brackets. This is particularly true with the standardisation of time:

> The calendar substitutes a linear homogenous, continuous time for practical time, which is made up of islands of incommensurable duration, each with its own rhythm, a time that races or drags, depending on what one is doing, that is, on the functions assigned to it by the actions that are performed. (Bourdieu 1990: 84)

This is why we can say that practice is temporalisation: practice makes time, it creates its own and specific time of the game, performing the future in the present of the action.

Habitus, situation and context

If the agent is not a 'subject', an individual with free will, he is also not a machine determined by his position in social space. As dispositions are 'virtualities' or 'potentialities', they are not fixed and habitus depends on a process of actualisation: 'There are acts that a habitus will never produce if it does not encounter a situation in which it can actualise its potentialities' (Bourdieu 1990: 295). In practice, questions are never posed in a purely formal and theoretical way. The coherence of things is always a question of pertinence in relation to the universe of practice: 'The same thing can, in different universes of practice, have different complementary properties and also, depending on the universe, contrasting, even opposite properties' (Bourdieu 1990: 144). Therefore, there is a strong interdependency between habitus and situation: 'According to the stimuli and the structure of the field, the same habitus can generate different, and even opposite practices' (Bourdieu 1997: 109).

The problem is that all the categories of thought the sociologists themselves use are also social and historical productions. Bourdieu often points out that it is difficult to distance ourselves from all the taken-for-granted categories that seem natural and objective. It is only when we consider our categories of thought from a historical point of view, that we are able to think through how they are determined: 'What is called social is history, through and through' (Bourdieu 1993: 74). Sociological analysis is a kind of photography of the meeting, and sometimes the conflict, between two histories: history objectified, as accumulated along time through lasting things, such as monuments, books, theories, rights and so on, and history embodied in human beings, as dispositions. Showing a forgotten history hidden in the taken- for-granted, sociology has a role to play in the objectification of necessity; it opens a possible liberty for the agent, if the analysis of practice demonstrates his historical and social background.

From this perspective, families' practices must be understood in their relationships to institutions and markets of goods and services in a historical context. Even though it does not cover all the range of practices between parents and children, the analysis of the (non-) use of home workbooks is particularly useful because it demonstrates the complexity of the social world in which family life is inscribed.

Family, institution, market: preschool home workbooks at the crossroad

The dynamic of social 'reproduction' has to be understood as the relationship between families and institutions, especially school, in Bourdieu's work (Bourdieu and Passeron 1977 [1970]). This dynamic is always inscribed in a historical context, which shapes the relationships between generations (Bourdieu 1993). The relationship between families and preschool institutions was studied in the 1970s by two of Bourdieu's colleagues, Chamboredon and Prévot (1973), when the institutional programme of the French nursery school aligned itself with a social definition of early childhood accorded to the middle and upper classes, that of a 'creative child' and 'cultural learner'. Since the 1970s, based on the idea that public educational policies have to ensure school success in a very selective French academic system (Duru-Bellat 2007), the organisation and the programme of the French nursery school have become increasingly academically centred. Nursery school in France is no longer a preparation for compulsory primary school, but it is considered as a school in its own right, giving priority to a cognitive and linguistic curriculum, and assessing pupils' scholastic competences (Garnier 2011). With a large public supply of places for all pre-schoolers from three to six years old, and a very small private sector (Rayna 2007), the problem of social and cultural inequalities arises both from what is done (or not) at nursery school and from family characteristics and educational practices.

In families, the use of educational goods and services also contributes to this dynamic of social differentiation. As Bourdieu stated many times about the social stratification of lifestyles, there is a homology between the field of production and the field of consumption. This is the case, for example, for children's books (Chamboredon and Fabiani 1977), according to the varying social definitions of childhood they involve. Home workbooks for young children can be considered as part of a growing market of early learning resources (Dahlberg et al. 2007), and more generally educational goods and services, aimed primarily at the middle classes (Ball 2003).[4] Marketers create specific products that respond to families' demands and also create that demand. Home workbooks for young children in France have been developed in relation to the institutional scholarisation of preschool education. They are somewhat hybrid and ambiguous in nature, somewhere between work and play, school and fun, or 'edutainment' mixing (formal) education and entertainment (Buckingham 2011).

Marketers seek to appeal to both young children and their parents. A direct appeal to the adult, and indirect appeal to the child, highlights the academic legitimacy of the product. The 'school' connotation is created by reference to the existence of a 'programme' with organisation by 'subject' or by 'activity', reproducing the social and institutional hierarchy of the nursery school curriculum system. At a more fundamental level, it is the very nature of the workbook that makes it scholastic, as a written form of relationship to the world (Goody 1977). A direct appeal to children as young consumers (Cook 2009), and indirect to adults, aims to attract via the recreational dimensions of the product, underscored by characters, worlds and stories familiar to young children, plus puzzles and games, colouring sheets and stickers of every kind. Another means of audience appeal now widely used in marketing strategies is the licensed use of well-known children's characters (Babar, Disney Princesses, Star Wars and so on), linking the workbooks to the worlds they represent in the same way as the vast collections of merchandising aimed at young children (such as toys, bags, clothing).

Between school and home, the workbook opens up a space in which the aim is to play '*like at nursery school*', a kind of second degree with children's mass culture. Between parents and children, the workbook opens up specific areas of hybridisation, translation and circulation between recreational and formal learning formats that the product descriptions link closely together: 'Explore the heart of the fairy tale world of Disney princesses! Follow Tania and her friends through the 2nd year nursery programme. ... You can spend magic moments with your child' (Hachette 2013). Clearly, these home workbooks illustrate composite assemblies between different pedagogic codes: on the one hand, an invisible pedagogy that emphasises play and, on the other, rigid forms of classifying and framing knowledge (Bernstein 1975). Insofar as these workbooks combine both play and school cultures, their meanings must be interpreted through the various ways in which families themselves use them (or not). If objectively, it is simple to say that they are used more in middle and upper class families and so contribute to social reproduction, we also have to take into account the meaning of their use in practice, looking carefully at the practices as the parents explain them.

The research design

This investigation into the use of home workbooks for young children is based on a survey conducted in two stages at three nursery schools in the Paris region (a gentrified area in Paris, a deprived area and a privileged environment in a Paris suburb). The first phase, a combination of classroom observation and interviews in first-year nursery classes, focused on the question of collaboration between school staff and parents (Garnier 2008). The second phase was conducted at the end of the third and final year of nursery school, two years later, and consisted of re-interviewing some of the parents interviewed during the first phase, with specific guidelines from the first interview. By referring back to that initial interview, our aim was to analyse how the experience of a child attending nursery school for three years had changed families' educational practices (Garnier 2010). It was during this second interview that parents of five-year-old children were systematically asked about their use of home workbooks. We showed the parents one of these products and asked if they had ever purchased or were planning to purchase such an item. We enquired as to when and why, whether the request came from themselves, the child or the teacher, and how the product was used in relation to the child. Although the interviews were limited in number, they were sufficient to achieve considerable social and cultural diversity between the families.[5]

The decision to interview parents again before the child moved on to compulsory primary school was intended to put into perspective their stance on pedagogical support for the child, for example as shown through the use (or non-use) of workbooks. At the same time, the question of the parents' reflexivity in regards to their own educational practices lies at the heart of the interviews and our analysis of their involvement with the school and relationship with the child. In the home environment, it is particularly important to guard against scholastic illusion and to be critically aware of the language used to describe educational practices so as not to invest them with a strategic purpose that is in principle alien to them. Similarly, we must be aware of an imposed issue that puts education and nursery school at the centre of parents' concerns. In this respect, the dual set of interviews not only creates a relative familiarity between the researcher and the parents but also offers them the possibility of distancing themselves from their earlier comments, thereby modifying the strategic nature of family educational practices. The process invites reflective feedback rather than an unequivocal interpretation of practices, and also serves to highlight any ambivalent meanings. As Bourdieu points out, particularly in *The Weight of the World* (1999), the interview is a social situation and what is said is always a co-construction, where the reflexivity of the sociologist him/herself is at stake.

Transactions and conflicts between parents and children

As preschool home workbooks are ambiguous, falling between play and school, and addressed to both parents and children, they may reveal tensions inside the family. Some of the parents who do not use workbooks express 'reservations' about them. For these middle and upper class parents, the absence of workbooks reflects an explicit refusal, an option that was ruled out. One of the criticisms levelled against home workbooks is the artificial nature of the play activity they offer the child. This goes hand-in-hand with a concern about protecting the child from educational pressure at too early an age, and about allowing opportunities for developing all his or her 'possibilities' (or abilities) and a wider range of cultural awareness. Tristan's mother spoke of how she suffered as a child from the pressure for academic results and of her refusal to consider nursery school as 'proper' school: 'For me, school begins in CP' (the first class of compulsory primary school), she says. So she did not buy a work-book for her son, as he wanted, but crosswords to play with. It is also possible to express reservations and, at the same time, to buy this kind of educational good, responding to the child's demand and letting him/her get on with it alone. In this regard, Leo's mother says: 'We've always said no to doing schoolwork at home; he gets on with his holiday workbook by himself. I buy it, and he does it when he wants to.' She refuses to look at what he is doing with it, relying on the autonomy of her son who, she says, has found 'his own way of learning.'

By contrast, the decision not to use workbooks may stem from the child's reluctance, a refusal that relates not to the workbook itself but to a relationship between a mother and her daughter: 'I know, because I talk to their mums, that she has friends who ask for work-books. I did suggest it to my daughter, but the answer was no; she doesn't want to. If it's her idea, she'll do it; if I ask her, she'll say no, she doesn't want to,' says Lea's mother. It seems all the easier, in this case, for the mother to accept the child's refusal: 'Since I can see that everything is fine on the whole, I let it go'. The mother's deci-sion not to use a workbook is accompanied by vigilance, support for the child at the everyday level that seeks to avoid anticipating more formal learning: 'I think if she were having more difficulty, I would intervene more; that's my role. But they are only in nursery school, I don't want to push her into being able to read by the end of the year; in fact, I don't want to push her too hard at all.'

Conflict can also take place when a child is experiencing difficul-ties. The teacher of the third year nursery school class, the last one before primary school, may ask parents to provide specific support at home. This was the case for one father, with low income and a migrant background, who was 'called up' to the school because his son had 'a problem with writing'. The boy was given 'big exercise books because he couldn't stay on the line', in order to practise what was expected of him in school, producing 'drawings' (loops and sticks) to help him learn to write. This insistence on the child system-atically practising at home, in complete ignorance of classroom activ-ities, is the cause of recurrent conflict between father and son: 'It's hard, because he always wants to watch TV and have fun, and I say no. He shouts…We have to find a way for him to accept that we should work together,' says the father. The school's failure to provide efficient support is accompanied by real school homework devoid of anything that might be amusing for the child. Work and play are thus pitted against one another, with no compromise possible.

These different cases show the resistance of children to parents or negotiations alongside a 'natural' process of acquisition of tastes, lifestyles.... Home, like all the social spaces in Bourdieu's theory, is a field of conflicts between children and adults. But explicit conflict may go with 'a practical mimesis (or mimeticism), which implies an overall relation of identification and has nothing in common with *imitation* that would presuppose a conscious effort to reproduce a gesture, an utterance or an object explicitly constituted as a "model"' (Bourdieu 1990: 73). The importance of these conflicts can be highlighted once again by the work of Merleau-Ponty (1988). For this philosopher, conflicts between adults and children are not only frequent in everyday life, they are inscribed in the inequality of their situation, culturally understood as 'natural domination', even though the identification of parents with their children also creates some complicity and solidarity. This constitutive inequality and these different identifications (inside and outside the family, and reciprocally between the child and his parents) provoke 'the contradiction, the ambivalence that characterises the adult-child relationship' (Merleau-Ponty 1988: 108). Even if they do not recognise it as such, with negotiations for example, parents have to take into account children's agency.

Vigilance: sense of present and future of the child, sense of the past of the parents

Because the conditions of families' practices often exclude distance, delay or detachment, a number of varying parental concerns overlap the use of home workbooks, sometimes in the same practice or at different moments: keeping a young child busy (or merely sitting still) while older siblings are doing their ('real') homework, offering a change of activity, stimulating or playing with the child, exercising his or her skills, and so on. This complexity makes it impossible to assert that concern for educational performance is the sole reason for the use of such workbooks; only one mother told us that she speaks with the teacher of her daughter about a workbook, and generally preschool teachers are against home workbooks. Furthermore, the support parents provide in using workbooks may vary between children. For the parent, this goes hand-in-hand with a practical knowledge of each individual child, a knowledge that the use of workbooks serves, in its turn, to develop. In a context where parents do not have a lot of the school's information concerning the results and, above all, the process of the child's learning, home workbooks can provide a closer understanding of the child's learning activity: 'Where you have to do noughts and crosses, for example, my son will do a nought and then put a cross on top of it. He knows it should be a nought, but what interests him is putting the cross on top and then seeing what we say about it. I get the feeling that talking to him consistently, logically, is not the way to get through to him', analyses Theo's mother.

This attentive support of the parent can provide a practical knowledge of how best to deal with the child, in the present and also for the future. The issue is not confined to the workbook itself; it also relates to how parents understand the situation and their relationship with the child. This support involves a strong reflexivity by the mother: how she positions herself in relation to the child and how she includes the child in overall 'family life'. Also how it makes sense of the 'personal histories' of each parent: 'in my husband's family, there was a lot of pressure to do well at school and, as a result, he tends not to want to apply any pressure at all; I would tend more to be all one way or all the other; but there is a graduation, all the same', says Theo's mother. This strong reflexivity, the attention to small details, brings into play both the sense of 'academic pressure' and the idea that, when it comes to anything that might indicate the child was experiencing educational difficulties, it is, she says, 'as if there were an *alert threshold* that, for now, has certainly not been reached.' In this sense, the workbook is not intended primarily to anticipate future school learning, or to help the child overcome difficulties. It is first and foremost a tool for parents' vigilance in the present, a source of reassurance against the risk of future educational difficulties, a kind of precautionary principle. Parents who play that kind of game are not planning the future of the child, they are 'engaged in what is about to come' (Bourdieu 1990). And because it takes time, these practices also show a division of labour between fathers and mothers in relation to the child, and sometimes with siblings and other family members or carers.

This stance calls for presence of mind and careful attention in the course of action: 'This exercise of vigilance avoids the need for an emergency response since it offers a way of dealing with upsets and disturbances as they arise and developing appropriate responses in the light of experience' (Chateauraynaud and Torny 1999: 78). For those from a privileged background, therefore, as long as it is 'just' nursery school, non-use of and reservations about home workbooks may go hand-in-hand with significant involvement in the child's learning, and also with an area of negotiation with the child and considerable reflexivity in postponing the influence of school pressure on family life. With this vigilance comes the possibility of keeping educational concerns in perspective, or at least preventing them from encroaching too far upon family life: 'To my mind, it's at school that it has to work out; because you can be doing other things during that time ... Ideally, it should *nonetheless* go as well as possible, so as to be able to do something else without it becoming a problem,' explains Theo's mother. For such parents: 'nursery school is still a hallowed place, where there is little at stake, the child is still very much protected and so, too, are the parents. *Nonetheless,* it is important to get the best out of nursery school because, for the child, it is the basis for all the rest,' emphasises Lea's mother.

At this nursery school age, parents have to be able to take both lightly and seriously the prospect of educational competition that will make itself felt too soon. Hence the frequent repetitions of 'nonetheless', in which it is easy to read both the imperative of future school success and the concern to retain a 'spontaneity' that is particular to a social definition of early childhood (Chamboredon 1975). Hence much of the publishing success of nursery school home workbooks whose hybrid mix of play and formal education allows users to, as it were, have it both ways. The dual nature of this kind of product sheds light on the uncertainty of the future, as well as on the ambivalent nature of childhood between becoming and being. It makes claims at the same time for adult responsibility for children's futures and care as mutual dependencies between children and adults in the course of family life.

Overall, some of the parents seem to be aware of a danger that all the practical family's life may be transformed into educational strategies. They try to control and limit the rationalisation of the life of their child because it also means a pressure upon them. As a result, socialisation becomes more and more an object of thinking. More precisely the effort of postponing school pressure creates a need for more reflexive practices, a paradoxical move toward rationalisation, in order to recover the immediacy and natural character of family life. Claiming for a release, parents create a new control upon their control of their child's life, which is a kind of compromise between the practical logic of family life and educational strategies. Frequently, the parents explain this position by their own family's pressure towards school success. They partially objectify their own history as an attempt towards auto-analysis of their habitus. This position needs a high cultural capital, including the resources of human and social sciences as tools for emancipation (Bourdieu 2004).

Conclusion

If statistics, as tools of totalisation based on institutional categories of thought, 'state thinking', offer a systematic view of the social stratification of educational practices in social space, it is important to put this alongside qualitative research that can show the 'mess' of practices, including the fact that children are themselves a source of uncertainty: 'Practice is always underestimated and under-analysed, and yet understanding it requires much theoretical competence, much more, paradoxically, than understanding a theory' (Bourdieu 2004: 39). The close attention to practices may avoid slipping, in Bourdieu's words (1977: 29), from the model of reality to the reality of the model. Through the example of activity books, I have shown that practices in families' homes involve more than interrelations between adults and children: they must be understood in relation to institutions and markets, and their history. Here, the differences between families' practices are not only economic; they are also influenced by parents' attitudes toward school pressure and by the abundant supply of edutainment productions which value children's agency as consumers, by conceptions of early childhood and its place between present and future. The close attention to families' practices not only reintroduces the importance of conflicts between 'young' and 'old' (Bourdieu 1993), it also shows that tension, contradiction and ambivalence lie at the heart of parent-child relationships.

Furthermore it raises questions of how differences are made (or not) between adults and children (Garnier 1995).

In family life, practices take into account the child as 'being' as well as 'becoming', and also the sense of parents' pasts. Considered as temporalisation, the notion of practice puts in question the choice of studying children's 'being' instead of children's 'becoming' (James et al. 1998). This theoretical dichotomy does not act counter to empirical data. On the contrary, Bourdieu's theory confronted by empirical studies invites us to rethink the concepts of age and socialisation in the light of situated practices. Through interviews, it shows the importance of the reflexivity and the symbolic mastery of parents' practices during the nursery school years. It emphasises the tension between educational strategies and a 'practical' family life, through the need of some parents to preserve it from academic pressure. It invites us to think about the dynamics of the relationships between adults and children, which take place within institutions and markets of goods and services in national contexts. In doing so, the age of children cannot be considered as a difficulty for the sociological analysis (James 2010), but as a social fact defined by relationships within institutions and markets. Studying practices opens the door to a sociological analysis of the different ages of children, far from a developmental approach (Garnier 2013).

The resources of Bourdieu's sociology will help us to emphasise our own critical reflexivity. In opposition to determinism, reflexivity is a condition of being aware of the necessity of our principles of perception and action, and thus gives us, up to a certain point, mastery over our reactions. It goes with the idea that the vocation of sociology is to be critically reflexive, not a narcissistic reflexivity, in the words of Bourdieu (2004), but a collective one, mixing cooperation and friendly conflict between scientists.

Notes

1. The colleagues of Bourdieu at EHESS *(Ecole des Hautes Etudes en Sciences Sociales)*, Chamboredon (1975), Chamboredon and Fabiani (1977) and also Boltanski (1969), among others, have worked in the field of childhood, dealing with nursery school, infant care, the field of production of books for children.... The key theoretical concept of these works was

'social definitions of childhood', meaning the diversity of the conceptions of childhood according to social classes.

2. Without all the considerations I should note in order to avoid a simple causal relationship between my theoretical choices and my own social trajectory, marked by a 'split habitus' to use Bourdieu's term, I would like to point out the kind of fascination and the necessity of distance I feel with Bourdieu's sociology that I discovered in 1981, with a former student of Bourdieu, Jacques Defrance. After completing my master's degree, I followed at EHESS the seminar of Bourdieu in 1987 and the seminar of Boltanski, the colleague and at that time competitor of Bourdieu. I completed my PhD in sociology with him, engaging his *Justification* framework (Boltanski and Thévenot 2006 [1991]) conceptualising the relationship between childhood and adulthood as a question of critique and justification in a historical perspective (Garnier 1995, 2013). More than 20 years later, the state of the field of sociology in France is quite different, and Boltanski (2011) intends to show the links between a critical sociology, like that of Bourdieu, and the pragmatic sociology of critique he has developed. This chapter represents the occasion to revisit my first sociological framework.

3. Bourdieu was aware of the difficulty of translating the phenomenological conception of our embodied-being-in-the-world into a sociological distinction between habitus and field which can be read as another intellectual dualism: 'This dualism, however, comes to haunt the very notion of practice that is supposed to render those disparate aims congruent or compatible.' (Butler 1999: 119). This critique can be understood in light of the differences between political philosophy's work and the sociologist's challenge to take into account empirical data systematically.

4. A dozen French publishers now offer home workbooks for nursery school children, each with its own collection ranging from the first to the third year of nursery school. Educational publishers are the main operators in the sector, but inroads are also being made by 'youth literature', comic strips and 'youth press', as well as by a company specialising in private home tutoring. For example, at the beginning of 2013, one educational publisher offered a catalogue of over 60 products for nursery school, in various collections, some general, some specific: math (or numbers), reading, graphics and/or writing, English.... I wonder if such nursery school activity books for three to six years old children are specific to France. Even the translation of the French, *'cahier d'activité parascolaire'* into English 'home workbook' is not entirely satisfying.

5. The sample of 12 families (each interviewed twice, more than one hour each time) is presented in Garnier (2010). We can notice objectively that six families from low-middle to upper classes use home workbooks, three from popular and migrant background do not (partly because this kind of product needs linguistic competencies) and it is also the case for three families with high cultural capital. Even though this sample is very small, this is in line with two previous studies about this topic at the age of primary and secondary school in France. Perhaps because this case study

is particular to early childhood in French context, I did not find a division between 'concerted cultivation' and 'the accomplishment of natural growth' as Lareau (2011) found in the United States. On the contrary, the analysis of practices shows that they are more complex, above all more ambivalent, than a dual conception of childhood.

References

Ball, S. 2003. *Class strategies and the education markets: The middle class and social advantage*. London: Routledge.

Bernstein, B. 1975. *Classes and pedagogies: Visible and invisible*. Paris: OECD-Centre for Educational Research and Innovation.

Boltanski, L. 1969. *Prime éducation et morale de classe*. Paris: Mouton.

Boltanski, L. 2011. *On critique. A sociology of emancipation*. Cambridge: Polity Press.

Boltanski, L. and Thevenot, L. 2006 [1991]. *On justification: Economies of worth*. Princeton NJ: Princeton University Press.

Bourdieu, P. 1977 [1972]. *Outline of a theory of practice*. Trans. R. Nice, first edition. Cambridge: Cambridge University Press.

Bourdieu, P. 1980. Le mort saisit le vif. Les relations entre l'histoire réifiée et l'histoire incorporée, *Actes de la recherche en sciences sociales*, 32–33, 3–14.

Bourdieu, P. 1984 [1979]. *Distinction: A social critique of the judgment of taste*. Trans. R. Nice, first edition. London: Routledge.

Bourdieu, P. 1990 [1980a]. *The logic of practice*. Trans. R. Nice, first edition. Cambridge: Polity Press.

Bourdieu, P. 1993 [1980b]. 'Youth' is just a word'. In P. Bourdieu, *Sociology in question*. London: Sage.

Bourdieu, P. 1998 [1994]. *Practical Reason*. (First edition: Raisons pratiques. Sur la théorie de l'action) Cambridge: Polity Press.

Bourdieu, P. 1999 [1993]. *The weight of the world: Social suffering in contemporary society*. Cambridge: Polity Press.

Bourdieu, P. 2000 [1997]. *Pascalian Meditations*. Cambridge: Polity Press.

Bourdieu, P. 2004 [2001]. *Science of science and reflexivity*. Trans. R. Nice, first edition. Chicago: University of Chicago Press.

Bourdieu, P. and Passeron, J.C. 1977 [1970]. *Reproduction in education, society and culture*. London: Sage.

Bourdieu, P. and Wacquant, L. 1992. *An invitation to reflexive sociology*. Cambridge: Polity.

Buckingham, D. 2011. *The material child: Growing up in consumer culture*. Cambridge: Polity Press.

Butler J. 1999. Performativity's social magic. In R. Shusterman (ed.) *Bourdieu. A critical reader*. Oxford, Blackwell Publishers, pp. 113–28.

Chamboredon, J.C. 1975. Infancy as an occupation: towards a sociology of spontaneous behaviour. Paris: OECD – Centre for Educational Research and Innovation.

Chamboredon, J.C. and Prévot, J. 1973. Le métier d'enfant. Définition sociale de la prime enfance et fonction différentielle de l'école maternelle, *Revue française de sociologie*, XIX, 295–335.

Chamboredon, J.C. and Fabiani, J. L. 1977. Les albums pour enfants. Le champ de l'édition et les définitions sociales de l'enfance. *Actes de la recherche en sciences sociales*, 13–14, 60–79, 55–66.

Chateauraynaud, F. and Torny, D. 1999. *Les sombres précurseurs. Une sociologie pragmatique de l'alerte et du risque*. Paris: Ed. EHESS.

Cook, D. 2009. Children as consumers. In J. Qvortrup, W.A. Corsaro and M.S. Honig (eds). *The Palgrave handbook of childhood studies*. London: Palgrave Macmillan, pp. 332–46.

Dahlberg, G., Moss, P., and Pence, A. 2007. *Beyond quality in early childhood education and care: Language of evaluation*. Abingdon: RoutledgeFalmer.

Duru-Bellat, M. 2007. Social inequality in France: Extent and complexity of the issues. In R. Teese, S. Lamb and M. Duru-Bellat (eds). *International study in educational inequality, theory and policy. Vol 2*. Dordrecht: Springer, pp. 1–20.

Frère, B. 2011. Bourdieu's sociological fiction: A phenomenological reading of the habitus. In S. Susen and B. S. Turner (eds). *The legacy of Pierre Bourdieu: Critical essays*. London: Anthem Press, pp. 223–46.

Garnier, P. 1995. *Ce dont les enfants sont capables*. Paris: Métailié.

Garnier, P. 2008. Des 'relais' entre école et famille: les ATSEM. In M. Kherroubi (ed.). *Des parents dans l'école*. Toulouse: Eres et Fondation de France, pp. 139–78.

Garnier, P. 2010. Deux ans après: L'école maternelle, les parents, les savoirs. In G. Brougère (ed.). *Parents, pratiques et savoirs au prescolaire*. Bruxelles: Peter Lang, pp. 73–91.

Garnier, P. 2011. The scholarisation of the French 'école maternelle': Institutional transformations since the 1970s, *European Early Childhood Education Research Journal*, 19 (4): 553–63.

Garnier, P. 2013. Childhood as a question of critiques and justifications: Insight into Boltanski's sociology, *Childhood* (on line 1 June).

Goody, J. 1977. *The domestication of the savage mind*. Cambridge: Cambridge University Press.

Hachette 2013. *Princesses. Maternelle moyenne section*. Paris: Hachette.

James, A., Jenks, C. and Prout A. 1998. *Theorizing Childhood*. Cambridge: Polity Press.

James, A.L. 2010. Competition or Integration? The next step in childhood studies?, *Childhood*, 17 (4): 485–99.

Lareau, A. 2011. *Unequal childhoods. Class, race and family life*. Berkeley: University of California Press (second edition).

Mayall, B. and Zeiher, H. (eds). 2003. *Childhood in generational perspective*. London: Institute of Education.

Merleau-Ponty, M. 1962 [1945]. *Phenomenology of perception*. Trans. C. Smith, first edition. London: Routledge.

Merleau-Ponty, M. 1968 [1964]. *The visible and the invisible*. Trans. A. Lingis, first edition. Evanston, Ill: Northwestern University Press.

Merleau-Ponty, M. 1988. *Merleau-Ponty à la Sorbonne 1949–1952*. Paris: Cynara.

Rayna, S. 2007. Early childhood education in France. In R. New and M. Cochran (eds). *Early childhood education: An international encyclopedia*. Westport: Praeger Publishers, pp. 1061–8.

Wacquant, L. 1992. The structure and logic of Bourdieu's sociology. In P. Bourdieu and L. Wacquant, *An invitation to Reflexive Sociology*. London: Polity Press, pp. 1–59.

Wallon, H. 1970. *De l'acte à la pensée*. Paris: Flammarion.

5

Early Childhood Education as a Social Field: Everyday Struggles and Practices of Dominance

Mari Vuorisalo and Leena Alanen

Introduction

In the dining room several small groups of children are sitting at their tables, having breakfast. The preschool teacher is also having breakfast, sitting at the adults' table. Every now and then the children get noisy. The teacher reminds them about keeping quiet during meals. She puts two fingers in front of her lips and signals that during meals you should keep quiet. The buzzing stops and the children continue their breakfast silently. Then Laura, sitting in her chair, starts a conversation with the teacher, telling her what's new. The teacher listens, answers and asks Laura for more. The children eat up their breakfast, get permission to leave the table and give their thanks. Two boys remain at one table, laughing and chatting loud. They have finished their breakfast and the teacher comes to them and says: 'Matti, why are you running so wild? You never behave like that!'

An appropriate opening question for any researcher attempting to identify a Bourdieusian *field* is to ask 'where is the fire' in the (at first only assumed) social field, in other words, which are the locations and the processes that show struggles of dominance going on (Swartz 2013: 27). In the short extract above, from the fieldwork notes of one of the authors,[1] 'fire' can be detected in Laura starting a conversation with the teacher. By doing so she contests the view of the teacher as a fair and equitable manager of preschool interaction, one who ensures, as part of her professionalism, equal opportunities for all children to take part in conversation. Despite the fact that the teacher had ordered children to be quiet during breakfast she allows Laura to start a conversation with her. And although the whole group had been restless during the meal, the teacher directed her question only to Matti, who she knew was not prone to restlessness. The case above demonstrates how essential it is to explore interaction processes in the preschool for gaining an understanding of 'what is going on here'. The scene shows that children clearly have quite different and even unequal opportunities to participate in preschool.

The aim of this chapter is to show how an analysis of preschool interaction in terms of Bourdieu's conceptualisation enables the identification of everyday *struggles* involving children in the preschool field, and how such struggles are constitutive of social and cultural practices of *domination* which in turn construct inequalities between children.

Field is a prime conceptual instrument by which Bourdieu constructs the objects of sociological research (Bourdieu and Wacquant 1992: 224–35; Grenfell 2008; Swartz 2013: 24). It is also our main instrument in entering the social world of the preschool. In the next section we present in more detail Bourdieu's analytical tools and his relational thinking which we employ in the study of a preschool as a social field. In the following section we sketch in relational terms the socio-political field of early childhood education and care (ECEC) which we believe is the worthy object of a (missing) sociology of early childhood education.

We then move our focus to a local setting of the broad (global and national) ECEC field and present glimpses of an empirical, ethnography-based study of two (micro-)fields functioning within one Finnish preschool, and make sense of the empirical findings by employing some further Bourdieusian concepts. We conclude with an appraisal of Bourdieu's 'thinking tools' for advancing a relational sociology of (preschool) childhood.

Doing field analysis

Bourdieu's theory of fields may be considered as his theory of 'society'. While in 'archaic' societies (such as the Kabyle, which Bourdieu studied in the 1960s in Algeria) there is only one field, in modern 'differentiated' societies their number grows: fields exist both hierarchically and vertically in relation to each other, they may inter-sect and subfields may emerge within larger fields.

Thus in Bourdieu's conceptualisation, modern societies are composed of multiple domains of action – fields – that are distinct from each other. A field is a relational historical formation: 'a network, or configuration, of objective relations between positions' (Bourdieu and Wacquant 1992: 125), a system of positions, or also a social 'space' structured by interrelated positions. Accordingly action taking place in a field (in Bourdieu's terms: 'practice') is to be under-stood and explained by locating the agents in their current social fields, in the structure of relations that both separate and connect them, and by identifying the logic of the 'game' that is taking place in the field.

Agents may be individuals, institutions or organisations, depending on the scale, or level, of focus. The 'game' of the field stands for struggles for control of the resources (*capitals*) that are valued and defined as legitimate in the field. Thus each field has its own rules, or *logic*, the game and the rules of one field being different from the games and the rules in other fields. A major point in field analysis, and a necessary step in providing a sociological understanding and explanation of social practice, is *to expose the very logic of the field's functioning*. While fields differ in their logic of practice they share a similar (homologous) structure, as all fields are structured by relations of dominance. Finally, fields are not static structures; they have their birth (genesis) and developmental trajectories, and the 'game' played in a field may change, or may even remain after the field disappears. The inter-field relations of influence also vary as fields have different degrees of autonomy.

Constructing a field

An example of a study of a large-scale field, and probably Bourdieu's best-known analysis of fields, concerns the field of cultural produc-tion (the production of arts and literature) in France. Bourdieu (1996) explains how this domain first struggled itself into an *autonomous* position in relation to the *heteronomous* forces of economy, politics and the state. His analysis was focused particularly on the struggles of nineteenth century painters and writers, such as Manet, Flaubert and Baudelaire, for freedom from the structural dominance of, first, the court and the church, then the salons and finally the Academy of France. Once autonomy was successfully fought for the field of cultural production, space was assured for artists' own game to develop.

The case of the field of cultural production in France, as analysed by Bourdieu, shows three stages in the development of a field. First, a field is born by way of separating itself from dominance by other, already existing fields. This move from a previous state of heteronomy to one of autonomy marks the beginning of a second stage in which the 'avant-garde' guarantees autonomy to the field. However, the accomplishment of autonomy is simultaneously also the beginning of internal, within-field differentiation, as the struggles within the field are reorganised and new strategies of action – a new logic – are established. The third stage in the development of a field is marked by diminishing autonomy. In the case of nineteenth century France, the field of economy was expanding its influence on the field of cultural production and a market for art objects was born, functioning on the basis of a logic different from the logic of the previously autonomous cultural field, and moving the field towards a state of heteronomy, albeit of a qualitatively different kind from its earlier stage of heteronomy.

According to Bourdieu, 'In empirical work, it is one and the same thing to determine what the field is, where its limits lie, and so on, and to determine what species of *capital* are active in it, within what limits, and so on' (Bourdieu and Wacquant 1992: 98–9). Field analysis implies the use – at least in the researcher's thinking – of several other concepts interrelated with that of *field*. Bourdieu's conceptual frame is a systemic one: all the concepts he developed through empirical work have a role to play in identifying and reconstructing a field and its functioning. The repertoire is shown in the list of the characteristics of fields that Bernhard Lahire has meticulously compiled (Lahire 2001: 24–6):

- Each *field* is a micro-world in a macro-world constituted by the whole social (national, global) space;
- Each field has its own *'game'* with specific *rules*;
- A field is a space structured by *positions*;
- Incumbents of positions are involved in a *struggle* about the *'stakes'* of the field, that is the conquering and/or definition of the legitimate field-specific *capital*;

- Capitals are unevenly distributed in the field and, accordingly, agents in the field divide into dominating and dominated groups;
- The uneven distribution of capitals defines the *structure* of the field;
- Agents in a field employ different kinds of *strategies* in field struggles that are oriented towards conserving or transforming the structure of the field;
- Agents in a field have an *interest* in preserving the field and they act according to this interest;
- Interests are specific to each field and they cannot be reduced to for example economic interests;
- To each field there is a corresponding *habitus*, a system of embodied dispositions to think and act in certain ways; actors' field-specific habitus develops when they participate in the game of the field, strongly believing in its significance;
- Once a field has emerged it has a certain *autonomy*. This in turn implies that the struggles conducted in a field have their own *logic*. However, the struggles in other fields (especially the fields of economy and of politics), and their results, also influence the internal power relations of other fields and they thereby may influence the development of these fields.

Bourdieu himself identifies three internally connected 'moments' in doing a full field analysis (Bourdieu and Wacquant 1992: 104; see also Grenfell 2008: 222–5: 'a three-level approach to studying the field of the object of research'). First, one must analyse the position of the field in relation to the *field of power*.[2] Next to analyse is the objective *structure of the positions* held by actors or institutions that compete for the legitimate form of *capital* specific to the field. Finally, the *habitus* of the actors are to be studied.[3] The preschool study presented later in this chapter concentrates on the second 'moment' in constructing a particular field.

Many of the fields that Bourdieu himself studied are cultural spaces, such as art, literature, religion, justice, education, academia and journalism, all of which are also institutionalised social domains in modern societies. Each of them can be shown to have a fairly large degree of autonomy, although they also constantly need to struggle to keep this autonomy. Also many of the fields studied by other scholars have focused on well established, institutionalised and 'public' arenas, such as the media, sports, economy and public accounting, policy and welfare services. Much less attention has been given to 'private' domains of practice, such as the household or family (but see Lenoir 2003 and 2008; Alanen 2011; Atkinson 2014). Domains of informally organised, voluntary networks of relationships such as children's peer-group relations have also been conceptualised as social fields (for instance, Connolly 2000). In addition, higher education, educational policy, educational research and teacher training, for instance, have been analysed as social fields (Ladwig 2004; Grenfell 1996, 2009 and 2010a; Grenfell and James 2004; Lingard et al. 2004; Benson and Neveu 2005; Rawolle 2005; Maton 2005).

The ECEC field: a brief sketch

In this study, Early Childhood Education and Care (ECEC) is understood as one of several subfields within the broader social field of education; these many subfields exist in relation to each other, on different 'levels' or also in parallel. As fields in the Bourdieusian sense, each of them has, at any point of time, a different and changing degree of autonomy in relation to each other as well as to further, more autonomous fields such as the economy and the field of power.

In educational research, 'education' is commonly treated as if it were nationally instituted and enjoying its (degree of) autonomy within the borders of a nation state. It is however becoming increasingly clear that the field of education is a truly *global* field, as supranational institutions, such as the UN and UNICEF, and organisations such as the OECD and the World Bank – each of them also conceivable as social fields – introduce transnational ideals, norms and models for nation states to transplant and adopt in their national institutions. Within the global ECEC field such norms and ideals are derived from, for instance, the UN Convention on the Rights of the Child ('equality', 'participation rights') and reports of global economic organisations ('investing in children', 'educational partnership'). Ideals such as these have also been transferred to the Finnish National Curriculum Guidelines on ECEC (Alasuutari 2010; Karila and Alasuutari 2012; Alasuutari, P. and Alasuutari, M. 2012).

Any institutional setting of ECEC is a minor component in the national ECEC field, which in Finland is operated mainly by municipalities. The municipal (local) ECEC (policy) field is embedded, and hierarchically ordered, within the state-wide as well as the increasingly global ECEC policy field referred to above. ECEC fields of different 'levels' interrelate among themselves and intersect with other policy sectors, such as schooling, social welfare and health services. Every field, including the preschool ('micro'-)field residing in each particular ECEC setting (in Finland: 'day-care centre') has some degree of autonomy in its functioning, and may impact on its interrelated fields, such as the family, and is in turn impacted on by them, for instance by schooling. To undertake a study of any minor field is therefore a highly complex endeavour, as in principle it would need to account for all interrelations between relevant fields and their impact on each other.

Individual agents in any field most probably belong, not to one but to a set of overlapping fields, and they move – often daily – within more than one field, occupying varying positions in each of those fields. In the case of young children, as in the present study, family[4] is a field of great importance. In modern times it is a significant formative field for a child's *habitus,* which begins to evolve from the day the child is born (if not earlier). In Finland in recent years the family has increasingly been made to engage with the ECEC field, by way of models of 'educational partnership'. This partnership is taken to mean 'a conscious commitment of parents and staff to collaboration for supporting children's growth, development and learning', and requires that ECEC professionals and practitioners reorient themselves in relation to parents and reconstruct their professionalism accordingly (Karila and Alasuutari 2012).

In the rest of the chapter we focus on analysing two specific fields that are constituted and upheld within the daily life of one preschool setting. As indicated above, these two fields are related, horizontally and vertically, to a number of other fields, up to the field of power. A full analysis of any of these fields and their interrelations, that is, the degree of their autonomy/heteronomy and reciprocal influence, is however beyond the scope of this chapter.

Fields in action in a Finnish preschool

In this section we present a few excerpts from a study based on extensive ethnography in one preschool (Vuorisalo 2013).[5] The excerpts have been chosen to exemplify the subtle dynamics of everyday interaction in a preschool, and to illustrate how a social field is daily constructed and reconstructed. We look at the forms of capital that emerge in the field and function as effective and legitimated means to use in the preschool 'game'. We are particularly interested in finding out how children come to utilise these capitals and what the consequences are for the (re)structuring of the preschool social space and the relations of power and domination amongst its agents (children and adults).

A field is constructed

Here is an excerpt from a morning circle assembly in the preschool:

> Teacher: Now we will have a game that some of you know and others don't.
> (In the game one child at a time moves like a particular animal, but without making any sound to indicate which animal she/he is being. The other children have to guess which animal is being performed. After a correct guess they all make the sound of the animal in question.)
> Laura is the first performer. She moves around and jumps like a bunny. Others quickly name the correct animal.
> Teacher: Now we have a problem. What kind of sound does a bunny make?
> Otto (shouts): It says bun-bun-bun.
> Teacher: I guess that's what it is.
> Taavi: I have heard bunnies screech.
> Teacher: But we are not able to perform a bunny's screech, are we?
> The teacher and the children sing 'I am a bunny and I say bun-bun-bun' while Laura is still acting like a bunny and jumping around the floor. When the song ends,
> Venla asks: Why didn't we sing instead 'rab-rab-rab' (referring to a rabbit).
> The next performer, chosen by the teacher, is Irina. She moves on the floor like a worm. Venla makes a correct guess.
> Teacher: Now it is time to end this game.
> Many thumbs are up. (By putting their thumbs up, children ask for a turn to give a performance.)
> Venla (who has not shown her thumb): I am thinking of a good one.

Teacher: Ok, show it to us.
Venla: You may think that this is a mouse, but it is not.
Teacher: Please Venla, just show it. Don't give too many hints.
The animal that Venla is imitating is a gerbil. Laura makes a correct guess.

This example represents a common beginning of the day in the preschool where data for this study were gathered. Children are sitting on their benches and the teacher steers the assembly. It is also a common situation for interaction between adults and children and a social space that we conceptualise as an *intergenerational social field* within the preschool setting, a preschool subfield that is separate but interlinked with *the (intra)generational field* of the children's peer group.

The idea in the game presented above is that when the animal is identified, the whole group sings a song which includes the sounds of the animal that has been performed. In the excerpt the bunny is a challenging choice. Otto's proposal is funny and it fits well with the song's rhyme. The teacher accepts his answer whereas Taavi's answer is discarded, even though it is acoustically more correct than Otto's. When the singing is over Venla continues to play with words just as Otto did. An important point to notice is that both Otto and Venla have made their proposals without asking for permission to speak which is against the 'thumb up' rule by which children ask for permission to speak, to answer or to take part in a game. Although several thumbs are up, demonstrating children's eagerness to take an active role in the game, Venla manages to gain a turn for herself although she is not following the accepted rule. The teacher is already moving on, but she nevertheless gives Venla one more turn to perform in the game.

In the excerpt the children and the teacher can be seen interacting simultaneously on *two different levels*. On one level, the children are involved in the game as part of their daily routine. The negotiation between the adult (teacher) and the children on the possibility of having a turn follows the group's explicit rules: children ask permission to perform and to present their guess. But there is also a second level of interaction as Otto and Venla negotiate with the teacher on the performance of the game and the whole situation. These two levels of child-adult interaction begin to make visible a process in which children use some of their resources and are able, as the situation arises, to convert them into *capital*, thereby contributing to the structuring of the preschool social field.

The definition of the field and particularly the struggle for power in the field takes place on the level where certain children take the initiative to discuss with the teacher, make suggestions and propose new ideas, as Venla and Otto could be seen to be doing. Thus, these intergenerational discussions are not only participation in activities organised for children; they are also part of the negotiations by which the field is constructed into being in daily action: whose ideas and what kind of ideas are accepted in the group (in most cases by the adult). All this generates for children positions in the field, and constructs for them relations of power and domination. Within these negotiations it is defined not only if and how each individual child may take part but also how the group functions as a social space of interrelated positions.

By speaking up and entering into discussion, Otto and Venla bring content to the assembly, which has an effect on the actions of the group as a whole. Hence, it indicates that *speaking up* functions as capital in the intergenerational field; in fact the preschool game is to a large extent played by speaking. This form of participation, always conditional on the situation, requires cultural capital, especially in its embodied form. Here we call this particular form of cultural capital *preschool conversation capital*.

A closer look at how children utilise conversation capital shows that there are two different ways of using it. In the excerpt above Otto and Venla, who get involved in discussions with the teacher, are rich in *free conversation capital*, whereas Taavi, who tries to follow the rules and give 'objective' facts (in the 'guess the animal' game), utilises *preschool conversation capital*. The difference between these two forms of capital is that the first one is used in a conversation between 'equals' (as far as this is possible in any interaction between participants in intergenerational, and largely institutionalised, positions), whereas the second form complies with the traditional structure of didactic preschool conversation in which the teacher asks and children respond.

Both forms of conversation capital are valued and have their strengths in the daily struggles in the preschool's intergenerational field of children and adults. However, and at the same time, there is also a tension between these two forms of cultural capital, which begins to bring out the way in which the struggles of *power* in the field appear.

The value of *preschool conversation capital* is quite obvious in an educational context such as preschool. By utilising it children implement the official structure of the preschool and this is generally highly valued by adults in the preschool, but not necessarily so by all children. The *free conversation capital* in turn represents power in the sense that children then tend to be treated, by the adults, as competent actors in educational interaction. This is why the teacher seldom totally ignores the initiatives of (some) children to start a discussion. In such situations an *intergenerational tension* arises because, on the one hand, the free conversation form of preschool interaction does not follow the explicit rules set ('from above') for the group of children and, on the other hand, such 'rebellious' involvement is highly valued by children and, consequently, the children who demonstrate this tend also to be well positioned within the field of peer relationships.

Moreover, the children rich in conversation capital are in the position of being able to reap further advantages. This is because the creation of spaces for interaction is an important part of a teacher's daily work in preschool. The teacher actually *needs* children's (competent) response to her/his own initiatives, and the children rich in (any form of) conversation capital provide the teacher with possibilities to create 'authentic' interaction with children, which is a master task in his/her work as an educator. Situations involving such interaction also tend to be enjoyed by the whole group, despite the fact that they strengthen the position of the children involved in the conversation and help them to take advantage of the situation and even to increase their own (field-specific) capital.

There are also children who lack both forms of conversation capital; they are clearly not able to negotiate how the field is constructed or to gain advantageous positions in it. Thus we conclude that conversation capital, in both of its forms, is a *legitimate* form of capital in the intergenerational preschool field. Therefore it also functions as *symbolic capital* in that field, by constituting 'good' positions for the children holding this capital. Moreover, the children who are rich in both forms of conversation capital are able to 'choose' which form of capital they will utilise in any particular situation, guided by their own embodied habitus. The children who are rich in just one type of conversation capital have to utilise the capital they hold in order to carve for themselves a position within the game taking place in the preschool field. All of this occurs within the flow of daily interaction and therefore positions in the field are constantly (re-)negotiated. Significant in these negotiations is that the position of children who lack any form of conversation capital is fairly permanent in the preschool field – an indication of the degree of stability of the field's game, despite constantly ongoing negotiations. It is therefore also an indication of the *social mechanisms* operating in the field – mechanisms that help to (re)produce a particular set of positions in the field and, consequently, a relatively stable and permanent social structure. For any individual child it is nearly impossible to evade the effects of this 'structuring structure' without struggling.

The positions formed in this structuring, according to the volumes and types of capital held by individual children, explain the distribution among the children of opportunities to participate as an agent in the field. The positions also indicate how power in daily practices is distributed. Children's relative positions in the preschool are reproduced as the everyday practices of the preschool are repeated and taken-for-granted (*doxa*). Consequently the children who hold 'weak' positions (in terms of legitimate capital) seldom expect to be offered opportunities to participate, and if they notice this lack of opportunity they do not know how to change the situation. This is a case of *symbolic violence*.

Children's positions and symbolic violence

So far, our Bourdieusian analysis of interaction in the preschool reveals a structural representation of two fields – the intra-generational field of children's peer relations, and the intergenerational field of ECEC professionals and children – with interconnections to and impacts on each other. Fields produce practices that are operated in and through the daily activities in preschool, and some of these practices tend to generate symbolic violence on and between children.

By using the concept of *symbolic violence* Bourdieu makes visible a form of everyday violence that generally goes unnoticed. Bourdieu describes symbolic violence as the violence which is exercised upon a social agent with his or her complicity (Bourdieu 2000, 164–205;

Bourdieu and Wacquant 1992: 140–8, 167–8). Linked to the concept of *symbolic power*, symbolic violence points to a stratified social order which however is not recognised as such (*misrecognition*). Significant of symbolic violence is its mainly unconscious nature: it is violence which is not recognised as violence. Instead, it is seen as normal or inevitable, and even legitimate, social action and for that reason dominated groups accept it without seeing or resisting its true nature as social inequality (Bourdieu and Wacquant 1992: 194–5; Swartz 2010.) In a preschool context the concept of symbolic violence indicates inequalities produced in and by the preschool's everyday practice.

Opportunities for participation are distributed among children differentially, according to their position in the preschool's intergenerational field. The two girls Elina and Venla will now be considered. Venla, as observed in the previous excerpt, holds a dominant position in the field, guaranteed to her as a child rich in conversation capital and also popular in the children's peer group. Elina, by contrast, is a rather quiet girl and not at all popular with other children.

The extract below is from a circle time assembly before lunch. During sessions like this an activity called 'this week's person' is carried out. Each Monday one child at a time is introduced to the other children as a 'special person' for the whole week. Preparing for this, the child, at home and with her or his parent(s), fills in a questionnaire and writes down answers to questions such as 'who are your best friends?' and 'do you have a pet?' The answers, with a few photos of the child and her/his family, are then glued on a poster and brought to the preschool. At the end of the 'introducing this week's person' session the child gets to choose a game of her liking.

Midday circle time

All of Elina's best friends are listed on the poster.

The teacher asks Elina to read aloud the names, but Elina will not, and so the teacher reads them. Out of Elina's preschool friends three names are listed (Siiri, Heidi, Titta), in addition to some other girls who are not in the same preschool group. (Elina had been asked many questions by the children in order to get to know her better.)

At the end of the session, as usual, the teacher asks Elina to pick her favourite game. Elina chooses 'The crane and the frogs'.

The teacher notes that it is a popular game for many of the children. She gives the drum straight away to Elina, which means that Elina will be 'the crane'. Other children join in on the floor.

In the first round Elina taps Matias and Meri and they are 'out'. .... In the beginning of the fourth round the teacher urges the crane to be attentive. In this round Titta, Otto, Laura and Tero are 'out'. Tero does not want to leave the game, but he is told that the crane 'has eaten' him. Tero thinks she did not. In the fifth round Henri and Matti are 'out', and in the sixth round Viola. In the seventh round Elina taps Venla on the back with the drumstick. Venla grabs the drumstick and pulls it to herself.

The teacher: 'Venla!'
Venla: 'I did not even move!'
The teacher comes to Venla, takes the drumstick and gives it back to Elina.
The teacher says to Venla: 'The crane has seen something.'
The last to remain in the game are Siiri and Heidi; Elina taps them in this order.
On the bench children are heard to say: 'Sure, her best friends...'
Heidi is told that of course she won, because she is Elina's best friend.
Heidi: 'I am not.'

The extract begins with the naming of Elina's best friends, three of whom are in her preschool group. The game which Elina chooses is very popular among the children, and nearly every time the 'week's person' chooses the same game.

The main idea of the game is that the leader, this time Elina, plays the drum and when she stops other children 'freeze' (stop moving). If the leader sees someone moving after he or she has stopped drumming, she is allowed to send that child out of the game ('the crane has eaten a frog'). The winner is the remaining child at the end of the game.

What happens here is that Elina, as leader of the game, uses the power that the situation opens up for her, instead of following given rules. Elina does not seem to take much notice of 'frogs' moving or not, and she clearly lets her best friend win. This is the way children tend to play this particular game anyway, so Elina is not doing anything unusual. But she is a girl in a minor position in both of the two preschool fields and does not occupy the kind of dominant position that 'the crane and the frogs' game now offers her. Other children, especially Tero and Venla, who hold dominant positions, protest against Elina's choices. But in this situation she is protected both by her position as the leader of the game and by the teacher who ensures that Elina may hold her position despite such protests.

Towards the end of the game the two girls who remain are those whom Elina had listed as her best friends. This is noticed by the other children and one of them says out loud: 'Sure, her best friends!' Heidi, however, does not appreciate being called that and denies that she is Elina's friend. This further testifies to Elina's weak position in the preschool field. A relationship with her is not one that other children are trying to achieve. With the help of the game she seemingly tries to confirm her relationships with other children, but what actually happens is that this is denied in front of the whole group.

This account can be read as a case of what a dominated position denies to the child. It is also a demonstration of how the field functions in a taken-for-granted way for the participating children. Even though the game momentarily, and exceptionally, offers Elina some power over the other children, the interaction within the game indicates that Elina does not hold the required capital, and therefore she does not reach above the possibilities that her current low position in the field provides her. Her sorry situation is accentuated by the way in which Venla and Tero – both of them occupying powerful positions in both preschool fields – behave as they find it difficult to accept Elina's orders as the leader of the game.

In a final excerpt the group of children is finishing the morning circle. There are only three children left sitting on the benches, among them both Elina and Venla, and they do not have any ready-made plans on what to do next.

Morning circle time

  Venla, Elina and Petri are sitting on the bench.
  The teacher suggests that the three of them play a game together. No one responds.
  The teacher then suggests that she could give Venla a game to play all alone: 'A bit of a tough preschool game (assignment).'

Venla gets excited.

The teacher: 'Would you two, Elina and Petri, like to play something together?'

A brief silence follows, then Elina says: 'I don't want to ...'

The teacher: 'Would you (Elina) rather like to play a game on your
own? If you do, then also Petri needs to do one.'

The end result is that all three children leave the room to take up
activities on their own. The extract shows how the teacher seems
to recognise the positioning of the children and follows their posi-
tional ordering in her management of the situation. This is a further
example of how distinctions are made between children in ordinary
preschool life. The basis for such distinctions is the way children's
opportunities to participate vary according to their positions in the
field. Children recognise this, as does the teacher.

First the teacher makes a suggestion that all three children join in
a shared board game. They do not respond to this in any way. Then
the teacher tackles the situation by starting with Venla, the one who
has a valued position in the field. What the teacher offers her is not a
common activity but something special – 'a tough preschool game'.
Children do not normally have access to such 'tough' games on
their own. The game equipment has to be fetched from the teachers'
room. By being allowed to play the game, Venla's special position is
recognised, lending support to her as one of the 'elite children' in the
preschool. Venla seems satisfied with the arrangement, so the teacher
tries once more to offer Elina and Petri a joint activity, but at this
point Elina refuses. The teacher then decides to offer them the same
game as the one Venla was given.

In this situation the three children find it hard to go beyond the
limits of their existing positioning in the preschool field. When the
teacher proposes that they could all play the game together, they all
remain quiet. It seems that this is an unthinkable proposal for the
children. What is also quite obvious is that the proposal is based on
the teacher's idea of treating children equally. The children's reactions however tell another story. They recognise the gaps between
their positions and are not ready to accept the teacher's proposal.
After a short moment the teacher submits to the power structure
existing in the intra-generational field and offers the children opportunities that are appropriate to their interrelated positions: Venla gets

something special (because she is 'special') and the situation seems to be over – for the teacher. When Elina then refuses to play with Petri (a boy in the same position as herself), the teacher offers both of them what Venla originally suggested. But before the episode is closed, the teacher reverts to the idea of equal treatment. She fails in achieving this, but what is achieved between her two efforts of equal treatment is the reproduction of the field positions of the children as either elite or minor participants. The ordering among children, as was seen in the previous episode, is once again renewed.

Episodes like these testify to the reality of *symbolic violence* in and through the 'normal', everyday practices in preschool. The two cases indicate how inequality is being produced in the quite mundane activities, even when the explicit ideal behind them is one of equal treatment.

Conclusion

The small-scale study presented in this chapter shows that conversation is a distinct and crucial practice in preschools and also a specific form of capital. By adopting Bourdieu's field analytic approach to study interactions in preschool we have been able to disclose the negotiations that take place in daily conversations in preschool and the hidden forms and mechanisms of social structuring that operate within and through such negotiations. While conversations are of sound pedagogic value in preschool they clearly end in not just 'schooling the child' (compare Austin et al. 2003): by conversing with adults, (some) children are able to acquire more eminent positions in relation to both other children and the adults in the preschool setting. Such positions in turn give the successful children more freedom; their actions also come to be seen as more valued and their ways of behaving justified. For these children, preschool interaction yields greater advantages than for those whose participation is more subdued.

Our first conclusion from the study is that preschools, through their everyday practices, actually help to produce social inequalities among children. Thus for instance the cherished principle of equality in treating children in preschool fails, causing social injustice and daily 'small suffering' (Bourdieu et al. 1999) for many children living through their preschool trajectory. This undoubtedly has a structuring impact on their emerging habitus, which will have further repercussions for the children's later life.

Our second conclusion is that by adopting and consistently applying a Bourdieusian relational methodology to study the social fields that children daily occupy, often together with adults, researchers can disclose the important social mechanisms that lie behind the relations of domination. These mechanisms take effect in and through the minds and the activities of 'real' children and adults; however, they are not available to superficial observation, as our analysis has shown. Because 'actors on social fields by and large misrecognize how cultural resources, processes and institutions lock individuals and groups into reproducing patterns of domination, *the task of sociology is to unveil this hidden dimension of power relations*' (Bourdieu and Wacquant 1992: 9–10; our emphasis). Being up to the task, we reassert, requires that a consistently relational approach is adopted for which we think Bourdieu's field analytical concepts are so far the most efficient tools. In this chapter we have focused on one part of the (Finnish) educational system and how the system, well-known for its emphasis on the equal treatment of all children, nevertheless uses and conceals practices that produce inequality among children. Moreover, instead of seeing the well-resourced children in our study as merely reproducing in their preschool life the socio-economic positions of their families, in our interpretation children's (inter)actions are more complex than a (simple) class 'reproductionist' theory would suggest.

Finally, we note that the microscopic scale of our study can only be a beginning of a relational analysis and of an understanding of children's social worlds. The Bourdieusian analytical view of social life is that any society is made of a large number of social fields, each having its own genesis and developmental trajectory. In this, fields unavoidably intersect and are continually (re)organised both internally and in relation to each other. Our focus in this chapter has been on one tiny micro-field and the logic of the specific 'game' played there. A much broader analysis of the manifold connections that link the preschool to a network of further social fields, both horizontal and vertical, and up to the field of (global) power, seems to us both possible and necessary.

Notes

1. The process of ethnographic field work for this study (Vuorisalo 2013) was conducted in a preschool group in one Finnish day care setting, during the whole preschool year, involving participant observation as well as interviews with children and staff. The preschool group was a full-time day care group with preschool activities in the morning (four hours), on its own premises. Some children in this group participated only in the morning part of the daily activities. There were 21 children in this preschool group; all except one participated in the study. Moreover, they were in the same age group; during the observation period they were all aged from five to seven years. Two preschool teachers and one nursery nurse worked with the group.
2. The field of power is not situated on the same level as other fields (the literary, economic, scientific, state-bureaucratic, and so on) since it encompasses them in part. It should be thought of more as a kind of 'meta-field' with a number of emergent and specific properties. (Bourdieu and Wacquant 1992: 18, note 32)
3. *Habitus* together with the concepts of field and capital form Bourdieu's principal conceptual triad, the three concepts being internally linked to each other. *Habitus* is a durable and transposable system of schemata of perception, appreciation and action and as it 'focuses on our ways of acting, feeling, thinking and being, it captures how we carry within us history, how we bring this history into our present circumstances, and how we then make choices to act in certain ways and not with others' (Maton 2008: 52). It is particularly the concept of *habitus* with which Bourdieu intended to transcend the series of sociology's deep-seated dichotomies, such as subjectivism-objectivism and structure-agency.
4. Family as a social field stretches long into history and broadly across spheres of politics, religion, morality and art. On the genesis of family as a social field see especially Lenoir (2003). For arguments on analysing family as a field in a Bourdieusian sense, see Alanen (2011) and Atkinson (2014).
5. See note 1.

References

Alanen, L. 2011. Capitalizing on family: habitus and belonging. In L. Alanen and M. Siisiäinen (eds), *Fields and capitals. Constructing local life.* Jyväskylä: Finnish Institute for Educational Research, pp. 91–123.

Alasuutari, M. 2010. Striving at partnership: parent – practitioner relationships in Finnish early educators' talk, *European Early Childhood Education Research Journal*, 18 (2): 149–61.

Alasuutari, P. and Alasuutari, M. 2012. The domestication of early childhood education plans in Finland, *Global Social Policy*, 12 (2): 129–48.

Atkinson, W. (2014). A sketch of 'family' as a field: From realised category to space of struggle, *Acta Sociologica*, 57(4): 223–5.

Austin, H., Dwyer, B. and Freebody, P. 2003. *Schooling the child: The making of students in classrooms*. London: RoutledgeFalmer.

Benson, R. and Neveu, E. (eds) 2005. *Bourdieu and the journalistic field*. Cambridge: Polity.

Bourdieu, P. 1996 [1992]. *The rules of art. Genesis and structure of the literary field*. Cambridge: Polity.

Bourdieu, P. 2000 [1997]. *Pascalian meditations*. Stanford, CA: Stanford University Press.

Bourdieu, P. and Wacquant, L. 1992. *An invitation to reflexive sociology*. Chicago: Chicago University Press.

Bourdieu, P. et al. 1999 [1993]. *The weight of the world. Social suffering in contemporary society*. Stanford: Stanford University Press.

Connolly, P. 2000. Racism and young girls' peer-group relations: The experience of South Asian girls, *Sociology*, 34 (3): 499–519.

Grenfell, M. 1996. Bourdieu and the initial training of modern language teachers, *British Educational Research Journal*, 2 (3): 287–303.

Grenfell, M. 2008. Methodological principles. In M. Grenfell (ed.), *Pierre Bourdieu: Key concepts*. Stocksfield: Acumen, pp. 219–27.

Grenfell, M. 2009. Applying Bourdieu's field theory: the case of social capital and education, *Education, Knowledge and Economy*, 3(1): 17–34.

Grenfell, M. 2010a. Working with habitus and field. The logic of Bourdieu's practice. In E. Silva and A. Warde (eds), *Cultural analysis and Bourdieu's legacy*. London, New York: Routledge, pp. 12–27.

Grenfell, M. 2010b. Being critical: the practical logic of Bourdieu's metanoia, *Critical Studies in Education*, 51 (1): 85–99.

Grenfell, M. and James, D. 2004. Change in the field – changing the field. Bourdieu and the methodological practice of educational research, *British Journal of Education*, 25 (4): 507–24.

Karila, K. and Alasuutari, M. 2012. Drawing partnership on paper: How do forms for individual educational plans frame parent-teacher relationship?, *International Journal about Parents in Education*, 6 (1): 15–27.

Ladwig, J.G. 1994. For whom this reform? Outlining educational policy as a social field, *British Journal of Sociology of Education*, 15 (3): 341–63.

Lahire, B. (ed.) 2001. *Le travail de Pierre Bourdieu. Dettes et critiques*. Paris: La Découverte.

Lenoir, R. 2003. *Généalogie de la morale familiale*. Paris: Seuil.

Lenoir, R. 2008. The family as a social institution: Struggles over legitimate representations of reality. In J. Houtsonen and A. Antikainen (eds), *Symbolic power in cultural contexts*. Rotterdam: Sense Publishers, pp. 31–42.

Lingard, B., Rawolle, S. and Taylor, S. 2004. Bourdieu and the study of educational policy, *Journal of Educational Policy*, 20 (6): 663–9.

Mahon, Rianne 2010. After neo-liberalism? The OECD, the World Bank and the child, *Global Social Policy*, 10 (2): 172–92.

Malsch, B., Gedron, Y. and Grazzini, F. 2008. On the paradox of social change and social reproduction in the field of public accounting. *Cahier de Recherche* 2008–01 E4. Grenoble: CNRS.

Mangez, E. and Hilgers, M. 2012. The field of knowledge and the policy field in education: PISA and the production of knowledge for policy, *European Educational Research Journal*, 11 (2): 189–205.

Maton, K. 2005. A question of autonomy: Bourdieu's field approach and higher education policy, *Journal of Education Policy*, 20 (6): 687–704.

Maton, K. 2008. Habitus. In M. Grenfell (ed.), *Pierre Bourdieu: Key concepts.* Stocksfield: Acumen, pp. 49–65.

Rawolle, S. 2005. Cross-field effects and temporary social fields: A case study of the mediatisation of recent Australian knowledge economy policies, *Journal of Education Policy*, 20 (6): 705–24.

Swartz, D. 2010. Pierre Bourdieu's political sociology and public sociology. In E. Silva and A. Warde (eds), *Cultural analysis and Bourdieu's legacy. Settling accounts and developing alternatives.* London: Routledge, pp. 45–59.

Swartz, D. 2013. Metaprinciples for sociological research in a Bourdieusian perspective. In P. S. Gorski (ed.) *Bourdieu and historical analysis.* Durham and London: Duke University Press, pp. 19–35.

Vuorisalo, M. 2013. Lasten kentät ja pääomat. Osallistuminen ja eriarvoisuuksien rakentuminen päiväkodissa. [Children's fields and capital. Participation and the construction of inequality in preschool.] University of Jyväskylä. *Jyväskylä Studies in Education, Psychology and Social Research* 467.

6

'A Fish in Water?' Social Lives and Local Connections: The Case of Young People Who Travel Outside Their Local Areas to Secondary School

Abigail Knight

Introduction

In this chapter, I demonstrate how I used Bourdieu's concepts of field, capital and habitus to gain insight into the experiences of young people who travel outside their local areas to secondary school, their social lives and sense of local belonging. The chapter is based on my doctoral study, carried out in England between 2006 and 2012, and including qualitative interviews with young people, parents and education professionals (Knight 2013). In England, most young people transfer to secondary school at the age of 11, where they stay until they are either 16 or 18.[1] England, like the rest of the United Kingdom, has a 'liberal welfare state', in which means-tested benefits and market-based approaches to welfare provision compete with the principles of universalism characteristic of a social democratic model of welfare seen in some Nordic countries, for example (Esping-Andersen 1999; Pringle 1998). As part of this liberal welfare regime, England has a complex, choice-based school admissions system. Education polices from the *Education Act 1988* onwards have introduced a system that claims to emphasise parental 'choice' of their children's schools and has fuelled the growing quasi-markets and commodification of education (Whitty et al. 1998; Ball 2003, 2008). Diversity in provision does not exist in many other European countries, where most children automatically attend their local schools (Weller 2007).

My study was carried out over the course of two UK governments, the Labour Governments under Blair and Brown and the Coalition Government since May 2010. Both governments have continued and increased the diversification of education provision; parental 'choice' of schools has therefore accelerated in recent years, alongside greater differentiation and fragmentation of provision. A child can now potentially attend a number of state schools outside a neighbourhood, including local comprehensive and community schools which recruit most of their students from the local area; selective schools, such as grammar schools, which select on ability; faith schools, which select mainly on the basis of religious faith; schools that are 'pseudo-selective', which select on the basis of a factor other than ability or faith, such as family connections with a European country; and private sector independent and fee-paying schools; also academies and free schools. The academy school programme was initially announced in 2000 by Blair's New Labour Government and was extended by the Coalition Government under the *Academies Act 2010*. Free schools have been promoted by Michael Gove, Education Minister under the Coalition Government and were also introduced by the *Academies Act 2010*, with the first one opening in September 2011. Both academies and free schools are state-funded but outside local authority control and are in charge of their own admissions policies. This latest process has increasingly diminished the importance of the local catchment area, thereby increasing the number of young people who do not attend their local school, and so potentially widening the distances many students travel to secondary school.

I start the chapter by briefly introducing my doctoral study, its main aims and objectives, and methods. I then outline some of the main concepts from Bourdieu's work I used to analyse the research data from the study. This is followed by an examination of the young people's and their parents' social lives, local connections and sense of local belonging in relation to the distance they were travelling to and from school, in order to show how Bourdieu's theories helped me examine this theme.

The study

The study explored the experiences of children and young people who travel outside their local area to secondary school. I asked what these experiences can tell us about their lives outside school, their social relationships, their levels of independent access to public spaces and places and their levels of agency in relation to choosing a secondary school and pursuing a social life. By analysing qualitative interviews with 26 young people, 12 of their parents and six education professionals, I sought to contribute to sociological understandings of children and childhood and child-adult relations in contemporary England. By exploring young people's journeys outside their local areas to school, I aimed to add to the understanding of what processes contribute to how childhood is subordinated to adulthood, through considering how relational processes between children and adults are negotiated in the context of national education policies and practices.

I aimed to address the following research questions: what are the implications for young people's social lives of travelling outside their local areas to secondary school? How far do young people participate in decision-making and exercise agency in relation to school choice and to their social lives outside school? What levels of independence or surveillance do young people experience related to their longer journeys to school, how do these young people view their neighbourhoods and localities and how connected do they feel to their local areas? In this chapter, I focus on the social lives of the young people, their views of their local areas and how far they felt a sense of belonging there.

The 26 young people I interviewed for the study were aged between 12 and 17. The 16 girls and 10 boys were recruited through professional and personal contacts. A variety of schools was represented: 12 young people attended private schools, five went to academies, two went to grammar schools, six to comprehensives and one to a faith state school. The young people lived in both urban and rural areas and were from a mixture of high-income, middle-income and low-income families. The majority (n = 16) were from White British backgrounds, three were from Other European backgrounds, two were Asian and five were Black. I interviewed 12 parents of the young people and six education professionals: these included teachers, a transport officer and a local authority education officer.

The study findings led me to argue that young people who travel outside their local areas to school are constrained by a number of powerful forces, such as intergenerational relations, both familial and extra-familial, educational policy, transport, habitus and by varying forms of capital. Yet the picture was not clear-cut: I also demonstrated in the study that some young people are able to resist the constraints placed upon them and that for some of the young people, their experiences of travelling to school outside their local areas provided them with greater opportunities than constraints.

The analysis of the interviews resulted in the examination of three main areas: young people's involvement in the school choice process; young people's journeys to and from school; and young people's social lives and local connections. Bourdieu's concepts of field, capital and habitus were applied to all three areas. In what follows, I will discuss the ways in which Bourdieu's ideas were used to analyse the young people's social lives locally.

Applying Bourdieu's concepts: field, capital and habitus

As with most sociological studies, I grappled with the tensions between structure and agency when analysing the data in relation to my research questions, that is, how far the young people's choices and experiences when transferring to secondary school and in their social lives outside school were determined by structural constraints. Bourdieu attempted to resolve the tension between structure and agency in sociological theory by incorporating them both within the same theoretical approach through his three concepts: habitus, field and capital. I therefore found these three main 'thinking tools' (Bourdieu and Wacquant 1992: 160) extremely helpful in analysing and framing the qualitative data for my study and will show how, throughout this chapter.

The study was also underpinned by a relational and generational approach to childhood (Alanen and Mayall 2001), which maintains that childhood is best understood, not as a separate, individual entity, but as a permanent component of the structural order contextualised in adult-child relations. Therefore, I thought the *relational* character of

Bourdieu's sociology, evident in the three key concepts, habitus, field and capital, was particularly relevant for my study. These relational and interdependent concepts are illustrated in Bourdieu's words: (Habitus × Capital) + Field = Practice (Bourdieu 1984: 101), and:

> Such notions as habitus, field and capital can be defined, but only within the theoretical system they constitute, not in isolation...And what is true of concepts is true of relations, which acquire their meaning only within a system of relations.... to think in terms of field is to think *relationally*. (Bourdieu and Wacquant 1992: 96)

And, in regard to the study of childhood, as Alanen (2009: 1) has argued: Bourdieu's 'distinctly relational thinking of the social world [is] useful for advancing the social study of children and childhood'.

Relational thinking like this emphasises the relations and systems of relations, and in this way connects the influences of structures on an individual's actions and vice versa. It is through the habitus and sources of capital that an individual transforms or reproduces society's structures or fields.

Maton (2008) uses the idea inherent in the phrase 'a fish in water' (Bourdieu and Wacquant 1992: 127) to explain Bourdieu's concept of the game and how habitus works. When we do not feel like this in a social situation, it is often because our habitus does not match the rules of the particular social field. In contrast, when we feel at ease in a social situation, this means our habitus matches the logic of the field because we are attuned with the unwritten rules of the game, or the *doxa*, as Bourdieu termed them. As Bourdieu explained:

> Social reality exists, so to speak, twice, in things and in minds, in field and in habitus, outside and inside of agents. And when habitus encounters a social world of which it is the product, it is like a 'fish in water': it does not feel the weight of the water, and it takes the world about itself for granted. (Bourdieu and Wacquant 1992: 127)

This means we may, as agents, avoid those fields in which there is a field-habitus clash and instead gravitate towards social fields that best match our habitus, that is, our dispositions and beliefs. Through these processes, we learn a particular place in the world which best matches these dispositions that we have acquired (Maton 2008). When the habitus matches the field, therefore, we usually behave unconsciously and without reflection; conversely when there is a lack of fit between habitus and field, and one feels like a fish out of water, the habitus becomes more accessible, rendering conscious what was previously taken for granted (Sweetman 2009).

Because Bourdieu insists that our dispositions are embodied, they are therefore territorially located (Savage et al. 2005b). As a consequence, habitus, having a 'sense of the game', feeling 'at home' or 'comfortable' are all embodied elements of habitus that are closely related to the importance of place and a person's strength of connection and belonging to a particular locality (Savage et al. 2005a, 2005b; Siisiäinen and Alanen 2011).

Bourdieu's theories of habitus, field and capital and his relational approach to social analysis enabled me to draw together two main elements of sociological thinking when considering my data: first, a generational approach that posits that adults and children and the relations between them are intrinsically interconnected; and second, the connection between agency and structure, allowing me to explore and explain the experiences of the young people and their parents in this study. For example, the concept of 'field' as applied to the family (when making decisions about school choice and social lives) and also the home-school space in my study (journeys and community relations), enabled me to conceptualise and understand the intergenerational social relations that occur in these 'fields'.

I used the concept of field to aid the analysis and understanding of the research findings, as a scholastic and heuristic device to help me make sense of the data (Thomson 2008). For the themes considered in this chapter, the social lives and local connections of young people who travel outside their local areas to secondary school, I viewed the family and the neighbourhood as fields in which power relations are played out and in which young people and adults are engaged in a struggle. As Bourdieu made clear:

> the family always tends to function as a *field*, with its physical, economic and, above all, symbolic power relations (linked, for example, to the volume and structure of the capital possessed by each member), its struggles for conservation and transformation of these power relations. (Bourdieu 1996: 22)

I also used the idea of correspondence or 'fit' between habitus and field to understand young people's sense of local belonging (Savage et al. 2005a, 2005b; Alanen 2011b) vis-à-vis travelling to school and their social relations. I will examine some of the study's research findings relating to the young people's social lives outside school and their sense of local belonging, using data from 12 of the 26 young people and their parents. In order to contextualise this data, the 12 young people discussed in this chapter are introduced briefly below. These young people were chosen for inclusion in this chapter because, compared to others in the sample, there was more to say about them in relation to their social lives and local connections. All the names are pseudonyms.

The young people: contextual information

Sara was aged 15, from a White British background and a high-income family. She lived in an urban environment and attended a private school six miles away from her home. She went to school each day by public transport, including a bus and underground train.

Elizabeth was aged 13, from a White British background and a middle-income, lone parent family. She lived in a socially and economically disadvantaged urban environment and attended a private school seven miles away from her home, after not receiving any of her choices of state secondary schools.[2] She travelled to and from school on public transport.

Anna was aged 14, from a White British background and a high-income family. She lived in a rural environment and attended a private school 12 miles away from home. She was driven to and from school each day in her parents' car.

Sally was aged 14, from a White British background and a high-income family. She lived in a rural environment and attended a private school 28 miles away from home. She was driven to and from school each day in her parents' car.

Faith was aged 13, from a White British background and a high-income family. She lived in a rural environment and attended a private school 27 miles away from home. She travelled to school on the school bus.

Catherine was aged 14, from a White British background and a high-income family. She lived in a rural environment and went to a private school 17 miles away from home. She was driven to and from school each day by her mother.

Peter was aged 13, from a Black British background and a low-income, lone parent family. He lived in a socially and economically disadvantaged urban environment and attended a comprehensive school six miles away from home, after not receiving any of his six choices of local secondary schools. He travelled to and from school each day on three buses.

Gill was aged 17 and was Peter's older sister. She attended a different comprehensive to Peter, five miles away from home, and this was also because she had not received any of her six choices of secondary school. She travelled to and from school on two buses.

Mark was aged 13 and from a White middle-income family. His parents were from European countries other than the UK and English was their second language. He lived in an urban environment and attended a comprehensive school 25 miles away from home, travelling to and from school on the train.

Emma was aged 13, from a White British background and a middle-income family. She lived in an urban environment and attended an academy nine miles away from home. She travelled to and from school by bus or her mother's car.

Ayotunde was aged 13, from a low-income Black African family. He lived in a suburban environment and attended an academy 13 miles away from home. He travelled to and from school by train.

David was aged 14, from a White British, middle-income family. He lived in an urban environment and attended a faith school eight miles away from home. He travelled to and from school each day on public transport, on a mixture of buses and trains, with the occasional lift from his mother.

In summary, of the 12 young people discussed in this chapter, there were six 13 year olds, four 14 year olds, one 15 year old and one 17 year old. Seven lived in inner city urban environments, one lived in the suburbs and four lived in a rural environment. Five were from high-income families, four were from middle-income families and three were from families with a low income. Six attended private schools, three went to comprehensives, two to academies and one to a faith school. Three travelled to and from school in their parents' car only, six travelled on public transport only (a mixture of bus and train), two travelled by a mixture of occasional lifts in the parents' cars and public transport and one travelled by school bus. Distances travelled to and from school each day varied from five miles each way to 28 miles.[3]

Young people's social lives and local connections: a habitus-field clash?

Apart from three, the young people mainly socialised with friends who lived long distances away, often near their school, rather than in their local areas. This led to the young people experiencing a strong sense of separation between their school life and their local life, with some feeling particularly isolated during the school holidays. Conducting a social life also required high levels of forward planning, often involving complicated travel arrangements necessitating lengthy negotiations with parents, and so making any spontaneous meetings, outings or sleepovers virtually impossible. This was particularly the case for young people from higher income backgrounds, travelling to school mainly by car.

Although the young people used mobile technology and social media to facilitate planning to meet friends, social networking did not substitute for face-to-face contact and some had been prohibited by parents from using social networking sites like Facebook. Many of the young people were, therefore, constrained and restricted both by the logistics of seeing their friends and by the reliance on their parents' goodwill to provide transport and/or money to see friends, and this reinforced the subordination of young people to their parents and reduced their possibilities for the independent management of their social lives.

Weller and Bruegel (2006) found that young people attending their local school were able to develop friendships and social networks locally, contacts which were potentially important for the formation of social capital. In contrast and perhaps inevitably for a group of young people who travelled several miles to school and back each day outside their local areas, the vast majority of the young people spoke about having two distinct groups of friends: school friends and local friends. So they expressed a strong sense of separation between their social and home lives. Only two young people from the sample of 26 were exceptions to this experience. The need for planning and help with transport restricted some of their social lives with school friends and meant that socialising with them had to take place near the school and never or rarely in the young person's local area. As Elizabeth (13, private school) explained:

> They (my school friends) don't really come here very often…. it would be quite a journey for them all to come here as opposed to just me going over there.

Emma (13, academy), in addition, said unequivocally that she never socialised near her home:

> No, I don't like to socialise in that area. I feel like I live in Hilltop (area near school) but I sleep in Derwood (home area), if you get what I mean. My whole life is in Hilltop but I sleep in Derwood.

Experiencing a sense of separation between school and local friends was not only linked to the long journey to school and the logistical difficulties of having friends over. It was also because some of the young people perceived a strong sense of social division between their school friends and the people who lived in their local areas. In these cases, Bourdieu's conceptualisation of the lack of fit between habitus and field is being operationalised. As Bourdieu maintains, when this lack of fit occurs, the habitus is brought to the fore and causes one to feel like a fish out of water, thus creating a greater self-consciousness and self-awareness (Bourdieu 1990). This experience was evident among the young people in the sample who were from the extreme ends of the social class spectrum – both those from high- income families who attended private school many miles from home and those who were living in a socially disadvantaged area but going to school in a more affluent area; both groups were likely to sense strong differences in class and values from local friends and neighbours.

For example, Elizabeth (13, private school), who went to a private school but lived in a socially deprived area, implied that she would feel uncomfortable with her school friends visiting her because:

> If they were to come here they would probably think 'Oh, someone's going to knife me in a minute, I'm going to die'.

Faith (13, private school) similarly described feeling 'cut-off' from young people in her local town because she went to a different school:

> I always see all these people outside, like all these young people my age, who I used to go to school with actually, erm walking down the streets together in groups, maybe going into shops, you know, and I don't ever get involved with them anymore.... I don't socialise with them anymore though if I see them in town they might come over and say 'hi'.

All the privately educated girls in the sample said they would sometimes keep quiet about which school they attended because they wanted to avoid inverted snobbery and conflict. Although this experience was not necessarily linked to travelling further to school and instead is an indication of the social division produced by an education system run on market principles and those of 'choice and diversity', the long distance travelled to school outside their local areas was likely to increase the young people's sense of social exclusion.

Catherine's mother had sensed a barrier between herself and her neighbours since Catherine and her brother started to be educated privately, although she found it difficult to articulate:

> I do think a bit that...there's a little bit...because they (the neighbours) do know that Catherine goes to an independent school and the other children don't go to independent schools and I sometimes feel that that creates a little bit of distance...it is just something that I feel.

Ayotunde (13, academy) felt socially excluded in his local area, complaining that he had no friends near his home, but for different reasons. His Black African family and he had moved to a white suburban area within the last two years and all the family members were commuting back to work in the inner city area they had left and where Ayotunde had attended primary school. Consequently, all his friends were near that school and this had left him socially isolated:

> All my friends are in Allenwood (area of primary school) and I don't make friends in my area because a lot of them are much

older than me or they are not part of my social group, so I don't talk to them and I don't really go out and if I ever do go out it will be to Allenwood...a lot of my life has been wasted by just being over there (where I live now) without being able to communicate with my friends.

Behaving differently with local people from a different background or school was a common experience described by these young people who perceived huge differences between themselves and local young people. As Catherine (14, private school) explained:

I feel different around...I'm part of friendship groups, almost, not deliberately, it just sort of happens and I find that I act differently around different people, so I could be different because people are different where I live...I've got this thing where because people don't talk to me where I live, I instantly sort of close off more to them but here because everyone knows me it's different.

Yet the experience of behaving differently with distinct sets of people, at school and locally, was not confined to young people who were privately educated. For example, Peter (13, comprehensive), who lived in a deprived area known for gang warfare, also described how:

I would rather live somewhere less violent, and less like this, some-where more posh, somewhere I'd feel more safe, and if I could go to a different school, I'd be even more safer. I can probably mix with any group, if I approached some people, I can listen to how their conversation, listen to how they speak, listen to how they think and I can mix with them, I know what to do. But if I moved, they'd be a different group.

Similarly Peter's elder sister, Gill (17, comprehensive) saw the social divisions between her school and local friends as an advantage; going to school in another place outside her local area (although she had not originally 'chosen' to) and behaving differently from the local girls had enabled her to 'break away' from the challenges of local territories and the difficulties associated with them. By attending a school in a different part of the city, away from her deprived home area, Gill felt that she was able to realise some aspirations that, she believed, she would not otherwise have had. She highly valued the 'wide variety of experiences' that she had at her girls' comprehensive school; she compared herself to local primary school friends and acquaintances, who, she felt, had not been lucky enough to have these experiences in their secondary schools and had instead been influenced by a culture of low aspirations and expectations.

The data show that many of the young people appeared to inhabit two different social worlds (Power et al. 2003) and this was the case for young people in private schools and for those who lived in areas very different in character from the one in which their school was located. Although the young people did not use the word 'class' in their accounts, their consciousness of social divisions created by class inequality was clear.

Using Bourdieu's concepts, we can see that the experiences of social divisions and contrasting social worlds described by the young people were illustrative of a habitus-field clash for the young people (Maton, 2008), and created circumstances in which they potentially felt at odds with their social relations in the 'field' of their local area. Yet for Gill, the habitus-field clash she experienced offered her an alternative to the acquisition of a habitus characterised by low aspirations and poor opportunities. In her case, therefore, we can see Bourdieu's idea of lack of fit between habitus and field in practice. For Gill, the clash between her habitus (the values and dispositions she had obtained from her local area) and the field (her school outside her local area where she obtained a different set of values and dispositions) had led to a greater self-consciousness and reflection about her habitus, thus bringing habitus to the fore. This enabled Gill to question her values and wishes and had provided her with greater cultural capital, raising her aspirations and thereby helping to change her life trajectory.

The next section will consider the young people's and their parents' links to their local areas and how these habitus-field clashes influenced their levels of local connections and sense of belonging.

Young people, parents and and local belonging

There was no link between how long the young people had lived in their areas and the level of local belonging they experienced, and this point adds weight to the idea of 'elective belonging' formulated by Savage et al. (2005b). In their study of adults in Manchester, they found that local belonging was not related to being born and bred in the area but was, instead, connected to factors such as social ties, neighbouring and being around 'like-minded' people; in other words the experience of feeling like a 'fish in water' (Bourdieu and Wacquant 1992: 127), as part of the embodied habitus that helps us feel 'at home' or 'comfortable' in our locality (Savage et al. 2005b; Siisiäinen and Alanen 2011).

We have already seen how some of the young people, such as Catherine, Gill, Peter, Ayotunde, Anna, Faith and Sally, experienced a lack of fit between habitus and the field (Bourdieu 1990) of their local area. This meant that these young people experienced social divisions relating to social class and race and consequently felt 'at odds' with the local area, leading to a low or absent sense of local belonging. Anna (14, private school), for example, agreed that there was a local community, made up of people of all ages, including her own age, in the area where she lived but that because she travelled so far away to school, she was not involved with this community and felt more comfortable in the area near school:

> There is a community where I live but I am not involved in it because I am more involved with the community in Summertown (where school is); I'm definitely more involved there because there's more people that I know here and I feel more comfortable in Summertown than I am at home.

Furthermore, Ayotunde said he had no friends in his local area and that he spent most of his weekends at home. When asked if he thought he 'belonged' to the local area, he replied: 'No, there's very few of my racial group'.

Importantly, both Ayotunde's parents travelled away from the local area every day for work and, like Ayotunde, did not socialise with local friends or neighbours. In addition to feeling 'at odds' with the local area because of the ethnic divide, the fact that his parents did not have local connections inevitably affected the level of local attachment that Ayotunde himself experienced.

I now turn to the subject of parents' local social lives and connections and how these affected and largely determined the levels of local belonging felt by many of the young people. Of great importance to how much the young people felt a sense of connection and belonging to their local area was the extent to which their parents had local friends and connections; young people whose parents also had a local social life and felt connected locally were themselves more likely to feel highly connected locally. Overall the parents who were connected locally the most by having friends and being involved with local groups were from the middle-income groups, (rather than the high- or low-income groups) and their children travelled outside their local areas to state schools of varying kinds, mainly on public transport. This finding contrasts with Alanen's (2011b) finding that local belonging in her Finnish study correlated to levels of economic and cultural resources that could then be transferred into social capital. The families who were most connected locally in my study held high levels of cultural and social capital but not necessarily high economic capital, although their incomes were not very low.

Sara (15, private school), who was from a high-income family, but travelled to school by public transport, had a lot of local friends and felt a high sense of connection to her local area. Her parents were similarly locally connected and were friends with several of Sara's local friends' parents:

> My parents and Eleanor's parents, they get on very well, so they go out to eat. Also we go away quite a lot in the holidays and they come so I see them a lot, also with Robert and Molly too (other local friends).

Mark (13, comprehensive) said that he knew a lot of his siblings' and his parents' friends locally and this helped him feel part of a community:

> I know quite a lot of people in the area ... I know my sister's friends, their brothers and stuff. I know loads of my parents' friends, we have a whole little trio. Everybody comes over to my house and says 'oh, let's have a meal' and they all bring food over and you sit in the garden and have it.

His mother described knowing a lot of 'interesting' people locally, saying that they had a 'big social life' with 'a big circle of friends'; this and the local facilities, such as the parks and cinema, had given them a very high sense of local attachment; she described a type of 'elective belonging' linked to one's life biography and trajectory rather than historical connections (Savage et al. 2005b).

> Abigail: Do you feel connected to this area?
> Mark's mother: Completely. I've never had such an amazing network of friends.

Some of the parents were involved with local organisations that connected them to the local area through their children and this thereby increased their sense of belonging, as found also by Bagnall et al. (2003). Sara's mother, for example, sometimes volunteered for the Parent Teacher Association (PTA) at her son's local primary school and David's parents were highly connected locally through friendships, the local primary school and church, and had also been involved in running children's groups. These links had helped David develop his own high sense of belonging to the local area. David himself (14, faith school) had been involved in the same events and organisations that his parents had close links with and he had also taken part in a local scouts groups and Woodcraft Folk.[4] His and his parents' local connections were inextricably linked. As his mother explained:

> We like Woodmere and I think it's quite unusual – you make a lot of links at different events, and meet people there. David has been used to being part of a lot of different social groups and had the benefit of being part of all these little groups where he belonged in his little area and now he makes his own way. He belongs in this skateboarding fraternity and it exists around here. It's just a natural progression, I think, from what we started and sometimes I find it difficult cos it's part of him growing up but I'm pleased he has that confidence. I think some of it's us but I think most of it's the nature of Woodmere; it's a place you can feel belonging.

David agreed, saying that he had managed to form friendships that bridged local connections with young people he had met through his journey to school; he saw this process as closely linked with his mother's connections locally:

> So through that long journey and just meeting people, I've met all these people and that tied in with people I knew through mum

and then people they knew through them and there's this massive group.

The connections that Sara and David's parents forged locally, therefore, served as forms of social and cultural capital in the 'field' of the local area, both for the parents and for the young people that then, in turn, facilitated their sense of local belonging (Alanen 2011b).

However, of the thirteen young people in the sample of 26 who felt a low sense of local connection, none had local friends and only two had parents who had local connections, in that they had a social life or other networks in close proximity. Catherine's mother's friendships and social life, for example, were centred both on the private school where she taught and that Catherine (14) attended, which was situated many miles from their home, and at home in contacts with her immediate family. She placed a high value on the privacy this exclusion from the local area gave her:

> My friends are people I work with here [at the school]. Because of the time I get home, I don't have time to go out...it doesn't bother me. One of the pluses for me is I can go shopping in the supermarket and not bump into parents or into children and I like that as it means I have some privacy.

The mother of Peter and Gill (who both attended comprehensives) also expressed a sense of social exclusion in their local area but for very different reasons. Many of her friends lived in other parts of London and she attended church outside her local area too. As noted earlier, the area where she lived was known for its violence and high rates of crime and this had resulted in her feeling scared and trapped, a world with which she felt no sense of local belonging:

> Here it's like living in 'The Bill!'[5] Since I lived here, it's been terrible, terrible. I come in and shut my door; you hear a lot of things, sometimes you see things, not that you can do anything about it, I mean I've reported certain things to the police, not that anything's done about it. I've got friends all over the place. It's completely different living here. I would use the word 'traumatised' living...because my eyes have seen a lot. On Sunday, there was a shooting right there (pointing to outside the house).

So feeling social divisions or a level of social exclusion in the 'field' of the local area can be experienced by people from very different ends of the social and economic spectrum. However for those people, such as Catherine's family, with social, economic and cultural capital at their disposal, being 'cut-off' can provide a sanctuary from the local area and provide peace and privacy after a long day at work. In contrast, because Peter and Gill's mother lacked the necessary levels of capital to move away to a less challenging area, her exclusion from local people was, for her, a necessary means of survival. For her children, therefore, travelling a long way to secondary school, as we have seen from Peter and Gill's accounts, was a way of changing their habitus and life trajectories in the fulfillment of their hopes and aspirations.

Conclusions

This chapter has examined some of the ways in which I used Bourdieu's concepts of field, habitus and capital to analyse a study about young people travelling long distances to school and their social lives and local connections. I used Bourdieu's concept of field to analyse the child-adult relations and power struggles in the sites relevant to the study: the family (where decisions about school and out-of-school activities were negotiated), and local neighbourhood (where young people and parents interacted with other families and local facilities).

The study suggested a number of implications of the daily travelling for young people's local attachments and sense of belonging. Overall, the young people who travelled to and from school by public transport experienced a greater sense of local belonging. This was because their journeys provided them with opportunities for mixing with other people of all ages from the local area, on the way to the bus stop or station, for example. However, many of the young people, instead of feeling like a 'fish in water' (Bourdieu and Wacquant 1992: 127), 'at home' in their locality (Savage et al. 2005b; Siisiäinen and Alanen 2011), experienced a great sense of separation between their home and school life as a result of having more friends many miles outside their local area. For some, this had created experiences of social divisions and exclusion in the local area with many experiencing a sense of being divided across two distinct social worlds or 'fields' of social relations (Bourdieu 1993) leading to a habitus-field clash, in which their habitus did not 'fit' within the field in which they were located (Maton 2008; Sweetman 2009; Alanen 2011b).

For a small group of young people, however, such as Peter, Gill and Elizabeth, (that is the young people who had been 'let down' by the system and had not been allocated a local state school of their choice) travelling outside the local area to school had enabled them to experience a different social milieu and broaden their horizons. For these young people, the habitus-field clash they experienced from their sense of inhabiting two distinct social worlds, leading to their low level of local belonging, served the purpose of changing their habitus and levels of cultural and social capital in the fulfilment of their aspirations. Although a habitus-field clash was uncomfortable for some young people, it also facilitated a change in their life trajectory, thus potentially increasing their prospects for social mobility. As Bourdieu (2002: 29, italics in original) pointed out, the habitus 'may be *changed by history*, that is by new experiences, education or training'.

In this chapter, I have demonstrated how Bourdieu's relational social theories have been applied to a small empirical study about children travelling to secondary school and their social lives outside school. Bourdieu's concepts of habitus, field and capital and his notion of a lack of fit between habitus and field leading to a more accessible and potentially changing habitus enabled me to obtain more sophisticated insights into the experiences of the young people in relation to their long journeys to school than I would have done without operationalising these concepts. The use of these interrelated concepts in the analysis also facilitated the avoidance of a number of sociological dualisms, notably structure-agency, autonomy-dependency and child-adult, thereby contributing to the continuing theoretical study of childhood within the discipline of childhood sociology.

Notes

1. A small number of areas in England have a middle school system, where children transfer to a middle school at the age of 9 and stay until they are 13, after which they transfer to secondary school. Some privately educated children do not move schools at all during their school career as the schools sometimes cater for all age-groups from infants to 18.
2. In the UK, young people and their families (unless opting for the independent sector) choose up to six state secondary schools in the autumn before they transfer to secondary school, with offers for school places received in the following March.

3. According to Burgess et al. (2006), the average secondary school journey in England is just over 1.7 km or just over a mile.
4. The Woodcraft Folk is a UK-based out-of-school hours educational movement for children and young people, which has local activity groups, usually led by parents, across the country.
5. 'The Bill' was a television series about police-centred stories broadcast between 1984 and 2010.

References

Alanen, L. 2009. Rethinking childhood, with Bourdieu. In A.-M. Markström, M. Simonsson and E. Änggård (eds), *Barndom och föräldraskap*. Stockholm: Carlssons Bokförlag.

Alanen, L. 2011a. Moving towards a relational sociology of childhood. In R. Braches-Chyrek, C. Röhner, A. Schaarschuch and H. Sünker (eds), *Kindheiten. Gesellschaften – Interdisziplinäre Zugänge zur Kindheitsforschung*. Opladen: Barbara Budrich Verlag, pp. 21–44.

Alanen, L. 2011b. Capitalising on family: Habitus and belonging. In L. Alanen and M. Siisiäinen (eds), *Fields and capitals: Constructing local life*. Finland, University of Jyväskylä: Finnish Institute for Educational Research.

Alanen, L. and Mayall, B. (eds) 2001. *Conceptualizing Child-adult Relations*. London: RoutledgeFalmer.

Bagnall, G., Longhurst, B. and Savage, M. 2003. Children, belonging and social capital: The PTA and middle class narratives of social involvement in the North-West of England, *Sociological Research Online*, 8 (4). http://www.socresonline.org.uk/8/4/bagnall.html Accessed on 24 March 2012.

Ball, S. 2003. *Class strategies and the education market. The middle classes and social advantage*. London: RoutledgeFalmer.

Ball, S. 2008. *The Education Debate*. Bristol: Policy Press.

Bourdieu, P. 1984. *Distinction: A social critique of the judgement of taste*. London: Routledge Classics.

Bourdieu, P. 1990. *In other words: Towards a reflexive sociology*. Translated by Matthew Adamson. Cambridge: Polity Press.

Bourdieu, P. 1993. *Sociology in question*. London: Sage.

Bourdieu, P. 1996. On the family as a realized category, *Theory, Culture and Society* 13 (3): 19–26.

Bourdieu, P. 2002. Habitus. In J Hillier and E. Rooksby (eds), *Habitus: A sense of place*. Aldershot: Aldgate, pp. 43–52.

Bourdieu, P. and Wacquant, L. 1992. *An invitation to reflexive sociology*. Cambridge: Polity Press.

Burgess, S., Briggs, A., McConnell, B. and Slater, H. 2006. School choice in England: Background facts. Working Paper No. 06/159. Bristol: The Centre for Market and Public Organisation.

Esping-Andersen, G. 1999. *Social foundations of post-industrial economies*. Oxford: Oxford University Press.

Knight, A. 2013. Young people travelling to school, social lives and local connections: constraints or opportunities? Unpublished PhD thesis, Institute of Education, University of London.

Maton, K. 2008. Habitus. In Grenfell, M. (ed.) *Pierre Bourdieu: Key concepts*. Durham: Acumen, pp. 48–66.

Power, S., Edwards, T., Whitty, G. and Wigfall, V. 2003. *Education and the middle class*. Buckingham: Open University Press.

Pringle, K. 1998. *Children and Social Welfare in Europe*. Buckingham: Open University Press.

Savage, M., Bagnall, G. and Longhurst, B. 2005a. Local habitus and working class culture. In Devine, F., Savage, M., Scott, J. and Crompton, R. (eds), *Re-thinking class. Culture, identities and lifestyles*. Basingstoke: Palgrave Macmillan, pp. 95–122.

Savage, M. Bagnall, G. and Longhurst, B. 2005b. *Globalisation and belonging*. London: Sage.

Siisiäinen, M. and Alanen, L. 2011. Introduction: Researching local life in a Bourdieusian frame. In L Alanen and M. Siisiäinen (eds), *Fields and capitals, Constructing local life*. Finland, University of Jyväskylä: Finnish Institute for Educational Research, pp. 11–28.

Sweetman, P. 2009. Revealing habitus, illuminating practice: Bourdieu, photography and visual methods, *The Sociological Review*, 57 (3): 491–511.

Thomson, P. 2008. Field. In M. Grenfell (ed.), *Pierre Bourdieu: Key concepts*. Durham: Acumen, pp. 67–81.

Weller, S. 2007. Managing the move to secondary school: The significance of children's social capital. In H. Helve and J. Bynner (eds), *Youth and social capital*. London: The Tufnell Press, pp. 107–25.

Weller, S. and Bruegel, I. 2006. *Locality, school and social capital: Findings report*. South Bank University, London: Families and Social Capital ESRC Research Group.

Whitty, G., Power, S. and Halpin, D. 1998. *Devolution and choice in education: The school, the state, the market*. Buckingham: Open University Press.

7

Childhood in Africa between Local Powers and Global Hierarchies

Géraldine André and Mathieu Hilgers

How do representations of childhood promoted and diffused by international institutions affect the social organisation of societies? Which type of schemata of practices and perceptions are disseminated through globalisation and the attempt to universalise a specific conception of childhood? What type of resistance do these discourses face? Do they reinforce a pre-existing system of social relations? Or do they shape a set of dispositions that leads individuals to behave differently? The theoretical apparatus developed by Bourdieu constitutes a powerful tool to approach these complex and decisive questions, to grasp childhood in the current neo-liberal era that contributes to reframing social dynamics of societies in the global South. Indeed, to tackle these questions, the main challenge consists of finding a way to analyse the transformative dialectic between institutionalised structures and embodied structures that shape the realm of childhood. Bourdieu theorised this dialectic through the relationship between two key concepts – field and habitus – at the heart of one of the most coherent and solid theoretical frameworks to engage in such an analysis.

Using Bourdieu's theory in non-western contexts raises several difficulties. Many major questions cannot be fully developed here (see notably Hilgers and Mangez 2014a). These difficulties can be partially dealt with through the concrete mobilisation of this type of model, as we shall do here. We aim not to discuss Bourdieu's work itself, but will just highlight some of the empirical and theoretical directions that raise a Bourdieusian perspective, which tackles the reconfiguration of agency and structure relations in the realm of childhood in a context shaped by an intensifying process of neo-liberalisation on much of the African continent (Hilgers 2012). For several decades, the African continent has been ever more affected by a deep dynamic of globalisation that impacts on both social structuration and individual dispositions (Hilgers 2013).

To illustrate this dynamic, we mobilise our empirical research: it is based on fieldwork on child work, the battle against child labour and associated development programmes, in the mining sector of three African countries: the DRC, Ghana and Burkina Faso (André and Godin 2013, 2014). The fieldwork was inspired by Burawoy's approach (2000, 2009), using participant observation, interviews with children and adults and ethnography. During three fieldwork periods (in 2007, 2010 and 2011), data were collected in turn in mining areas of the three countries, in each of which differing stages in the process of liberalising the mining sector are in operation, involving programmes aimed at ending child labour and transnational mining companies' investment.

Here we aim to identify the impact on social structures and individual dispositions following the diffusion of a global conception of childhood. In order to do so, we shall present two main components in the framing of childhood in numerous modern African societies: the seniority system and social group structuration. Both play a major role in the shaping of local structures of legitimacies that design the role, function and position of children within the society and that are internalised by agents. Whatever is the diffusion and progressive imposition of a globalised narrative of childhood – that is the result of a long historical process marked out by symbolic struggles between competing discourses – it is affecting local conceptions and practices of childhood. The second part of the chapter focuses on the original synthesis that results from the encounter of these forces, and analyses the way in which it affects lifestyle and legitimacies, and reinforces social class stratification through the consolidation of symbolic boundaries and the perpetuation of certain types of domination. A Bourdieusian perspective is particularly useful to identify how the current social configuration attracts, stimulates and reinforces some dispositions instead of others when the local and global narratives on childhood meet and mesh.

In other words, this chapter uses Bourdieu to analyse the impact of globalisation of childhood on individual dispositions and on domination dynamics in the current neo-liberal moment that shapes sub-Saharan Africa.

A dispositionalist perspective on childhood

Much of Bourdieu's work consists in showing that the most spontaneous or involuntary behaviours, like the most considered behaviours, spring from the habitus: a matrix of representations and practices that constitutes a system of durable, transposable dispositions acquired by an individual in the course of his or her socialisation. Some socialising agencies exert a decisive influence on this process of incorporation: school, state and family. The habitus works as a matrix of perceptions, appreciations and actions that integrates past experiences and leads agents to develop a regular and regulated behaviour, without being the result of obedience to rules. The habitus shapes not only a 'predisposition', a 'tendency', a 'propensity' or an 'inclination' to act but also a conatus, agents' tendency to persist in their social being because they perceive the world through a system of dispositions – in other words, a set of schemes of perception, appreciation and action that result from their socialisation – which is the most decisive during childhood – and that they transpose analogically from one experience to another.

This perspective leads us to consider child workers in Africa as social beings who have incorporated – within the frame of their family and community – schemes of behaviours, perceptions and representations, which then shape their ability to act and their work initiatives, such as mining-related activities. During their socialisation process children internalise a vision of childhood and of the role of the child in the society where they grow up. This is the generalisation of perception, hierarchisation, evaluation and the practice of childhood-related activities that build a stable practical and cognitive framework. This practical sense of childhood is reproduced by children when they become adults. Of course they do not act as children any more but it continues to shape their behaviours and notably the relation that they will have with children as a function of their social positions. These perceptions and practices of childhood (children's behaviours and behaviours with children) result from the internalisation of a set of principles that establish and structure hierarchies, social divisions and legitimacies within the social space. Beyond all the small and multiple variations that differentiate social groups, the seniority system and social stratification are central to child work in the African mining context where we have worked. Naturally these dimensions are not frozen. On the contrary, as we shall show in the last part of this chapter, they have been affected by the globalisation of a specific narrative which aims at altering the matrix of representations and practices of childhood in the global South.

The seniority system

In many places in Africa, the institution of seniority is a central component of the dynamic of social structuration. This has many implications for children's work. Meillassoux (1975), for example, has shown that the elders' authority, which is based on control of the meals, marriageable women and other means of prestige that play a key role in alliances, involves young men working for the elders, to whom they give the result of their work. In exchange, the elders redistribute food to all the members of the family and community as well as women to the juniors. Elson (1982) and Nieuwenhuys (1994) show that this institution entails the 'social construction of an age hierarchy'. The subordination based on the absence of seniority does not correspond to a default of juniors' capacity for autonomy or personal initiative. It corresponds to the absence of 'the public means for recognition of the right to autonomy; and the lack of public means to sustain and extend autonomy' (Elson 1982). According to Nieuwenhuys (1994: 23), the consequence of this is that 'children's work is valued less since it is performed by children'.

But while Marxists such as Meillassoux and post-Marxists such as Elson and Nieuwenhuys insist on the material sphere for defining the consequences of the seniority system for child labour, the Bourdieusian approach makes it possible to keep the advantages of this perspective and simultaneously underlines the importance of the symbolic dimension: the distinct and distinguished representations of work, childhood and parenthood correspond to different positions within the seniority system. It also emphasises the importance of the relational properties of such a system, that is, the fact that social groups of juniors and elders result respectively from the conjunction of a 'shared position' and 'shared dispositions' (Wacquant 2008).

Within the seniority system, the various groups and individuals of the various groups, for example the group of children and the group of elders, see their positions (and their tasks) defined within a reciprocal set of duties, gifts and responsibilities.

The same type of structures organises the families and communities where we carried out our research. This organisation shapes and structures dispositions for work according to the positions of children as the youngest within the system. For example, children consider it their duty to help their elders by carrying out various work-related activities according to their gender, and also following their social position. In the process of socialisation within their families and communities, children internalise other objective social divisions, notably those directly related to the position they occupy within the social structure.

Social class structuration

Habitus is a system of dispositions produced by the internalisation of objective conditions. The singularity of social trajectories, experiences and their chronology particularise individuals, and each individual system of dispositions constitutes a structural variant of the others, but sociological analysis establishes that a set of agents placed in similar conditions of existence that impose a similar type of socialisation leads to homogeneous systems of dispositions and these generate more or less similar practices, a set of common properties and unquestioned beliefs expressed in their lifestyle and class habitus (Bourdieu 1979: 112 [1984: 101]). Class habitus is produced through the internalisation of the conditioning induced by a common social class condition. In other words, even if they do not know each other, children who are educated in similar conditions share similar experience, conceptions and perceptions. Bourdieu argued for a correspondence between social structures and mental structures that agents mobilise to act in the world. In so far as the members of the same class share class experiences and situations, they will have distinctive habitus and lifestyles. Developing a genetic structuralism, Bourdieu shows that oppositions in cultural matters reappear at all levels of social life: in food, cosmetics and dress, musical preferences and interior decoration. These oppositions make it possible to establish emic systems of classification and to show that 'taste classifies and it classifies the classifier' (Bourdieu 1979). The spontaneity of such judgements induces the illusion that they spring from a free choice and often leads to denial of their social character. The agent's disposition constitutes the expression of a social position in relation to the other positions in the social space.

In Africa, the experience of child work is central to the process of social differentiation and stratification. The distinction between children who spend time in a work-related activity in the domestic economy (Nieuwenhuys 1994; Bass 2004; Spittler and Bourdillon 2012) or with the subsistence economy (Abebe 2013) and the ones who do not work is a key feature distinguishing social groups, their experience, their relationships to the world and their perceptions of labour. In families from the upper and middle classes, there is stronger separation between the realm of family and the sphere of labour, between the realm of adults and children, to the point that children are barely perceived as producers or providers to the domestic income. This is so, even though in middle-class homes work-related activities such as fetching water or washing clothes are still, according to the lines of the seniority system, deemed valuable activities for children, since they have strong socialising virtues.

To sum up, children's ability for action is formed by social structures embodied through processes of socialisation shaped within families and communities and related to seniority systems and social class. However this process is now affected by the dissemination of a competing conception of childhood in the global South.

The field of child protection in Africa

Nowadays it seems impossible to analyse childhood and the socialisation of children without considering the pattern of globalised childhood diffused through the media, NGOs and international institutions. A relatively uniform conception of childhood seems to emerge from various institutions that compose a true field of worldwide child protection. To grasp the process of dissemination of this standardised conception of childhood and its impact it seems particularly useful to return to one of Bourdieu's most important concepts: field.

The theory of social field draws on classical sociological theory. A field is a realm of relatively autonomous activity, a space of relative positions within which actors and groups think, act and take up a position. The growing differentiation of the domains of human activity that accompanies societal modernisation engenders the creation of social spaces endowed with legitimacy and a functioning of their own, such as religion, politics, art and so on. A field responds to rules of functioning and institutions specific to it which define the relations among the agents who compose it. Agents' positions within the field are defined by the volume and structure of their capital (including the form of capital specific to the field). In taking their 'positions', persons and groups pursue (however unconsciously) interests linked to their field positions, which may consist in preserving or transforming the position they occupy in the field and the resources associated with it. What is ultimately at stake in the struggles that constitute the history of a relatively autonomous realm of activity is the maintenance or transformation of the social structures and/or the structures of the field and the orders of legitimacy that prevail there.

While internationalisation is profoundly affecting many domains of activity and has led some researchers to question the relevance of Bourdieu's field theory in the context of globalisation (Lemieux 2011), in social spaces where public policies concerning childhood are enacted, the dynamic of globalisation has contributed to strengthening and structuring the field of child protection in Africa. Indeed, the United Nations' adoption of the Convention on the Rights of the Child (UNCRC 1989) has led to a relatively autonomous realm of activity within which specialists discuss and define a conception of childhood and politics for protecting children around the world and this has affected many societies in the South. It is animated by numerous protection professionals and practitioners working all over the world to resolve various problems that affect children. The structuration of the field of child protection is determined by the main agents who structure it and who participate in its development: international institutions, NGOs, the state and the private sector.

This realm of activity is dominated and governed by international experts, mainly trained in western international institutions, who have the legitimacy to intervene and to promote specific conceptions of childhood presented as universally legitimate. As Bourdieu and Wacquant (1999: 42) have shown in their analysis of the international diffusion of dominant ideas in the age of globalisation, dominant conceptions are reproduced in the media, the development agencies and development programmes, and they constitute a new global common vulgate, a 'universal common sense' that manages 'in the end to make one forget that they have their roots in the complex and controversial realities of a particular historical society, now tacitly constituted as model for every other and as yardstick for all things'.

The dominant and increasingly globalised conception of childhood results from symbolic struggles within the field that opposed a diversity of institutions and NGOs each competing to impose their own narratives about children's rights.[1] The current dominant discourse is the result of long processes of discussions and coalitions among groups and institutions, resulting in the naturalisation of a historical and contextual narrative of childhood. This is not the place to describe the milestones along the way to this so-called universal conception of childhood, now dominant in the field of child protection and in development programmes related to child welfare (Boyden 1990). We are concerned here to focus on the effects of this conception of childhood on societies.

To apprehend these impacts, it is important to underline that the relative autonomy of this field allows people to present this conception as objectively depoliticised. Yet this narrative of childhood has direct ties and relations with the economic, political and development spheres. It is part of a broader implicit philosophical anthropology. The dominant conception of children's rights is rooted in a capitalist perception of the world and reproduces the principal values on which the neo-liberal order has been erected (Stephens 1995; Evans 2005: 10). In Western countries many influential analyses have emphasised the relation between similar discourses, the diffusion of this specific conception of the family and the expansion of a (neo-)liberal governmentality (Donzelot 1977; Rose 1989; Wells 2009). Global discourses that frame a teleology of childhood – that imply the necessity for societies in the South to reach the modern final stage of childhood – encapsulate an anthropology of the family and the society that focuses on the responsibility and autonomy of children and parents. This philosophical anthropology tends to hold biological parents as principally accountable for the needs of their children (nutrition, health and education, conceived mainly as schooling) and aims at making 'ignorant parents' aware of their responsibilities regarding their children. Indeed the principal goal is not to make them responsible citizens able to develop a public critique and to take position in the public sphere but to convert them into rational economic units able to be economically autonomous and entrepreneurial. They are urged by developers, sensitisation programmes and government campaigns to be the heads of the household whose duty is to satisfy their family's needs through their labour.

In Africa, this anthropological conception is promoted by a constellation of institutions as the right, fair and teleological conception of modern childhood in a world ever more globalised. The necessity – always presented as ineluctable – for conversion to a market economy is supported by the diffusion of a relatively standardised conception of nuclear family and childhood. International institutions, NGOs and governments discuss, conceive and disseminate international conceptions or standards of childhood and parenthood that fit with the dynamic of neo-liberal capitalism and through this they play a historically unprecedented role in the making of childhood in Africa. They contribute to the elaboration of public policies, establish standards and control and give birth to the sub-field of child protection in Africa. In parallel to the implementation of structural adjustment programmes encouraged by international institutions such as the World Bank and the IMF, national African governments have been led to promulgate their own laws on child protection under the influence of experts on the UNCRC.[2] Despite the official African appropriation of the UNCRC at national or continental level,[3] the influence of international institutions in this field is great, notably through the role of NGOs and local agencies of international institutions. In other words, the globalisation of childhood facilitates and is facilitated by the globalisation of the neo-liberal economy. To use Bourdieu's and Boltanski's terms (1976) the function of the dominant ideology associated with this global narrative is to orientate action and maintain cohesion, to give an interpretive framework through the ritual affirmation of its relevance and its necessity.

Implementing such global conceptions is presented as a struggle against the weight of an archaic tradition or, in euphemistic terms, the 'local culture'. The ambition to adapt African populations to capitalism took place during the colonial period and continues today through a neo-liberal proselytisation which aims to convert poor people into entrepreneurs.[4] Long-term fieldwork observations of the mining sector and development projects related to child-miners show how projects developed by international institutions, such as ILO and UNICEF, and supported by states that hope to benefit from their support, aspire to reframe African families and adapt them to the dynamic of contemporary capitalism. All these multiple and often uncoordinated processes are supported by a conception of childhood which becomes progressively the only legitimate conception globally, the most coherent, fairest and the most rational way to educate and raise children. As Bourdieu and Wacquant put it, 'cultural imperialism rests on the power to universalize particularisms linked to a singular historical tradition by causing them to be misrecognized as such' (1999: 41). But how does it work on the ground and how does it affect social structuration and social life in Africa?

Symbolic struggles

Bourdieu's theoretical tools help to catch analytically the structural forces that shape the realm of childhood in Africa, but also to identify the effects of their entanglement. As noted above, the conversion to market economy is supported by diffusing a relatively standardised conception of childhood where international institutions are playing a historically unprecedented role. They contribute to the elaboration of public policies, and establish standards and control to implement this child protection conception. However, the attempt to implement this conception does not occur in passive social space. To identify the impact of the conception of childhood produced within the field of child protection and to grasp how the diffusion of this narrative reshapes relationships between agents and groups, Bourdieu's relational epistemology and approach to social stratification appear useful. Indeed they make it possible to identify how the impact of this diffusion varies according to the position of groups in the social space and it is fruitful to apprehend in the same analytical gesture the dynamics of reproduction and change of social structures as well as the concrete representations and practices of childhood.

Refining Bourdieu's classification for Africa

The notion of class used here should be understood in the relational perspective that differentiates social groups in relation to their position within the social structures. Indeed the difference between Africa and Europe requires substantial conversion work to make all the complexity of Bourdieu's framework on class useful (Hilgers and Mangez 2014b). Bourdieu retains from Marx the idea that the distribution of capital defines objective positions and from Weber the idea that membership of a status group (*Stand*), and the life-style that this membership implies, affects class situation. In other words he expands the notion of capital by considering, in addition to its economic dimension, social, cultural and symbolic dimensions. According to him, the social space is marked by a distribution of economic capital symmetrical but opposite to the distribution of cultural capital. On the basis of this distribution of capital, Bourdieu reconstructs the positions of groups and individuals in the social space. These positions are established according to the volume of their capital and the structure of this capital, mainly the relative weights of economic capital and cultural capital. The latter is composed of objectified properties (possession of goods and objects), incorporated properties (dispositions, schemes of perception and action, savoir-faire and competences) and institutionalised properties (qualifications, titles, medals and marks of recognition).

All this appears obvious in the case of child labour in Africa. The family occupying a high position in the social structure does not need or wish to put their children to work. However, the problem of such analyses is that they are framed in a particular context. In contrast to French republican society, where the educational hierarchy is always a decisive element in the evaluation and profitability of this capital, where the educational system establishes what Bourdieu calls 'a unified market for all cultural capacities' and guarantees 'the convertibility into money of cultural capital acquired at a determinate cost in time and labour' (Bourdieu 1976: 125), in most African countries it seems difficult to identify absolute cultural reference points within the local horizon. In other words there is no unification of the market in cultural capital (or at least not equivalent to the ways in which it is fashioned in France). The overlapping of different sets of norms means that several hierarchies coexist and appear as more or less legitimate depending on the context. Aside from extreme cases, where individuals accumulate (or are totally deprived of) all the legitimate facets of cultural capital or where children are fully obliged to work or fully forbidden to work – it is difficult, but not impossible, to identify precisely the value of the specific components of an individual's overall cultural capital (including its incorporated and therefore dispositional form). The multiplicity of these legitimacies results notably from the difficulty of establishing a state institution which could, as in the French case, constitute a 'meta-field', that irradiates the other fields (Bourdieu 2012: 488–9).

Second, the principles that establish and structure hierarchies, social divisions and legitimacies in Africa are different from the French context. Other factors are at play in addition to cultural and economic capitals, for example the capital of autochthony or the degree of urbanity. The 'capital of autochthony' refers to a set of advantages and networks that benefit groups who claim precedence in a city's territory (Hilgers 2011). In the case of childhood, the division between rural and urban areas, between the rural villagers and farmers and the city dwellers, is also decisive. Even if this opposition is not very well fixed, since the exchanges and ties between villages and urban areas are numerous, it involves symbolic conflicts, and processes of distinction between villagers and city dwellers which lead, for example, to people's wish to demonstrate a high 'degree of urbanity', that is, the capacity to manipulate codes, representations and practices proper to the city (Hilgers 2009: 135–79). The distinction between rural and urban can precisely be perceived as a hierarchy than can cross over almost all the social space.

In this chapter we take into account these multiple variables at the family level – capital of autochthony, economic capital and cultural capital (conceived here as relational degrees of schooling and urbanity) – in order to distinguish analytically children coming from families with lower-class or middle-class backgrounds. This provisional reconceptualisation of the social classes makes it possible to refine perceptions of children's work. In the case of the DRC for example, it highlights the fact that sometimes extremely diverse dispositions lead children to work at the mines; the rate of children involved in the mining sector is quite high because a period of unprecedented social, political and economic crises in the 1990s has led to low public investment in education (Poncelet et al. 2010) and financial difficulties for parents to send their children to school. This period of crisis explained the diversity of sociological profile in the mining sector and the presence of families with middle-class backgrounds.[5]

Next we analyse sensitisation programmes against 'child labour' (such as children's small-scale mining-related activities) addressed by development agents to rural and urban lower-class communities in Ghana, the DRC and Burkina Faso. We will show that the dissemination of this global conception of childhood triggers symbolic struggles to 'gain control over the classificatory schemata' (Wacquant 2008: 272), used to define social realities and governing people and things: symbolic struggles between social classes, through which lower-class and rural-class childhood is stigmatised; and conflicts between juniors and elders, through which the elders try to maintain their dominant position, when the new legitimacy promoted by the global conception of childhood gives more advantage to younger people.

The attempt to adapt African populations to the dynamic of modern capitalism is particularly visible in development projects related to children working in artisanal mines that we have studied in Ghana, the DRC and Burkina Faso. The first step in these programmes concerns the re-enrolment of child-miners within the school system. Quite often this first phase positions and tasks family members in relation to the principles and representations of what we call 'responsible parenthood': parents are urged to be the head of the household without receiving any help from the child, and especially when this help is related to artisanal mining-related activities (André and Godin 2013, 2014). The second step consists most often in a phase of sensitisation against the so-called 'worst forms of child labour', such as mining-related activities. Secondarily, it helps to criminalise artisanal mining activities on sites recently bought by transnational mining corporations. Many of these institutions and development projects spread dispositions and representations of the market which attempt to turn people into active entrepreneurs in their community and household. In the mining sectors, for example, after evictions necessary to occupy the land where farmers had been cultivating and, according to the seasons, practising artisanal mining-related activities with their children, parents received an 'economic kit' (as a form of compensation for the loss of revenues from the mining sector) and special training in order to be able to produce suitable income-generating activities. In addition, for each child successfully reintegrated, a 'school kit', made up of money for the payment of school fees or school furniture, is provided. The school kit is to be given only during the first year of the programme: after one year of transition (from the child-miner to the re-enrolled child), parents are supposed to become self-sufficient and to be able to pursue their 'family duties'. What are the impacts of these attempts to convert the conceptions and practices of childhood and parenthood on the ground?

Symbolic struggle as class struggle

Our analysis of the development programmes that fight against the so-called 'worst forms of child labour', such as mining-related activities, show that differing positions concerning child protection and children's rights can be correlated to the differing positions that people occupy in social space. Middle-class individuals easily adhere to the representations of childhood and parenthood that children's rights legislations and programmes convey. During sensitisation programmes and campaigns against child labour, national development agents diffuse and promote the international legitimate representations of childhood and parenthood. These agents, who generally feel they belong to the middle class (or to avoid the problem of this notion and phrase it another way, generally feel that they don't belong to the bottom of the social structure) do so in ways directly related to their own position within society. They generally stigmatise representations and dispositions of lower-class and rural backgrounds that they consider 'less civilized', 'rural', 'uneducated' and 'not adapted to the modern world'. These agents, in tune with the representations of childhood promoted by the sensitisation campaigns (Invernizzi 2003; Nieuwenhuys 1994; Boyden 1990; Twum-Danso 2008), develop arguments and discourses which tend to present and condemn parents as the main cause of the 'worst forms of child labour'. Their pedagogic awareness campaign reproduces the mainstream argument of a global conception of childhood that emphasises child protection.

The development agents regard children as exploited by adults. The campaign focused on the difficult working conditions of children 'forced' to undertake mining-related activities. Thus they perceived children as only in need of protection and the only social space valued as able to provide such protection is the nuclear family. While lower-class and rural-class children have worked on mining sites to support their households, such campaigns stressed the family ruptures induced by such child labour.

Basically, parents' social role is henceforth defined within the children's rights framework. NGOs' justifying narrative for acting against child labour relies on a legal representation of childhood based on human rights and more specifically on children's rights, as well as on what 'parenting' should be, in the context of neo-liberal categories. Parenting tends to be limited to the role of protection and to duties such as accountability for the schooling of children. Children are perceived as passive social agents who need to be protected by responsible adults and not as producers and providers for the household. This vision of the 'passive-child' versus the 'active-parent' corresponds to the spatial and time organisation of the family in capitalist economies to which national development agents somehow adhere, and not to the representation of the child as a key-provider of the household.

Middle-class families adopt an understanding of child mining activities more in line with notions of 'child labour' as understood and practised by the development agencies. The discourses of middle-class fathers rely mainly on an ideal of social roles (particularly sensitive to ideals of the nuclear family, the breadwinning father and the school-going child) which somehow prevent their households from coping better with child mining-related activities. But also and paradoxically, individualistic social values that characterise middle-class families are pushing some children to go to work in the mines more for themselves than for their parents. In middle-class families, children are less aware of having a potential role as producers or of the obligations that such representations imply, such as sharing earnings with the family. In effect, in the DRC, middle-class children, who generally went to school before going to the mines, began to work there not so much for their parents as for themselves (André and Godin 2013, 2014).

Children go to the mines with varying social representations and dispositions and the way children used their pay from the mines differed according to the representations of childhood dominant in their families. Of course family configuration does not constitute a homogeneous microcosm, but refers to 'particular structures' of 'plural co-existence' through which children develop their dispositions (Lahire 1995). In the case of the DRC, while children can be influenced by the father figure's dispositions and representations of work related to the industrial, capitalist world, young people also have dispositions to work transmitted by the mother, who is more concerned with the family's daily survival and thus more connected to the informal world of work that implies child labour (see Lahire 1995). In most lower-class families, children are considered more as producers and have a duty to contribute to the family's revenue in their own way. A homologous logic organises domestic and mining work and the moral obligation to contribute to the households.

Contact with the development programmes did not change the representations of childhood and parenthood underlying their strategies for survival or the functioning of their domestic economy. In lower-class and rural-class families, the closing of the artisanal mining site, combined with the NGO programme, has frequently caused the oldest children to migrate to other artisanal mining sites. Young people have decided to go away to find new artisanal and small-scale mining sites and thereby to continue providing for their family.

Thus how social groups receive and interpret the global narrative of childhood is directly correlated to the social group's position within the social structures. The symbolic struggles that take place to impose this narrative as the most legitimate conception of childhood vary according to the social configuration and the area of the social space where these conceptions are promoted. Though this narrative benefits from the support of the higher and middle classes it faces resistance from those at the bottom of the hierarchy.

Symbolic struggle as seniority struggle

In the artisanal mining sectors studied, child mining-related activities are structured by reciprocal structures like other child work-related activities carried out at home: many children perform mining activities because they consider it is their duty to support their parents or their elder relatives. In such a perspective, small children (and girls) carry out many tasks such as selling water or tomatoes in the streets or small-scale mining or farming. Because they are more dependent on their parents for their survival and activities they work more than older boys. Though international child rights campaigns depict their work as one of the worst forms of child labour, children consider that what they do helps their elders. The same logic of the child as worker lies beneath both forms of activity: domestic work and work at the mines. These children respect the moral obligation to put their earnings back into the domestic economy, and simultaneously acquire decision-making power in the home – by planning meals, for example. In this case children's work in the mine (even if not encouraged by parents) does not lead to a change in terms of how solidarity is organised.

According to the global rhetoric of parenthood, parents should care for their children without receiving any help from them. Consequently, awareness campaigns focused on the so-called dramatic side-effects of child labour: behavioural risks related to drug abuse, precocious emancipation, a lack of respect to elders and a loss of adult authority over the young. By doing this the discourse strategically activated and reinforced fears that elders already have vis-à-vis the young. Indeed, though children generally carry out activities in order to help their parents, parents and elders worry that work-related activities and access to money will generate a noxious process of radical individualisation and affect asymmetrical relations between parents and children. During development programmes that aspire to end child labour and to redefine childhood, parenthood and work according to the global field of child protection, parents and elders appropriate children's rights rhetoric according to their positions within the seniority system; and thus with their own concerns and with the goal of keeping their advantages in the system. From this perspective, children's rights may be perceived by the elders as a threat to their position in the seniority system unless it maintains a clear distinction between child work and child labour. Consequently, elders emphasise this distinction in order to maintain advantages. For them, child labour is work carried out not for the community, nor in order to help the elders; but child work is good because it helps and supports the elders. The obligation to assist the elders is so well embodied that, during an enquiry in Ghana, a common answer given by the children, when asked what does child right mean, was precisely 'the right to help the elders'.

In this context the expansion of children's rights legislation does not always contribute to children's growing autonomy. On the contrary it may be used by elders to distinguish good activity (child work) and bad activity (child labour) to consolidate the seniority system. This follows exactly what Bourdieu and Passeron (1970) aim to theorise with their notion of symbolic violence; this designates the imposition of a cultural arbitrariness (that is, authority discourse) in the name of a social legitimacy (a man's status) that masks the power relations on which it is based (the asymmetrical relationship). So in this case the local dominant power perpetuates its domination by mobilising children's rights in a way radically opposed to the globalised conception of childhood in principle inspired by these rights.

Conclusion

Over recent decades, media, international organisations and NGOs, in the wake of the UNCRC 1989, have drawn attention to the sufferings and vulnerability of children living in developing countries. This has resulted in children being identified as victims more than as driving forces towards social change. In contrast, the renewed interest in childhood and children in social sciences since the end of the 1980s is characterised by a strong will to make visible the 'lifeworlds' of children (Nieuwenhuys 1994), to study the strategies that the youngest deploy for managing their own survival (Reynolds 1991; Hecht 1998), and to highlight their own perspectives and their words regarding social life (Montgomery 2001, 2009). African children have been perceived as key agents who play a crucial role in the shaping of social, political and economic processes (Honwana and De Boeck 2005) and African child workers' capacity for action has been analysed in the social sciences (Abebe, 2013. Yet in taking a specific stand regarding the international rights rhetoric on misery and pain, researchers have tended to put the emphasis more on the young people's energies, than on the domination that African child labourers have to face. Bourdieu's sociology of domination has been especially useful to analyse this three-fold domination. First, located in a generational structure, African child labourers are dominated by adults: their capacity for action and their autonomy are not recognised on the public stage and their symbolic creativity is constrained by the viewpoints of their elders. Second, belonging to the rural masses or to the lower classes of urban areas, they are generally positioned at the bottom of the social hierarchy. Finally, they are members of societies considered to be poor nations, or still perceived and labelled as 'developing countries', affected by a history of colonial domination and subordination. In other words, they are members of societies whose symbolic references and institutions take place in a network of power relations with dominant nations which tend to impose hegemonic cultural values (Friedman 1994). This last dimension is especially important in order to understand the progressive diffusion of a dominant representation of childhood since the end of the Cold War.

Bourdieu's critical approach helps us to relocate this process of dissemination within global and local structures of domination. It uncovers the anthropological conception that underlies the global narrative on legitimate childhood. It shows that the global narrative on legitimate childhood is part of a global neo-liberal process that impacts on social structuration and social changes, on the structure of socialisation and on childhood. It helps to uncover the extension of relations of domination that such dynamics involve.

In our global age, international institutions play a decisive role in the dissemination of symbolic representations of childhood that carry a cultural arbitrary directly related to the logics of capitalism. This dissemination of a global discourse on childhood affects representations and practices all over the world. The framework offered by Bourdieu to apprehend the dialectical relationship between agents and structure constitutes a powerful resource for broadening the traditional approach to childhood and to engage in comparative analysis of the transformative dialectic between institutionalised structures and embodied structures that shape representations and practices of childhood. To understand these dispositions produced by structural changes, we must describe the symbolic operations that give rise to government-enabling representations as well as to categories that support and are propagated by them. This task requires us to account for the historicity of the spaces in which these global conceptions are diffused and put into action, the intentional constructions and unconscious historical processes, in which they become entangled, and the transactions, negotiations, associations, working misunderstandings and chains of translation that give their flexibility and support their deployment. The implementation of a global conception of childhood cannot be reduced to the application of a programme or to institutional changes. It becomes real when it is embodied in the agents and representations through which it is put into action. Through a historical process, the dispositions that it generates become, as Bourdieu would say, durable and transposable, as well as increasingly autonomous from their initial conditions of production.

Notes

1. Invernizzi (2003) has shown that, regarding child labour, the abolitionist perspective is not the only position amongst NGOs and international institutions promoting children's rights. There is also a position that promotes movements of child workers. Nevertheless, while the second one is not very well considered, the former is dominant.
2. For example, Ghana, after the liberalisation of its economy from the mid-1980s, ratified the UNCRC in the early 1990s and enacted the Children's Act 1998. In the DRC, because of an unprecedented period of economic, political and social crises, a new law on child welfare, which introduced the concept of children's rights, was implemented in January 2009.

3. The African Charter on the Rights and Welfare of the Child (ARCWC) was adopted by the Organization of African Unity (OAU) in July 1990, and came into force in December 2000.
4. Bourdieu has analysed the impact of the diffusion of capitalist economy at the end of the 1950s and the early 1960s in Algeria. For a more detailed analysis of the attempt to reframe African family in function of capitalism dynamic see Cooper 1996.
5. This appears clear when one compares different neighbourhoods in the DRC. The distance between each neighbourhood and the mines helps account for the contrasts between them. In Matoléo, a central area of La Ruashi which is relatively far from the mines, the population is generally older and more at ease in manipulating urban codes and styles. People there have had direct experience with the wage-based culture of the former national mining companies, or they worked in occupations that led them to adhere to representations of the nuclear family. In contrast the population of Kalukuluku, located closer to the quarries and characterised by hastily built mud residences, is relatively recent, as is its experience of urban codes. It has less cultural and economic capital than Matoléo. These differences affect the way in which adults and children perceive child labour.

References

Abebe, T. 2013. Interdependent rights and agency: The role of children in collective livelihood strategies in rural Ethiopia. In K. Hanson and O. Nieuwenhuys (eds), *Reconceptualizing children's rights in international development: Living rights, social justice, translations.* Cambridge: Cambridge University Press, pp. 71–92.

André, G. and Godin, M. 2013. Children's rights in the DRC and neoliberal reforms: The case of mines in the province of Katanga. In A. I. Twum-Danso and N. Ansell (eds), *Children's lives in an era of children's rights: The progress of the Convention on the Rights of the Child in Africa.* London: Routledge, pp. 72–91.

André, G. and Godin, M. 2014. Child labour, agency and family dynamics: The case of mining in Katanga (DRC), *Childhood*, 21 (2): 161–74.

Bass, L. 2004. *Child labor in Sub-Saharan Africa.* Boulder, Co: Lynne Rienner Publishers.

Bourdieu, P. 1976. 'Les modes de domination'. *Actes de la Recherche en Science Sociales*, 2 (2–3), 122–32.

Bourdieu, P. 2012. Sur l'Etat. Paris: Seuil.Bourdieu, P. and Passeron, J.-Cl. 1970. *La Reproduction.* Paris: Les Éditions de Minuit.

Bourdieu, P. and Boltanski L. 1976. *La production de l'idéologie dominante, Actes de la recherche en sciences sociales.* 2 (2/3), 3–73.

Bourdieu, P. and Passeron, J.-C. 1970. *Reproduction in Education, Science and Culture.* London: Sage.

Bourdieu, P. 1979. *La distinction. Critique sociale du jugement.* Paris: Les Éditions de Minuit.

Bourdieu, P. and Wacquant, L. J. D. 1999. On the cunning of imperialist reason, *Theory, Culture and Society*, 16 (1): 41–58.

Boyden, J. 1990. Childhood and the policy makers: A comparative perspective on the globalization of childhood. In A. James and A. Prout (eds), *Constructing and reconstructing childhood: Contemporary issues in the sociological study of childhood*, London and Washington, DC: Falmer Press, pp. 190–229.

Burawoy, M. 2000. *Global ethnography: Forces, connections and imaginations in a postmodern world*. Berkeley, Los Angeles and London: University of California Press.

Burawoy, M. 2009. *The extended case method: Four countries, four decades, four great transformations and one theoretical tradition*. Berkeley, Los Angeles and London: University of California Press.

Cooper, F. 1996. *Decolonization and African society: The labor question in French and British Africa*. Cambridge: Cambridge University Press.

Donzelot, J. 1977. *La police des familles*. Paris: Editions de Minuit.

Elson, D. 1982. The differentiation of children's labour in the capitalist labour market, *Development and Change*, 13: 479–97.

Evans, T. 2005. *The politics of human rights: A global perspective*. London: Pluto Press.

Friedman, J. 1994. *Cultural identity and global process*. London: Sage.

Hanson, K. and Nieuwenhuys, O. 2013, *Reconceptualizing children's rights in international development: Living rights, social justice, translations*. Cambridge: Cambridge University Press.

Hecht, T. 1998. *At home in the street: Street children of Northeast Brazil*. New York: Cambridge University Press.

Hilgers, M. 2009. *Une ethnographie à l'échelle de la ville. Urbanité, histoire et reconnaissance à Koudougou (Burkina Faso)*. Paris: Karthala.

Hilgers, M. 2011. Autochtony as capital in a global age, *Theory, Culture and Society*, 8 (1): 34–54.

Hilgers, M. 2012. The historicity of the neoliberal state, *Social Anthropology*, 20 (1): 80–94.

Hilgers, M. 2013. Embodying neoliberalism: Thoughts and responses to critics, *Social Anthropology*, 21 (1): 75–89.

Hilgers, M. and Mangez, E. 2014a. Bourdieu's theory of social field: Concepts and application. London: Routledge.

Hilgers, M. and Mangez, E. 2014b. Field theory in the postcolonial age. In M. Hilgers and E. Mangez (eds), *Social field theory: Concept and applications*, London: Routledge.

Honwana, A. and De Boeck, F. (eds) 2005. *Makers and breakers: Children and youth in postcolonial Africa*. Oxford, Trenton and Dakar: James Currey, Africa World Press and Codesria.

Lahire, B. 1995, Tableaux de familles. Heurs et malheurs scolaires en milieux populaires. Paris: Gallimard/Seuil.

Invernizzi, A. 2003. Des enfants libérés de l'exploitation ou des enfants travailleurs doublement discriminés? Positions et oppositions sur le travail des enfants, *Déviance et Société* 27 (4): 459–81.

Lemieux, C. 2011. Le crépuscule des champs: Limites d'un concept ou disparition d'une réalité historique. In M. de Formel and A. Ogien (eds), *Bourdieu. Theoricien de la pratique.* Paris: EHESS, pp. 75–100.

Meillassoux, C. 1975. *Femmes, greniers et capitaux.* Paris: Maspero.

Montgomery, H. 2001. *Modern Babylon: Prostituting children in Thailand.* New York and Oxford: Berghahn Books.

Montgomery, H. 2009. *An introduction to childhood: Anthropological perspectives on children's lives.* Malden, Oxford and Chichester: Wiley-Blackwell.

Nieuwenhuys, O. 1994. *Children's lifeworlds: Gender, welfare and labour in the developing world.* London: Routledge.

Poncelet, M., André, G. and De Herdt, T. (2010) 'La survie de l'école primaire congolaise (RDC): héritage colonial, hybridité et résilience', *Autrepart*, 54: 23–42.

Reynolds, P. 1991. *Dance civet cat: Child labour in the Zambesi Valley,* London: Zed Books.

Rose, N. 1989. *Governing the soul: The shaping of the private self.* London and New York: Free Association Books.

Spittler, G. and Bourdillon, M. (eds). 2012. *African children at work: Working and learning in growing up for life.* Zurich and Berlin: Lit.

Stephens, S. 1995. *Children and the politics of culture.* Princeton: Princeton University Press.

Twum-Danso, A. 2008. A cultural bridge, not an imposition: Legitimising children's rights in the eyes of local communities, *The Journal for the History of Childhood and Youth,* Vol. 1, No. 3, pp. 391–413.

Wacquant, L. 2008. Pierre Bourdieu. In R. Stones (ed.), *Key contemporary thinkers.* London and New York: Macmillan, pp. 261–77.

Wells K. 2009. *Childhood in a global perspective.* London: Polity Press.

8

'Those Who Are Good to Us, We Call Them Friends': Social Support and Social Networks for Children Growing up in Poverty in Rural Andhra Pradesh, India

Virginia Morrow and Uma Vennam

Introduction

Ideas about 'social capital' (variously derived from Bourdieu 1986, Coleman 1988 and Putnam 2000[1]) continue to circulate in research literature across a spectrum of disciplines, including sociology and development studies, despite numerous critiques (see Fine 2010 for a summary). It is broadly accepted that social networks and social resources, and social support (social capital), in the form of personal, familial and community-level relationships are crucially important to children as they grow up (Morrow 1999, 2001). Yet this is an under-researched topic in developing countries, where the unprecedented pace of change puts pressure on children to pursue particular trajectories through formal schooling, while traditional values simultaneously insist that they follow pathways constrained by norms that are patterned by gender, class, caste and ethnicity and intergenerational norms of reciprocity and responsibility. Drawing on qualitative data gathered from children from the 'Young Lives' study[2] in Andhra Pradesh, India, we analyse children's descriptions of sources of support, whom they turn to when in difficulty, and why. This chapter is a preliminary attempt to use Bourdieu's distinctive theoretical ideas about social capital as relational, interconnected and underpinned by economic capital, to explore patterns of inequality in developing countries in the twenty-first Century. Sociological concepts are important here, not least because traditional societies are modernising rapidly. In a Bourdieusian sense, the number of fields grows, all of which have their own logic – institutions (such as formal schooling, social welfare provision, social protection schemes) and modern states are evolving rapidly. Bourdieu developed his ideas about social capital to explain the operation of social class and social reproduction in a specific time and place – 1980s, France. However, his earlier work, based on ethnographic research in Algeria where he developed the concepts of habitus and field, is also relevant here (Bourdieu 1979).

First, we summarise Bourdieu's ideas about forms of capital, field and habitus. Then we briefly review research on children's social relationships and sources of support in developing countries, before turning to some empirical examples from two sites in rural Andhra Pradesh (AP). We analyse the role that social capital may play in supporting or constraining children and young people over time. We find that parents, siblings, extended family and friends are crucial, and that while new social policies, like the expansion of formal schooling and the increasing 'institutionalisation' of children, are successful in enrolling children in school, other poverty-reduction schemes may be vulnerable to manipulation by higher status groups to benefit themselves.

Bourdieu: capital, field and habitus

As summarised elsewhere (Morrow 1999 and 2001), Bourdieu distinguishes between cultural and social capital, in *Distinction* (1984) and more explicitly in 'Forms of Capital' (1986). Cultural capital can exist in various forms: institutional cultural capital (that is, academic qualifications); embodied cultural capital (particular styles, modes of presentation, including use of language, forms of social etiquette and competence, as well as a degree of confidence and self-assurance); and objectified cultural capital (material goods such as writings, paintings, and so on). Social capital consists of social networks and connections, and the sociability needed to sustain networks:

> Social capital is the aggregate of the actual or potential resources which are linked to possession of a durable network of more or less

institutionalised relationships of mutual acquaintance and recognition – or in other words, to membership in a group – which provides each of its members with the backing of the collectively owned capital, a 'credential' which entitles them to credit, in the various senses of the word. These relationships may exist only in the practical state, in material and/or symbolic exchanges which help to maintain them. (Bourdieu 1986: 51)

The reproduction of social capital presupposes an unceasing effort of sociability, a continuous series of exchanges in which recognition is endlessly affirmed and reaffirmed. (Bourdieu 1986: 52)

Bourdieu's theorising is primarily concerned with how economic capital underpins these other 'disguised' forms, how these forms of capital interact with wider structures to reproduce social inequalities, and how the day-to-day activities of social actors draw upon, reproduce and sometimes challenge structural features of wider social systems.

In his discussion of field, Bourdieu uses the term 'space' to mean not only physical space, but also in a metaphorical sense, social space.

In this latter sense, actors are conceived of as occupants of multiple places within multiple relatively autonomous domains – *fields* – that together constitute the total social space. These multiple fields in turn constitute the status, class and social positions of the actors, their place in society. (Alanen and Siisiäinen 2011: 16)

In what follows here, we see the fields of family and school, interconnecting. Bourdieu's concept of *habitus,* developed in his research in Algeria, is also useful. Habitus is defined as:

A set of dispositions, reflexes and terms of behaviour people acquire through acting in society. It reflects the different positions people have in society, for example whether they are brought up in a middle class environment or in a working class suburb. It is part of how society reproduces itself. But there is also change. Conflict is built into society. People can find that their expectations and ways of living are suddenly out of step with the new social positions they find themselves in. ... Then the question of social agency and political intervention becomes very important. (Bourdieu 2000:19)

Habitus is revealed in practices: 'the nature of various habituses can be detected and tested in the practices of distinct social fields' (Alanen and Siisiäinen 2011: 21). For Bourdieu, field, and not individuals, is the true object of social science.[3]

In earlier research within the UK, it was suggested (Morrow 1999) that a conceptualisation of children could be used to explore how children themselves actively draw on, generate or negotiate their own social capital, or indeed make links for their parents, or provide active support for parents. Siblings may support each other (which we see below). Many of the studies that 'measure' social capital seem to assume that individual children are influenced only by family structure and school (see Coleman 1988, and see Chapter 6); such studies use an individualistic notion of social capital, as opposed to Bourdieu's relational conceptualisation. They do not give an account of local social context, friends, social networks, activities such as paid work, and children's membership of clubs and associations. Nor do they pay much attention to structural constraints and how these impact on social capital, or how these constraints may be differentiated according to gender, ethnicity and location.

Bourdieu is not noted for his attention to gender relations in childhood, though he recognised that women are responsible for maintaining affective/familial relationships (Bourdieu 2001). In many majority world countries, there are powerful gender norms whereby experiences of puberty, rites of passage, and social values related to family honour and reputation operate to structure girls' social and physical mobility (that is, whom girls marry, as well as the extent to which girls may travel independently). At the same time, modernity requires girls to go to school, and this raises questions about how the two fields – family and school – intersect. Here, we focus some of our analysis on gender relations in childhood and youth, since this is both a somewhat neglected area and also timely, given the unprecedented focus in developing countries on girls' education as a means of raising the social status of families and future generations (Koffman and Gill 2013).

Bourdieu is 'good to think with' and his concepts are useful heuristic devices, because he is concerned with how

the routine practices of individual actors are determined, at least in large part, by the history and objective structure of their existing social world, and how…those practices contribute – without this being their intention – to the maintenance of its existing hierarchical structure. (Jenkins 1992: 141)

Bourdieu does not focus on 'community' in his formulation of social capital. (The word 'community' in French has rather negative connotations, meaning a small, closed society.) Rather Bourdieu uses the concepts of social space and field, where capitals reside. Fields are analytic notions, and do not refer to everyday notions of (institutional) arenas or domains of activity. They are determined through research (e.g. Bourdieu and Wacquant 1992: 94–110) and their 'influence' therefore needs to be demonstrated. Specific sorts of cultural capital may be valued in one field, and less valued in another. In what follows, the physical as well as the social 'spaces' and 'fields' in which children are located are clearly influential in profound ways to their experiences.

There is very little research on children's social capital in the form of social networks in developing countries, yet 'social capital' was (and to some extent still is) expected to help people to survive in or indeed enable them to move out of poverty (See Fine 2010 for a critique). The literature on social support networks for children and young people is mostly limited to children growing up outside parental/familial homes, such as street children (see, for example, Ennew 1994; Mizen and Ofosu-Kusi 2010) and children affected by HIV/AIDS (Ansell and van Blerk 2004; Bell and Payne 2009; Evans 2011; Payne 2012) or conflict/genocide (Pells 2011). However some studies on social support include: Ansell (2004) on rural young people in Lesotho and Zimbabwe, Camfield (2012) on urban children in Ethiopia, Morrison et al. (2005) on girls' access to information in rural Jamaica, and Punch (2002) on children's relationships in rural Bolivia. Dyson's (2010) research on children's friendships and foraging work in rural Himalaya shows how the creation of the category of 'youth' in many parts of the world means that girls now have opportunities for close relationships for example, if the age of marriage is delayed, partly through extended schooling. Jones and Chant (2009) in research with young people in Ghana and The Gambia find that educational qualifications are by no means a clear route to employment and suggest that finding work is 'a matter of "know who" not "know how", with the "knowing who" involving a complex array of familial, ethnic and religious contacts' (Jones and Chant 2009: 192–3). From a Bourdieusian perspective, this is how social inequalities are reproduced. Hulme and Moore (2010, drawing on Putnam's notion of social capital) note that in international development discourses,

> the role of the family and informal civil society institutions in poverty alleviation and reduction...tends not to be adequately recognised...informal action and institutions are undervalued because they are difficult to measure and to programme...At the same time, we need to move away from the tendency in contemporary development policy thinking to uncritically laud civil society and to see social capital automatically as favourable and in need of 'building'. Civil action can be beneficial to the poor, but it can also keep poor people poor. (Hulme and Moore 2010: 93)

The next section of the chapter explores what these points might look like in interpreting data from young people growing up in poverty in Andhra Pradesh (AP), India. On the whole, parents and children have embraced the dominant discourse about education via formal schooling as the route to development, with vastly raised expectations about the capacity for cultural capital in the form of educational qualifications to lift children and their families out of poverty. This is a global phenomenon, though the capacity of schooling to deliver what it promises seems to be in doubt. At the same time as expressing an acute awareness of the importance of education, and a desire to succeed, as we will show, young people also describe a strong sense of filial duty to their parents, especially sons to their mothers, a reflection of what may be understood as 'traditional' values (see Morrow 2013). In a Bourdieusian sense, children are ambiguously positioned at the intersection of the fields of school and family.

Case study examples

Here we present longitudinal qualitative data[4] from two sites in Andhra Pradesh, and case studies of children and the role their friends, family and other people have played in helping them, supporting them or, indeed, constraining them. In 2010, young people aged 16–17 were asked, in individual interviews and in group discussions, to map their social networks, and to discuss who provides support, what kind of support, gaps in resources, opportunities for reciprocity and barriers to using available resources. Children had previously been interviewed at age 12/13, and 13/14. Here, a case-study approach has been utilised, by examining all interviews with children over the successive data collection rounds. In this chapter, to enable comparison, we focus on one tribal (remote rural) site and one rural site. The two sites reflect a diversity of cultural contexts in rural AP, and a boy and a girl have been selected from each site to enable exploration of a range of experiences illustrative of the kinds of social relationships and resources that are available to children. The experiences described are reflected in trends from Young Lives survey findings – in other words, these are more-or-less typical cases. Young Lives research has been conducted at a time of rapid social change, and, in order to make sense of the children's accounts, it is important to understand the context of shifting social policies. Numerous government programmes are in place in both communities.

Patna, a remote tribal community

The first examples are two young people from *adivasi* (tribal) backgrounds in Patna, a very poor rural community in Srikakulam district of AP. The two tribal groups living in the area are Savara and Jathapu. Jathapu people speak Telugu, but Savara have a different language and script, and some children find school difficult. Produce and goods are traded through a barter system, though the introduction of the Mahatma Gandhi National Rural Employment Guarantee Scheme (NREGS), guaranteeing adults 100 days of work a year for a minimum wage, has meant that a cash economy is rapidly developing. Numerous government programmes and interventions, including schools, are run by the ITDA (Integrated Tribal Development Agency). The *sarpanch* (head of the village *panchayat* or council) represents the opposition party and thinks that the flow of public funds and the sanction of programmes are limited compared to the *panchayats* represented by the ruling party. Children attend local primary schools, then move to nearby towns in order to continue in secondary school, staying in hostels. The ITDA is a source of employment for young people, who are being recruited as community teachers, even those who have only basic schooling (ten years) and no further training.[5] There are now more educational opportunities for children – new schools and hostels, and more seats in residential schools; and increased private transport means children can travel to school (see also Behera 2007). Younger cohort children attend residential schools and as we see below, some older cohort children are moving on to higher education.

Two cases: Yaswanth, and Santhi

Yaswanth's father died when he was in the first grade (about seven years old) and he had always helped his mother by fetching water and buying provisions. His mother had high hopes for him finding a 'small job'. By 2010, when he was 16, his sister was married but the family had incurred debts for the dowry, and Yaswanth worried: 'If we don't repay them they will mortgage my house'. When interviewed in 2007 and 2008, he wanted to continue to study and go on to university but realistically could not afford it and struggled at school. By 2010, he wanted 'anything that will earn me and mother to lead a happy life...anything, like repairing vehicles...We must have the capacity to earn'. He anticipated that when he married, his wife would come from a poor family and he would not ask her family to pay a dowry, because of his own family's experiences.

Yaswanth described how two years previously, he had been ill with jaundice and tonsillitis, and his mother paid for an operation to remove his tonsils. At the time of his sister's wedding his paternal uncle and his maternal aunt helped his family with cash gifts that were used as dowry for his sister. Other relatives gave her some gold, some cooking pots, and household appliances like a TV, gas stove and a steel *almirah* (cupboard). If they had not helped, his mother would have had to borrow from money-lenders at very high interest rates. As it was, she secured a loan from the local Self-Help Group (SHG). Because of this he was strongly opposed to the dowry system: 'it is a bane for...families'.

Yaswanth recounted how his friends helped him to pay school fees whenever his mother was out of the village, and sometimes gave him pens and pencils. Some of his friends had helped him study at exam time. He too supported his friends, sharing food with them, and even though he was poor he paid the examination fee for a friend whose parents had temporarily migrated for work. He also felt that teachers were encouraging children to score good marks, and said he had helped his teachers, getting tea, breakfast and lunch for them. He helped his mother to learn how to sign her name, and he was able to explain to her the details of the SHG.[6] Just as Bourdieu reflected on his own 'split' habitus, as the son of a rural postman who became a member of the French intellectual elite, so Yaswanth's description of helping his mother reflects his own advancement. Notably, Bourdieu also speculated that at times of rapid social change this split would become more common (Bourdieu 2004).

The ways in which children's knowledge and skill, for example, in literacy, has implications for generational relations was discussed by Yaswanth, who also talked about the Indiramma housing scheme,[7] and said that poor, Backward Caste and single parent families and widows did not get the help they were entitled to, because government officials and political leaders were 'corrupt, partial and cunning' – favouring their relatives and Forward Caste who had wealth and influence.[8] Rajesh, another Scheduled Tribe boy, complained that despite having a letter sanctioning the building of a new house, and demolishing their old house, they had still not got the money and were struggling to live in a small hut – and during the rainy season, he and his older sister went to his relatives' house to sleep. All the young men in the group complained about corruption and bribery related to getting jobs, and felt that this kind of corruption is a barrier for poor children. Yaswanth complained that a minister had sanctioned mines located in Patna to his own son, and because of examples like this, poor people missed out on opportunities and were exploited by politicians. Both Rajesh and Yaswanth complained that caste discrimination means that capable and worthy candidates are not getting employment. On the other hand, the young men spoke favourably about the Rajiv Udyoga Sri (employment for youth) scheme where the ITDA provides training and placements in different trades where there is a demand. Yaswanth said that if he failed tenth class, he would attend this training. He also mentioned that the Self-help Group (SHG) gives women whose children are studying ninth grade and above a scholarship.

For Yaswanth and his mother, the main sources of social capital seemed to be extended family, with some support from a local SHG. Yaswanth expressed an acute awareness that powerful people in the community (who are also more affluent) have access to services that he and young people like him are excluded from. Their difficulties are underpinned by their lack of economic capital – their precarious financial situation, which is exacerbated by debts incurred because of Yaswanth's sister's marriage.

Santhi is also Scheduled Tribe, but 'middle class'. Her father is a teacher in a Government school, posted to a tribal area about 30 km away. Her uncles and cousins are engineers. The family moved to a town about 13 km away from Patna to take advantage of better schools. In interviews in 2007 and 2009, she said she wanted to be a paediatrician. Santhi described the great pressure she felt from her parents and family to succeed:

> They worked hard and got me admitted into this college...so the only way to repay their support is to study well, score good marks and achieve a good position in society about which my parents feel proud, and be happy without any worries.

Her comment resonates with Bourdieu et al.'s (1999) exploration of intergenerational debt. She did well at school, despite experiencing ill-health and a great deal of anxiety about her tests and examinations. During tenth grade, she suffered from chest and stomach pains for six months, and missed school, which caused her anxiety: 'the pressure was mounting on me more as I fell behind'.

By 2010, Santhi was studying at an intermediate college, and staying in a hostel. Initially, she was studying Biology, Physics and Chemistry for medicine, but had been ill on joining college, so had shifted to Maths, much against her will. Her parents had been worried that if she studied medicine she would work too hard, and fall ill again. She was upset about this, but after talking with a sympathetic teacher, had modified her ambitions. After 12th class, she planned to study Engineering, and then look for a job. She describes how indebted she felt to her parents, who sought out a college with a good reputation.

The family had financial difficulties, because of ill health (Santhi described how her brother had been very ill), and Santhi's schooling was no longer free because there were tuition and hostel fees. The family had received marriage proposals for Santhi, but her mother said: 'We told them it is not possible for 4–5 years because she is studying'. Santhi constantly worried that her studies will be stopped for marriage, and refused to discuss the possibility with the interviewer.

Santhi listed a range of sources of social support including her friends, her chemistry teacher and her uncle. She described how she sought his guidance on which college to go to. Initially he wanted her to go to a nearby town to study, but Santhi was worried that it was far away from her parents, in case her health deteriorated. 'He agreed and told me to join anywhere... My father said he will let me join only if my uncle agrees'. She talked at length about how her parents have supported her, but her uncle was clearly very important. The interviewer asked why:

> From [when I was] small, my uncle does everything I need about my studies, health, and what will suit me...he takes the decision, so I like him very much. ... Elders will have a brief idea about their children and what they like and what suits them, what they will be able to study, and how much stress and pressure they can handle... In every matter, I consult him only.

Her uncle also encouraged her to seek advice from others 'He told me if I...doubt what he said, he asked me to consult my sister too, but I believe his decision, so I took MPC (Maths Physics and Chemistry). ... he thinks and knows all things'.

Santhi described how she offered support to her friends:

> When they are not feeling well, I write fair notes and give to them. I go and ask them if they have any problem. If they are not well, I go to the hospital and visit them... and tell them about the class and lesson details.... we use each other's support.

She had also helped her father with correcting homework (though this had stopped, presumably when she had too much homework of her own to do and she was living in the hostel). She described receiving good support from her teachers in the past:

> The Maths teacher, he gave me good support, like if I miss class also if I go and ask him...he will clarify without any scolding. There is another [teacher] who taught me from 5th class to 7th class, he even now comes and enquires about me...he is such a nice person.

At her current College, she turned to her Chemistry teacher for support:

> She is special to all of us, if we have any problems we go to her only first. We don't see her as madam [a teacher] we all treat her as mother. She also takes care of us more than other teachers. She tells us to treat her as our mother. We have stopped calling her madam, we call her mother. She tells us if she has any problems in her house…She not only understands us, she understands everything, whether it is small or big, any type of problem, she understands and gives suggestions.

Santhi's social networks can be interpreted as acting as social capital – in this case, the social capital that resided in her extended family, particularly her uncle who seemed to be a vital source of information and advice about schooling. Santhi also had access to a range of 'role models' within her extended family. By moving away from the tribal site, where there was a perceived lack of connections, her family enabled Santhi to expand her networks and possibilities (though whether she is able to continue and to resist marriage remains to be seen). Yaswanth, on the other hand, remained in Patna with a powerful sense of responsibility to his mother, and his priority was to find a way to look after her.

Poompuhar, a poor rural community

Poompuhar is a poor rural community in southern Telangana region of Andhra Pradesh. The main occupations are in agriculture and daily wage labour. Children are involved in cotton seed pollination work which has meant they miss school for two to three months each year, though this declined between 2007 and 2010 (Morrow et al. 2014). A new local secondary school recently opened, on land donated by the *sarpanch*, and by 2010 children were attending school regularly. The *sarpanch* and the local government were keen on reducing child labour in cotton seed pollination. The Mandal Revenue Officer, the school headmaster, *sarpanch* and teachers went around the village telling parents not to send their children to work. The headmaster has also introduced a small fine for every day of absence from school, or children had to clean the school premises. In order to avoid this, children pleaded with their parents not to send them to the cotton fields. Seasonal migration (February/May until June/July) was common, but the introduction of the national rural employment guarantee scheme (NREGS) means that wages have risen. There is plenty of work in public works (a railway track and canal work) as well as subcontract work on small farms, but this has unintended consequences for children, as they may substitute for parents by working on family land while their parents undertake wage labour.

Two cases: Harika and Ranadeep

Harika is the only daughter in her family. She has a younger brother. When interviewed in 2007, her father was unable to work because he had injured his leg, and Harika's mother spent most of the day working at the family fields. Harika did most of the household work, while also working at pollinating cotton (see Morrow and Vennam 2010). She found it difficult to manage school and work. Harika said: 'If I go to the fields, I won't get an education.' A year later, there had been several changes in Poompuhar, and in Harika's situation. She had obtained a scholarship of Rs 6,000/a year, conditional on completing school, that is, continuing education beyond Class 10.[9] Generally, children were undertaking less cotton pollination work. Harika's situation had improved, and she was attending school more regularly, because her father had recovered, and 'he is going to the field now...I used to go in his place every morning'. She occasionally monitored the wage labourers while attending to work herself, effectively replacing her mother when she was away at the market selling vegetables. She explained that she is absent once in two or three weeks: 'when my mother goes out somewhere, when she goes out of the village. I have to go to the farm...'.

In 2010, aged 16, Harika had passed tenth grade and was attending a college in a nearby town, staying in a hostel. She described how at first her parents did not want her to continue her education, but with the help of her older brother and her mother's elder sister's daughters, she was able to persuade them:

> They told my parents that it will be good to send me for further education. In case, if they plan to get me married in between, than to stop my education after 10th grade, otherwise to send me for further education. Also now my parents are sending me for further

studies. I feel I am studying because of them [my cousins] and that makes me feel good.

She described a number of sources of social support – her younger brother was a support to her because he accompanied her everywhere:

> He is with me the entire time... he comes along wherever I go. This is the first time I am staying away from all of them [family]... he used to come with me when I would go to the fields or school. When he is with me, I am not scared.... when I go alone, I get scared, but when my brother is there, I feel confident.

He also did some of her errands and domestic work. Harika also explained that when she wasn't sure about something at (intermediate or secondary) school, she felt confident enough to go to teachers to ask for clarification. Her Headmaster at Poompuhar school was a support to them when they were doing exams.

> We did not know about the National Talent Test, he told us and explained about it. Even though I was the only girl who signed up for it, he gave me assurance and confidence that he is behind us and we should take the test. Sir helped to open an account in the bank. He did everything for us... Sir bought us the books, from 7th to 9th class.... gave us coaching, after the last class, he would take half an hour to coach us.

At college, there was another girl, 'my sister who is related to me...' (a cousin from Poompuhar) who was studying for the final year of her degree there.

> When we would go to her and tell that we are scared here and want to go back (home), she told that till we feel accustomed to the Hostel, we can sleep in her room, and she gave courage and confidence.... in College, I get scared to ask the lecturers... maybe because I am new, so I ask my friends in the hostel and they clear my doubts.

Harika described how the family turns to 'our brothers, my mother's elder sister's sons, if we need any money they are there to help us'.

She said: '[people] cannot do anything alone, they learn what to do on the basis of others' advice'. Reflecting back on the time when she missed school to work because of her father's injury, she said she 'knew that there was a shortage of money in the house, so I didn't ask for things'.

Thus, Harika recognised the importance of sources of support, advice and information. In her case, an interested head teacher seemed to have been the catalyst for her academic progress. Her wider kin networks supported her decision to continue in school, and there was a tension for her because her parents will want her to marry. Apart from her teacher, her social connections seemed to be limited to familial networks, and these networks operated as capital insofar as they supported her aspirations and her decisions about education.

When interviewed in 2007 and 2008, Ranadeep was ambitious to migrate away from Poompuhar, to run his own business and open a small shop. By 2010, he had failed his tenth grade exam. Five of his friends had also failed. Ranadeep was now farming. He still aspired to go to college, and had applied to retake his exam. He had worked pollinating cotton, but his uncle had told his parents not to make him work. The family needed labour because the National Rural Employment Guarantee Scheme had pushed up the price of local wages. Ranadeep described how his uncle, who was a teacher at a college in Gadwal, was teaching him in preparation for the exam in March. 'I am learning and working at home, my uncle comes and he is teaching me'. His uncle had told his parents not to make him work on the land, but

> my parents never listened to him... there is nobody to work in the fields, and there is no labour coming, and we need to pay Rs100/- as wages every day, and we were not able to afford it, so they stopped me from going to school. (My parents) told me I need to do both work and studies.

This had led to friction and arguments since he failed, because his father blamed his mother for sending him to work:

> My father knows, he has studied so he knows the importance of tenth class, but my mother is not educated... so she does not know... she will not listen.... she says we will not get jobs even if

we study, so she will tell us to come to the fields and work. I told her 10th class is important, and I will be a waste if I don't complete my 10th class, ... still she will not listen. My mother never listened. So my father took me to the fields to work, they stopped me from going to school for a month. During that time they (fellow school-mates) covered most of the chapters (syllabus).

Here, family operates as a social field, with family members taking differing approaches to cultural capital in the form of educational qualifications. Informal social networks in the form of friends also operate as social capital. Ranadeep described how his school friends helped him when he missed school to work:

> I used to borrow the notes from my friends in the night, and used to say the answers when the teachers asked me. I used to ask my friends what they learned in school that day, and used to update myself...my friends helped me a lot.... Those who are good to us, we call them friends.

He described how he is now closer to his friend Prahalad,

> he also failed, he told us that in our fate it is written that we must only do agriculture (be farmers). There is no way we can go to college. He also felt bad....

When asked specifically about sources of social support, he mentioned his friends helping him with exams and school; his family supported him financially, within limits; his paternal uncle taught him maths. He mentioned relatives providing emotional support, and 'I am expecting help from the government in the form of a scholarship for continuing my higher education'. He abandoned the idea to open a shop – he said he didn't want to tell his family and, like Harika, he didn't want to ask for help: 'I know they are struggling in the house, so how will I ask?' A recent crop failure meant further debts. However, we know that by 2012, he had successfully passed his tenth grade exams, and was at college.

From a Bourdieusian perspective, then, Ranadeep was acutely aware of the importance of school qualifications (a form of cultural capital), and saw himself as a 'waste' if he did not continue in formal education. He saw his family's poverty as the explanation for not asking for financial support. Yet his uncle had the resources to support him in resitting his exams and indeed, this strategy was successful in the short term because it enabled Ranadeep to continue in college. Further rounds of data will show whether or not he is able to escape from a life of farming.

Discussion

In a Bourdieusian sense, powerful norms, values and social hierarchies govern people's capacity to negotiate systems. The economic situation of children and young people only partially determines what happens to them – the relationship between cultural, social and economic capitals, and how these interact and are translated into other forms of capital, is the important point here. These forms of capital are always specific: some are legitimate in some fields, some in other fields, and they intersect dynamically. So, for example, it remains to be seen whether Santhi can convert the social capital in her social networks into cultural capital in the form of qualifications, which will then lead to a well-paid and rewarding job and career. Somewhat counter-intuitively, her acquisition of qualifications may inhibit her marriage prospects, if she has 'too much' schooling. This is where fields are in contradiction or tension, as modernising institutions of education and schooling intersect with the traditions of patriarchal societies.

Thus, children and young people's location in specific fields is also significant for mobility and access to markets, other livelihoods and services such as health and education. Formal schooling (another field) has expanded exponentially over the past 15 years and vast numbers of children are now enrolled in primary school. But how formal schooling operates to enable some children to progress and others to be left behind, and what processes of discrimination lie behind this need to be better understood. Despite numerous social policies aimed at reducing discrimination, social status according to caste and poverty status is still acutely felt and experienced. The young people described here do not lack social capital (in the sense of strong social networks) but the social capital they do have is bound up with other forms of capital and this is likely to inhibit their capacity to escape from poverty and disadvantage

In Patna and Poompuhar, and for all four young people described here, parents, brothers, sisters and extended family seemed to be the first line of support that young people and their families turned to. Our interviews with them led to numerous mentions of uncles, cousins and so on. This has implications for social reproduction – if wider networks linking young people to more powerful or more affluent others and to sources of information are not available, then this limits young people's possibilities. Family-based sources of social support/social capital will not help young people to move on and up out of poverty unless they include kin who have managed to escape the cycle of poverty and secure more affluent and respected positions, like Ranadeep's uncle. The young people provided detailed descriptions of reciprocal support, mostly family- and friendship-based. This is structured by gender – the young men's expressed desire to support their parents or mothers highlights the interdependency of family members, and the ways in which boys' contribution to the domestic economy extends into adulthood. This also has (hitherto) unexplored implications for relationships between generations, because children's knowledge (cultural capital) will exceed that of their parents, leading to possibilities of 'split' habitus and *'déclassement'* (the process whereby individuals leave their social situation/milieu).

In the case of the two girls, Santhi seemed to be well-connected socially, Harika less so, though she appeared to be have overcome initial difficulties, with the support of extended family and the head teacher at her primary school. The girls mentioned some individual teachers as vital sources of support, and in Poompuhar, the *sarpanch* seemed to have played an important role in encouraging children to go to school. Indeed, some social policy interventions appear to be experienced positively. However, this has to be balanced by descriptions of corruption and discrimination, at least in the case of Patna, where Yaswanth described how more affluent, higher caste villagers use their power to favour their own kind and thus exclude poorer families. In Poompuhar, it seems that the *sarpanch* has been instrumental in bringing about an improvement in children's lives in that more children now go to school.

However, in emphasising children's social networks and social support systems, there is a risk that we overlook the powerful impacts of other constraints on children's lives, such as the provision of educational opportunities, as well as economic factors relating to persistent poverty and widening inequality, that underpin their accounts. Simplistic understandings of social capital may inadvertently pathologise children in poverty, constructing them as deficient because they lack supportive and/or constructive social networks and contacts at the level of family. A more nuanced understanding based on Bourdieu's interconnected forms of cultural, social and economic capital combined with sociability, that is, the capacity to sustain and utilise social networks, as demonstrated by Santhi and, to an extent, Ranadeep, can advance our understanding of the practices of everyday life that children describe, and helps to explain how these practices constrain or enable young people to move out of poverty. By coupling Bourdieu's formulation of social capital as in relation to other forms of capital and as rooted in the practices of everyday life, with a view of children as having agency (albeit constrained) we can link micro-social and macro-social structural factors. We can use 'social capital' as a tool or heuristic device for exploring processes and practices that are related to the acquisition of other forms of capital (see also Morrow 1999).

Finally, Bourdieu's conceptualisation of social space seems to be crucial, and is arguably underplayed in his formulations of social reproduction as being mostly family-based. However, in *Weight of the World* (1999), Bourdieu documents the ways in which social spaces have effectively marginalised poor sections of (French) society. He suggests that we need to go beyond seeing 'material poverty as the sole measure of all suffering' because this

> keeps us from seeing and understanding a whole side of the suffering characteristic of a social order which, although it has undoubtedly reduced poverty overall ... has also multiplied the social spaces and set up the conditions for an unprecedented development of all kinds of ordinary suffering .... (Bourdieu 1999: 4)

Similar processes appear to be taking place on a global scale, as societies modernise and develop in highly uneven and iniquitous jumps and starts, and as 'traditional' and modern notions of self and identity collide, causing some to be left behind in what they see as undesirable situations.

Notes

1. The turn of the twenty-first century witnessed a wave of 'social capital' research based on Putnam's conceptualisation of social capital as consisting of formal, informal and community social networks, levels of trust, reciprocity, civic engagement and community identity. Putnam's work did not focus on children and youth. Coleman's research on youth in the US focused on social capital within families and communities and the causal effects on individual children's outcomes. See Morrow 1999 for a review.

2. 'Young Lives' is a 15-year study investigating the changing nature of childhood poverty in four countries, Ethiopia, Peru, the state of Andhra Pradesh in India and Vietnam. The study aims to improve understanding of the causes and consequences of childhood poverty and the role of policies in improving children's life chances, in the broad context of the Millennium Development Goals. Young Lives collects data from two cohorts of children in each country: 2,000 children born in 2000–1 (the younger cohort) and 1,000 children born in 1994–5 (the older cohort). A survey is carried out every three years with the full sample of children and their caregivers, and is complemented by qualitative research with a sub-sample of 50 children in four communities in each country, their parents/caregivers, and other key figures in the community, including teachers, local health workers and community leaders. See www.younglives.org.uk, and Crivello et al. (2013) for further details.

3. In development studies, the concept of social capital received a vast amount of academic attention during the late 1990s to early 2000s (see Fine 2010), though this did not focus on children and young people, who remain somewhat marginal subjects of study in international development, where human capital models dominate. However, social capital research with or related to children and young people in the UK underwent something of a boom period during the 2000s, and a more refined approach can be seen, for example, see Knight (this volume), Allan et al. 2009, Weller 2006, Reynolds 2010).

4. We draw here on data from three rounds of qualitative longitudinal research, conducted in 2007, 2008 and 2010, with 25 children born in 1994–5. Fieldwork is conducted by local research teams, fluent in local languages. A range of qualitative research methods are used, including one-to-one interviews, group discussions and creative activities. Interviews are conducted in homes, fields or in village community premises, and are voice recorded, transcribed and translated. Interviews are structured around specific questions, and last from 30 minutes to 2 hours. Data are coded by themes, using Atlas.ti qualitative data analysis software. Data are divided into different domains such as education, work and aspirations, and creating a narrative for each domain (see Crivello et al. 2013 and www.younglives.org.uk for details of methods, ethics and analysis). Names of children and places are pseudonyms.

5. Passing the tenth grade exam is necessary in order to proceed to the next stage: intermediate college.
6. Self-Help Groups: groups of 10–15 poor women who save together and lend each other money from a common fund. The aim is to reduce poverty by enabling women to have access to credit without needing collateral. The Government gives credit to these groups, on certain conditions, to assist them with lending. SHGs are a deliberate attempt to 'build social capital'.
7. Rural housing scheme to build *'pukka'* houses.
8. Scheduled Castes (SCs) are the lowest in the traditional caste structure and were earlier considered to be 'untouchables'/*dalit*. SCs have been subject to discrimination for years and have had no access to basic services, including schooling. Backward Castes or Classes (BCs) are people belonging to a group of castes who are considered to be 'backward' in view of their low level in the caste structure. Scheduled Tribes are indigenous communities, who are traditionally disadvantaged and live in forests and mountainous areas.
9. These scholarships are to encourage education and are given to various groups (SCs, girls) through different programmes. This particular scholarship was based on an aptitude test for which Harika was coached by the head teacher.

References

Alanen, L. and Siisiäinen, M. (eds). 2011. *Fields and capitals. Constructing local life*. Jyväskylä: Finnish Institute for Educational Research.

Allan, J., Ozga, J. and Smith, G. (eds) 2009. *Social capital, professionalism and diversity*. Rotterdam: Sense.

Ansell, N. 2004. Secondary schooling and rural youth transitions in Lesotho and Zimbabwe, *Youth and Society*, 36: 183–202.

Ansell, N. and van Blerk, L. 2004. Children's migration as a household/family strategy: coping with AIDS in Malawi and Lesotho, *Journal of Southern African Studies*, 30 (3): 673–90.

Behera, D. 2007. In between two cultures: the process of educational institutionalisation of tribal children in Orissa, India. In K. Malone (ed.), *Child space: An anthropological exploration of young people's use of space*. New Delhi: Concept.

Bell, S. and Payne, R. 2009. Young people as agents in development processes: Reconsidering perspectives for development geography, *Third World Quarterly*, 30: 1027–44.

Bourdieu, P. 1979. *Algeria 1960: The disenchantment of the world: The sense of honour and the Kabyle house or the world reversed: Essays*. Cambridge: Cambridge University Press.

Bourdieu, P. 1984. *Distinction: A social critique of the judgement of taste*. London: Routledge.

Bourdieu, P. 1986. The forms of capital. In J. G. Richardson (ed.), *Handbook of theory and research for the sociology of education*. New York, Greenwood Press.

Bourdieu, P. 2000. The politics of protest. An interview. *Socialist Review*, 242: 18.

Bourdieu, P. 2001. *Masculine domination*. Cambridge: Polity Press.

Bourdieu, P. 2004. *Esquisse pour une auto-analyse*. Paris: Raisons d'agir.

Bourdieu, P. and Wacquant, L. 1992. *An invitation to reflexive sociology*. Chicago: University of Chicago Press.

Bourdieu, P. et al. 1999. *The weight of the world. Social suffering in contemporary society*. Cambridge: Polity Press.

Camfield, L. 2012. Resilience and well-being among urban Ethiopian children: What role do social resources and competencies play? *Social Indicators Research*, 107: 393–410.

Coleman, J. 1988. Social capital, human capital and investment in youth, *American Journal of Sociology*, 94 (Supplement): S95–S120.

Crivello, G., Morrow, V. and Wilson, E. 2013. Young Lives Longitudinal Qualitative Research: A guide for researchers. *Young Lives Technical Note 26*. Oxford: Young Lives.

Dyson, J. 2010. Friendship in practice: Girls' work in the Indian Himalayas, *American Ethnologist*, 37 (3): 482–98.

Ennew, J. 1994. Parentless friends: A cross-cultural examination of networks among street children and street youth. In F. Nestmann, and K. Hurrelmann, (eds), *Social networks and social support in childhood and adolescence*. Berlin: de Gruyter.

Evans, R. 2011. 'We are managing our own lives....': Life transitions and care in sibling-headed households affected by AIDS in Tanzania and Uganda, *Area*, 42 (4): 384–96.

Fine, B. 2010. *Theories of social capital: Researchers behaving badly*. London: Pluto Press.

Froer P. 2011. Education, inequality and social mobility in Central India, *European Journal of Development Research*, 23: 695–711.

Hulme, D. and Moore, K. 2010. Thinking small, and thinking big about poverty: Maymana and Mofizul's story updated, *Bangladesh Development Studies*, 33 (3): 77–96.

Jenkins, R. 1992. *Pierre Bourdieu*. London: Routledge.

Jones, G. and Chant, S. 2009. Globalising initiatives for gender equality and poverty reduction: exploring 'failure' with reference to education and work among urban youth in The Gambia and Ghana, *Geoforum*, 40: 184–96.

Koffman, O. and Gill, R. 2013. 'The revolution will be led by a 12-year-old girl': Girl power and global biopolitics, *Feminist Review*, 105: 83–102.

Mizen, P. and Ofosu-Kusi, Y. 2010. Asking, giving, receiving: Friendship as survival strategy among Accra's street children, *Childhood: A journal of global child research*, 17 (4): 441–54.

Morrison, S., Howard, R., Hardy, C. and Stinson, B. 2005. Social capital, health and HIV awareness of girls in a rural Caribbean community, *International Electronic Journal of Health Education*, 8: 135–45.

Morrow, V. 1999. Conceptualising social capital in relation to the well-being of children and young people: A critical review, *The Sociological Review*, 47 (4): 744–65.

Morrow, V. 2001. Young people's explanations and experiences of social exclusion: Retrieving Bourdieu's concept of social capital. *International Journal of Sociology and Social Policy*, 21, (4/5/6): 37–63.

Morrow, V. 2013. Whose values? Young people's aspirations and experiences of schooling in Andhra Pradesh, India, *Children & Society*, 27: 258–69.

Morrow, V. and Vennam, U. 2010. Combining work and school: The dynamics of girls' involvement in agricultural work in Andhra Pradesh, India, *Children & Society*, 24: 304–14.

Morrow, V., Tafere, Y. and Vennam, U. (2014) Changes in rural children's use of time: Evidence from Ethiopia and Andhra Pradesh. In J. Boyden and M. Bourdillon (eds), *Growing up in poverty: Findings from Young Lives*. Palgrave: Basingstoke.

Payne, R. 2012. Agents of support: Intra-generational relationships and the role of agency in the support networks of child-headed households in Zambia, *Children's Geographies*, 10 (3): 293–306.

Pells, K. 2011. 'Keep going despite everything': Legacies of genocide for Rwanda's children and youth, *International Journal of Sociology and Social Policy*, 33 (9/10): 594–606.

Punch, S. 2002. Youth transitions and interdependent adult-child relations in rural Bolivia. *Journal of Rural Studies*, 18 (2): 123–133.

Putnam, R. 2000. *Bowling alone. The collapse and revival of American community*. New York: Simon and Schuster.

Reynolds, T. 2010. Editorial introduction: Young people, social capital and ethnic identity, *Ethnic and Racial Studies*, 33 (5): 749–60.

Vennam, U. and Andharia, J. 2012. Chronic poverty amid growth: Insights from long-term poverty trajectories. *Young Lives working paper 84*. Oxford: Young Lives.

Weller, S. 2006. Skateboarding alone? Making social capital discourse relevant to teenagers' lives, *Journal of Youth Studies*, 9 (5): 557–74.

9
Struggling to Support: Genesis of the Practice of Using Support Persons in the Finnish Child Welfare Field

Johanna Moilanen, Johanna Kiili and Leena Alanen

Introduction

Bourdieu has often – and we believe mistakenly – been regarded as a theorist of social reproduction rather than a theorist of transformation. Along with many others, we consider the Bourdieusian approach a particularly valuable means for studying social change. For Bourdieu history appeared as 'a privileged instrument for breaking with received views that strike the uncritical observer as self-evident, commonsensical, and only natural' (Bourdieu and Wacquant 1992: 238; Swartz 2013: 22). His own studies on social transformation often focused on such large-scale *fields* as the French academic world (1988 [1984]), the *grandes écoles* (1996a [1988]), art (1996b [1992]) and economy (2005 [2000]). Gorski delineates Bourdieu as an eminent theorist of historical change in that his master concepts 'can be elaborated into a more general framework for describing various forms and levels of socio-historical change and tracing out causal interconnections' (Gorski 2013b: 327; also 2013a).

Field is a key concept among Bourdieu's 'working tools' when analysing social change. In this chapter[1] our focus is on one social field – state-organised child welfare in Finland – and a change in its practices from the early 1970s up to the present. The study presented here is based, and expands, on our previous work (Moilanen et al. 2014) in which we adopted a Bourdieusian frame to study how a particular practice is currently operated in one location. The practice of *using support persons* (in short: PSP) as an 'open care' method in child welfare social work is today well established in Finland. In the study we conceptualise child welfare work as a social *field* and as a subfield of the broader state-organised social work field, which is interconnected, horizontally and vertically, with a range of other social fields, including the field of power. Here the scale we focus on is however smaller as we explore the *genesis* of that particular practice, given the changes in its many interconnected fields. We do so by embedding the emergence of the idea of 'support' – the key novel idea of the practice – within the struggles in the child welfare field.

We start with a brief and condensed review of the results of our previous analysis (Moilanen et al. 2014) of a local case of operating the PSP. Building on this, the following section is an exploration and a descriptive account of how the practice came into being – its *genesis* (for instance, Gorski 2013b). The data available to us do not allow us to follow year by year the transformation of the PSP from the early 1970s to its present usage. Instead, we juxtapose a current case of operating the PSP with the practice previously dominant in the field, and analyse the emergence of the first forms of the PSP as new objectives of child welfare work were locally adopted. By asking 'What has the present been made of?' we aim to generate a better understanding of the current state of operation of the PSP and the (new) tensions that over time have emerged as an effect of changes in the child welfare field's autonomy.

Practising support in child welfare

Agents and relations

The practice of using *support persons* has been part of municipal child welfare in Finland since the early 1970s, although it only became official with the Child Welfare Act 1983. There is, then, more than 40 years of experience in this practice. Despite this, and rather surprisingly, we lack experiential and research knowledge and even descriptive statistics on the practice.[2] Clearly, a question to ask is why so much trust is being placed in the practice as a presumably effective open care method in child welfare, and what in fact is contained in the 'support' that is 'given' to selected children? In our previous paper we aimed to give this question at least a partial answer, by disclosing its working in a local child welfare field. What follows in this section is a résumé of our earlier study's results (Moilanen et al. 2014).

The current Child Welfare Act (2007) stipulates that the municipal body responsible for social services *must, wherever necessary, arrange a support person (or family) for the child deemed to be in need of support*. A child welfare social worker should, then, assess and decide on the need for provision, and an official decision must be made about the terms and conditions under which a support person will be working with a particular child. Also a support person cannot be appointed against the will of the child or parent(s), and children must have the opportunity to present their own views and wishes on the relationship before entering it.

The PSP service was originally meant to be provided by the municipal child welfare agency. At present, however, the municipal agency may also purchase the service from private for-profit or non-profit organisations. Non-profit child welfare organisations in Finland have a history of organising various forms of support services, and several of them have developed novel practices which closely resemble those of the 'municipal' PSP. Most recently the 'market' has entered the welfare service arena as a service provider, including in its repertoire also support person services (Moilanen 2011). Often the support services provided by for-profit organisations are based on employing variously trained professionals from the social and health care sectors, whereas in the case we studied the support work is delivered by *volunteers* – as was also the fundamental idea when the practice was originally introduced (see the next section).

The operation of the practice can be described, in Bourdieu's field analytical terms, as follows.

The *agents* in the local child welfare *field* within which the volunteer support person practice is operating, include, first of all,

- the municipal *welfare agency* (child welfare social workers), and
- the *volunteers* who actually perform the support work.

Clearly, to fully account for the operation of the PSP, the *children* (and their families) who are clients of the child welfare agency and inducted into a relationship with a support person, also have to be reckoned with. The local case we studied involved an additional party mediating between the municipal agency and the volunteers:

- the *child welfare NGO* that provided the service as a purchase-service for the municipality.

Thus the local child welfare field was one in which 'the market' had entered as one of its agents.

The explicit aims of the practice, according to our documentary and interview data (see Moilanen et al. 2014), were

- to promote the well-being of children and families,
- to support families in raising their children, and
- to prevent children from getting into 'risky situations'.

A support relationship is established by a child welfare social worker who, after assessing and confirming, together with the child and his/her parent(s), the need for the service, delivers a support person application to the NGO (the service coordinator). The NGO then recruits a volunteer to act as the child's support person. The child, the parent(s), the volunteer, the social worker and the coordinator sign an official agreement to start the relationship. Our study showed that the key aspects of the support relationship (its rationale, goals and time schedules) were mostly decided upon by adults (especially when the child is young). In our case the agreement was valid for one year, as the municipality allots funding for support person services for one year at a time.

The PSP relies to a great extent on the interest and commitment of individual *volunteers*. They are recruited via several channels, and can in principle have varied educational, occupational and other backgrounds. Volunteers are expected to report regularly to the NGO on progress made in their relationship with 'their' child. They are also required to be present at the biannual assessment meetings along with the child, the parent(s), the social worker and the service coordinator. In addition, volunteers are instructed to report their child-related concerns to the coordinator, who in turn is legally bound to submit a child welfare notification if needed.

The social workers monitor the operation of the practice and oversee the rights of children and parents. Thus they are holders of the political and legal authority in organising the child-support person relationships. In Bourdieusian terms they have considerable *political* and *juridical capital* although this is constrained by the municipal budget (decided upon by the local field of power). Moreover, the municipality depends on the NGO (the only local service provider), which therefore also holds considerable power resources (capital).

Symbolic capital

We found evidence of a broad consensus on the *valued cultural (and social) resources* that volunteers were seen to need in order to be able to produce a 'good' support relationship: she or he needs to be a caring, trustworthy and safe adult, and provide enjoyment and novel experiences for the child. Importantly, a support person should be 'just his or her ordinary self', unburdened by the duties and obligations of a child welfare professional. Thus a support person's *'ordinariness'* was believed by all respondents, as was evident also in the documents, to be effective in supporting children in their various needs (compare Ward 2004: 211–12; Regner and Johnsson 2007). We interpret this 'ordinariness' to be a specific form of *cultural capital* and one that 'bureaucrats' (social workers) do not hold when working in the professional field (compare Halliday et al. 2009: 420–1). Thus, 'being ordinary' was, for the volunteers, the required 'admission fee' to the child welfare field.

More than half the support persons interviewed had a professional background in education, social or health care; nevertheless, all those interviewed strongly emphasised the value of 'ordinariness'. Thus support persons are expected to clearly distinguish their position from that of the child welfare professionals as well as of the child and his/her family members. To ensure this, the value of *being an ordinary adult* was underlined.

However, when the volunteers expressed the felt worth of their support work, they frequently used the more professional-bureaucratic welfare discourse of 'risks', 'prevention' and 'cost-effectiveness'. Obviously the use of the practice itself has been influenced by professional notions of 'good parenting' and 'child well-being'. Also administrative protocols and legal obligations are constantly mediated to the field through established child welfare channels, leading both the volunteers and the professionals to define what is 'normal' and what is not, in enacting the PSP.

There was unanimity in both the documents and the interviews on the way 'normality' is understood in the field and on the goal of the practice: to bring 'normality' and 'ordinariness' into children's *family relations*. Both data sets could also be read as underlining and supporting the notion that because of their 'inadequate' family life the children's social and emotional environment requires improvement. The idea of 'normality' in a child's life and of the 'naturalness' of family seemed to be the foundational belief (*doxa*) in the PSP field: the 'right' kind of 'ordinariness' is gained by living within 'normal', 'ordinary' familial contexts, and this is what the support practice aimed to provide.

Consequently the valued social and cultural resources within the PSP were those needed to emulate close familial relations and to nourish (familial) values, such as commitment, caring and loyalty, and the child's proper upbringing (compare Webb et al. 2002: 22; Kendrick 2013). Such resources – a species of *family capital* – could therefore be seen as a stake in the contestation of what constitutes legitimate capital in the child welfare field; in Bourdieu's terms: *symbolic capital*.

The expressed need for more *male* support persons to compensate for absent fathers gives additional support for this interpretation. In some cases, absent fathers were even mentioned as risking their children's (especially boys') healthy development and growth (see also Regnér and Johansson 2007: 322). This further reflects the privileged position that the nuclear model of family relations occupies in Western culture (Uhlmann 2006: 47; Alanen 2011) thus providing the PSP with its key *interest*.

Field-specific habitus

What are the motivations for working as a volunteer? Especially the younger volunteers in our study expressed a desire to 'help people'. These altruistic motives seem to be connected to the volunteers' own life *trajectories* over social space and time. Often specific life histories and situations had encouraged volunteering, for instance volunteers may have started after some transition point in their personal lives, such as taking to independent living as students or retiring from paid employment. In other cases a change in the volunteers' social networks, such as leaving behind their childhood family, friends or colleagues at work, may have prompted them to do voluntary work, as if to fill a void in their social life. Similarly some of the older volunteers referred to their earlier life experiences, such as having lived in a large family, which had a formative effect on their habitus (dispositions).

Dispositions to volunteer also have a civic aspect as they may simultaneously derive from Finnish legislation which stipulates that child welfare is a concern for all public authorities. Thus all public services are responsible for promoting children's welfare. Volunteers often come from these (professional) domains and from a broad mosaic of civic associations in which children's welfare issues are addressed and information on opportunities to promote them as (responsible) *citizens* is disseminated.

Volunteering at field intersections

The volunteers strongly believed that the PSP generally accomplishes its stated objectives. However, despite the general belief in positive effects for children, half the volunteers simultaneously expressed scepticism about the real effects of the practice, given that their meetings with the child were infrequent. As laypersons drawn into the child welfare field, without the authority or resources that are available to social workers, volunteers easily face a human dilemma: they are engaged in activities for the good of children and they do this voluntarily. They also clearly value the support practice, and sense that they are valued by the public for engaging in civic work. But their involvement in the PSP also induces some misgivings on the outcomes and the meaningfulness of the practice.

The PSP is not only located in the professional child welfare field: the logic in 'playing the game' in which the volunteers are involved is in many ways different and distinct from professional child welfare work, and the practice is partly also civic action. Furthermore, by modelling the practice according to familialist notions of (adult) responsibility and caring it is also connected to the family field (for instance Lenoir 2003; Alanen 2011; Atkinson 2014). The significance for the PSP of such an *intersectional* location in and between several fields becomes obvious by looking more closely at the effects of the practice, as experienced by the interviewed support persons. This leads to our interpretation that the scepticism derives from the *shifting value of field-appropriate capital* in the intersecting fields in question. This becomes manifest in the volunteers' questioning of the value of the *cultural* and *symbolic capital* they retain: in their experience its value is underrated in the total symbolic economy in the child welfare field as well as in the family field. Professional social workers enjoy greater symbolic capital, since their capital, gained via university qualifications and positions of relative authority in child welfare matters, is objectified and bureaucratised in law (compare Halliday et al. 2009.) They also know what 'needs' to be done when treating cases, whereas 'ordinariness' implies resources that cannot be legitimately used in the professional field. The expected and enacted 'ordinariness' also connects to the ideal of 'normal' family but the volunteers are not to act as if they were members of the child's family. All of this leaves them in a paradoxical (contradictory) position at the intersection of, or between, the fields of family and child welfare work proper, and with feelings of reservation and scepticism as to the real effects of their contribution.

Overall the aims imposed on the PSP seem rather demanding, especially given the civic nature of the practice. These ambitious aims may originate in the heritage of social work and child welfare as charity work, but we propose a different kind of explanation. What at first seems to be contradictory may in fact provide the best outcome in that the resources and the control provided by child welfare authorities may guarantee the effectiveness of a practice based primarily on volunteer work. We thus suggest that volunteers are positioned as 'softeners' in the child welfare field: their function is to mediate between the field of (institutional, 'bureaucratic') child welfare and the family field, these being somewhat natural opposites to each other. How did such a situation come into being? In the next section we give a descriptive account of the genesis of the practice in the 1970s.[3]

Genesis of the practice

Reorienting child welfare

Until the 1960s, Finland was a comparatively poor and mainly rural nation. An extensive in-country migration during the late 1960s and early 1970s caused major social transformations which were also felt in the field of social welfare. Critique was voiced in the public domain towards the fundamental/basic grounding ideas and the style in social welfare work which, relying on the traditions of poor relief, were criticised for being stigmatising, patronising and controlling (Kröger 2011; Urponen 1994: 240–3).

The reform of social care and the expansion of social services in the late 1960s and 1970s implied setting new goals for social work, including efforts to turn the field into one based on science and to increase the number of professionals in social care and child welfare. (Satka 1994: 303–7; Pulma 1987: 241–3). Completely new, *open care* (non-residential) methods and public services (including public day care) were developed (Pulma 1987: 220). Up to the 1960s in many municipalities there were only laypersons acting within social care. Now they were seen as blocking the professionalisation and modernisation of the field (Satka 1994: 316–17; Rauhala 2001: 308–10). The distinction between criminal sanctions (*control*) on the one hand and services provided by social welfare (*support*) on the other hand was strongly underlined in public discourse, and it was argued that social problems would be effectively prevented by redistributing income and targeting public services at families with children (KM 1973: 86; Harrikari 2008: 105–7.) Since the *zeitgeist* stressed the negative sides of control and low tolerance of difference, the main aims of social work were redefined as 'the building of a trustworthy care-relationship' and 'exclusiveness of support' (KM 1973:86: 56, 96–7).

A key aim of the 1970s reforms was to revise the whole ideology of social welfare. Existing practices were to be changed to help implement the principles of orientation to service: *normality, freedom of choice, confidentiality, prevention and the promotion of independence* (KM 1971: A 25; KM 1973: 86). A reorientation was also taking place in the social work profession and the child welfare domain. An ideological turning point was reached in the late 1960s and early 1970s, crystallised as a 'turn from child protection policy to child policy', and promotion of children's rights (Pulma 1987: 243; Satka et al. 2002: 246).

The 'old' Child Welfare Act (1936), based largely on applying criminal justice doctrines in child protection, and including the measure of 'setting the child to protective supervision', was still in force. According to the Act (10 §), a 'protective supervisor' was to

> carefully monitor a child or youngster under supervision; to supervise and guide her/him in behavioural and attitudinal matters with instructions, advice and actions; to help parents in nurturing and upbringing their children; and to have an eye on parents' duties to their children.

'Protective supervision' was now regarded as bureaucratic, control-centred, stigmatising and even detrimental to its clients, with elements of unregulated sanctions performed by non-professionals with no expertise in child welfare. A Committee of Protective Education was set up in 1971, and took on the recommendation to remove the practice from the new child welfare law under preparation (KM 1972:B135; KM 1973:86: 96–7). The main aim of the new practice (PSP) would be *freedom of choice*, and it was to provide *normality, prevention* and *personal support* for minors with social and psychological troubles. As an open care method the PSP would also support families and parents in raising their children. The Committee Report portrayed a support person as an *adult whom the child could trust* – a trustful relationship was to be a key goal and resource for the child in overcoming a difficult life situation (KM 1972: B135: 98, 101; also SHYK B52/1974/lv).

The transition from protective supervision to the PSP took place before changes in the legislation due to the pressure on the municipalities to develop new open care methods (Helasvuo 1974: 100; LSJ 19.2.1979: 80 §; GI). State authorities actively promoted the adoption of the PSP by allocating funds for the development of open care methods and making clear that funds were not to be used for protective supervision. The national guidelines now strongly emphasised that the aim of the PSP was not to replace trained social work professionals and that support persons needed training and supervision.[4]

Struggling to support: the practice comes into action

In our local case study, a group of social workers in the child welfare agency also recommended, in their proposal to the welfare board (1972), rejection of protective supervision: because firstly, it did not work, and secondly, it did not include any (professional) elements of personal support and guidance for the child and his/her family (SLK 21.6.1972: 254 §). The local authorities were already in favour of giving up protective supervision, and a new generation of university-educated social work professionals had entered the field, fully embracing the new client-centred and supportive approaches (GI). The new PSP model of work was presented, on the one hand, as lay activity, and on the other hand, as a valuable open care method that filled a gap in existing professional resources. Along with the emphasis on working *personally* with an individual child or youngster, supporting the *whole family* was underlined (also SLKVK 1973: 10; YOK 29.8.1973: 325 §).

The PSP was put into practice locally in 1973. It was not the support persons' occupational or educational background that was the issue but their *willingness to work with children and families* and *to create a trustful relationship with them*. The support person candidates were provided with 20 hours of training by social work and other helping professionals. They were expected to keep regular contact with social workers by participating in monthly meetings which functioned as a form of collective supervision of the practice. The decision was made in the social welfare board to grant the support persons a relatively small monthly compensation, despite some moaning about 'paying for voluntary work' (SLK 21.6.1973: 260 §; GI).

Two main agents were involved in putting the PSP into local action: the *social workers* who worked in the municipality under its child welfare division which in turn was subordinated to the local social welfare board,[5] and the *volunteers*. A child welfare *social worker* was expected to take the initiative of setting up a support relationship for a child after first assessing the need for provision.[6] The municipal child welfare division was then to decide on the support person for the child. In practice the framework was not as strict as that, as support relationships were often confirmed only after forming them. Still, a formal decision was necessary in order for the volunteer to get her/his activities financially compensated. The social workers were to follow up each case of support, and the support persons were obliged to make formal reports to the social worker in charge of their case, but again procedures were not followed strictly: some volunteers compiled their reports regularly, while others did not, or merely reported orally (HA 1–2, 6, 15–16; also GI).

In summary, in new social conditions the field of child welfare sought to strengthen its professional quality and its autonomy in redefining the value of child welfare work. The implementation of the PSP meant getting rid of the earlier links with protective supervisors and layperson-based social work and relying on a relationship between professionally educated social workers and volunteer support persons trained by them (compare Noordegraaf and Schinkel 2011: 117). The sharp demarcation between the 'old field' and the 'new field' implied furthermore that the field's *doxa* – what is taken for granted in the field – became contested (see also Saurama 2002: 233–4). 'Support' was the emerging new *doxa* that as a symbolic form of power would hold the child welfare field together (cf. Deer 2008; Gorski 2013b: 332).

Symbolic capital emerging

We traced in our data the valued cultural and social resources that volunteers were believed to hold in accomplishing a successful support relationship with a child. In the early years of the new practice, ideological differences between old and new were strongly emphasised: the support person was considered to be in many ways the reverse of the protective supervisor, as manifested in an excerpt from a trade journal article:

> A support person is not a supervisor nor an advisor or instructor. S/he is a trusted person and an equal partner in co-operating with the young person and her/his family, and above all respectful of the confidentiality that is built up with the young person. (Hiltunen 1974: 304)

An overriding issue also was not to appoint a support person against the wishes of the child. In the case of protective supervision this was not considered important at all; now it was accepted that a child could refuse a support person. Such a change in the significance of a child's own wishes appears clearly in what social workers wrote in the case records, and in the initiatives they submitted to the child welfare division, for example: 'the issue has been discussed with both the mother and the boy, and they have both accepted the idea' (YOK 12.11.1974: 863 §; see also Saurama 2002: 196).

Because the cornerstone of the new practice was to establish a confidential and open human relationship between the child and the support person, the support persons were absolutely not meant to be used by the child welfare agency to supervise or maintain control over clients. (KM 1972: B 135: 99, app. 5; also Helasvuo 1974: 100–1; Hiltunen 1974.) In practice however, despite aims to eliminate the monitoring and controlling elements specific to the 'old' field, new (more hidden) mechanisms of control were created. They appeared, for instance, in support persons' obligations to make formal reports and to keep regular contact with the social workers.

Our data show how appropriate support relationships were described, for instance 'being a child's mate' or acting as a 'mother/father figure'. The rationales for such model relationships clearly followed the discourse of developmental psychology and the conviction that 'a growing child needs at least one unbroken and safe relationship based on personal familiarity and mutual trust' (Saloranta 1974: 349; also KM 1972: B 135: app. 5; Helasvuo 1974: 101).

Towards the end of the 1970s the need for male support persons surfaced more strongly in the discussion around the PSP; in fact the lack of male support persons was jeopardising the development of the practice (LSJ 19.2.1979: 73 §). Case records occasionally point to the belief that a particular child needs a 'father-figure', alternatively a 'safe adult', in her life, to compensate for a missing ('good') parent. This is exemplified in an account of the progression of a support relationship: The mother had ... was discontinued. (LSJ 14.9.1977: 277 §)

The support persons also recognised this 'parental expectation' in their assessments of what a child 'needs' (for instance, HA 7–8, 11, 15, 17.) At times the support person was positioned as a peace-maker, whose task was to mediate between the child and her/his parent(s) and help to settle disagreements in the family (e.g. HA 1–3, 6–8, 15). Thus she or he was to step also into the contested 'family arena':

> I have considered my central tasks to improve, among family members, communications skills, the ability to express oneself and one's needs and to receive message from others as 'objectively as possible'... For this purpose I have started a new activity: a joint session. A joint session is a discussion, to be arranged every four weeks. Everyone needs to be present and the idea is to deal with all matters concerning family members. One of the principles is that each member presents his/her view on the matter at hand. Disagreement is allowed and even necessary, but no one should be insulted by it. (HA 6, a support person's report from 1977; a male support person working with a single father and his three children)

The emerging symbolic capital in the early operation of the PSP derived fairly straightforwardly from the idea of the 'naturalness' of familial relations (see also Satka 1995: 127–8). The support persons were expected to provide both family-like caring and non-controlling and enriching relationships for the children which were assumed also to support the well-being of children and their families. The required personal qualities of a support person were not distinctly specified; reliability, trustworthiness and safety in their everyday sense, sufficed.

Emerging habitus, intersecting fields

More than half of the support persons in the 1970s had a professional background, such as in social work, psychology, education, youth work or parish work, or they were studying for a profession (YOK and LSJ 1973–80). Thus it comes as no surprise that several support persons described support activities in highly professional terms, in their reports to social workers. Even specific professional methods or tests were reported as being carried out with children, such as psychological tests or specific family work methods (for instance HA 3, 6–7).

A further boost to the 'professionalisation' of the support persons' position was their often close cooperation with the child welfare social workers – a cooperation resembling collegiality, for instance through joint home visits or meetings with other professionals. Some support persons also kept regular contact with a child's teacher or other professionals, aiming to support the child's schooling (HA 2–4, 6–9, 12, 14–15; GI). Often, then, the network of professionals with whom a support person was working was not limited to social workers only. The following excerpt demonstrates the cooperation between the support person and the child's teacher, but also the 'parental expectation' of support persons:

> I had an excellent opportunity to familiarize myself with [the boy's] schooling during a parents' meeting arranged by the teachers of his school. I met there both his class teacher and his English teacher. Both told me that (the boy's) school work was really not going well. ... I told these teachers about [the boy's] background and factors that evidently had an impact on his school work (conditions at home, his big brother's 'aiming at power' and so on). (HA 8, a support person's report from 1975; a male support person to two school age boys)

In their reports to social workers support persons often gave quite inclusive and comprehensive evaluations of the everyday situation of the children and the factors that in their view caused their problems.

Some also presented fairly educated solutions to the children's problematic situations and behaviours, as reported in this excerpt:

> All the disturbances probably originate in his childhood and the conditions that then prevailed in his home. A reform school has been considered, but I want to wait until next autumn, because my therapy takes place over a longer time-frame. (HA 3, a support person's undated report; a male support person to a school age boy)

In summary, examples in our data suggest a considerable degree of *ambiguity* in the relations between child welfare professionals and volunteers and consequently in the content and scope of volunteering. Child welfare social work was in the process of professionalisation, pressuring the field's main agents (social workers) to accommodate their (professional) dispositions and to redefine the field-specific value (capital). Simultaneously, several laypersons recruited as support persons were already oriented towards the field as they had a professional background or were studying for a profession.[7] Recruitment may well have contributed to favouring persons with roughly similar backgrounds with professionals, that is, with dispositions to behave according to the emerging new logic of the field. Thus a 'good' volunteer was 'well-adjusted to the objective set of relations in which he or she occupies a position', and had developed 'a right feel for the game' (Noordegraaf and Schinkel 2011: 100; also Woolford and Curran 2013).

Every social field 'constitutes a potentially open space of play whose boundaries are *dynamic borders* and also the stake of struggles within the field itself' (Bourdieu and Wacquant 1992: 104). The boundary struggles thus concern the always changing interdependencies between the agents of the field – here: social workers and volunteer support persons. The endeavour of the former was to establish for themselves an independence which however can only be achieved in and through dependence (compare Noordegraaf and Schinkel 2011: 116; Bourdieu 1987: 829).

Conclusion

In this chapter we have presented our analysis of the genesis of a new field – a subfield within the broader field of state-organised child welfare in Finland. A field in the Bourdieusian sense is created through struggles among its members as they compete with each other to produce and be recognised for producing its distinctive value (Calhoun 2013: 50). The 'value' that members of the emerging field in the early 1970s sought to define and produce was *support* as a specific intergenerational relationship. In the governmental and state administrational fields 'support' was introduced as a new, more humane and caring discourse and an antithesis of the then domi-nant practice of protective supervision with its core idea of *control*.[8] Legitimised by the state agents, the transforming of the child welfare field was left to its local agents in municipalities. The focus of our analysis has been on the local level and on the way the field-defining value ('support') was brought to life in actual relations between two categories of agents in the field: social workers and volunteer support persons.

One of our conclusions concerns the PSP as an arena in which 'professionalism' became contested as symbolic field-specific capital (compare Schinkel and Noordegraaf 2011). Support persons' work became filtered through principles of professionalism and the new practice formed one channel to form these principles and enact them in the social work field. Thus the recruitment of volunteers with an appropriate professional background served as an (implicit) strategy of professionalisation.

Social work has now achieved a degree of professionalisation, and the position of the volunteers in relation to professionals is much more demarcated compared with the early days of the PSP. Today volunteers' most valued capital is their *ordinariness* – being neither too professional nor too family-like. Such an ambiguous resource cannot easily be turned into field-appropriate capital and legitimately used in the current professionalised child welfare field, as was possible in the 1970s when the content and scope of the PSP and the position of the volunteers in relation to professionals was not as clear as it is today. By linking this observation to the location of the PSP at the intersection of several fields, we inter-pret present day volunteers' scepticism as to the actual effects and the experienced value of their activities resulting from the *shifting value of field-appropriate capital* in the field of (professionalised) child welfare.

However, although the position of support persons in relation to social workers has changed over the decades, it seems that the idea of the 'normality' and the 'naturalness' of the nuclear family model as the *foundational belief* of the PSP still stands. The social and cultural resources that within the PSP are held valuable are thought to help in bringing normality into children's troubled family relations. As a species of *family capital* these resources constitute legitimate capital in the child welfare field – in Bourdieu's terms: *symbolic capital*. The ordinariness (or 'normality') that support persons are expected to 'deliver' to children is believed to be convertible into *familial resources* – resources that professional social workers cannot deliver. This conviction also probably helps to explain the popularity of the PSP over the decades, notwithstanding the remarkable lack of research evidence on the practice. On the basis of a study of a contact family programme (somewhat similar to the PSP), Swedish researchers recommend that, instead of aiming to provide nuclear family-like models, the practice should target the support in the direction of the children's schooling – one of the most important developmental factors influencing the future of children, especially clients of child welfare (Brännström et al. 2013: 413).

Today the field of child welfare is changing again, and so are the 'rules' of the 'game' played in the field, as new strategies (for instance, inspired by New Public Management) are introduced to the field and privatisation and outsourcing of social services to the private sector is increasing. New agents are entering the field (such as the NGO in our local case), causing the logic of practices in the field to change (Höjer and Forkby 2011). Public services are being offloaded to the non-profit and for-profit providers, which however depend on the public sector for funding (Woolford and Curran 2013: 49). As a likely result the interdependencies between the agents operating in the (child welfare) field need to be renegotiated according to the renewed logics of the field.

A Bourdieu-inspired approach represents a contribution to study both of (the history of) a social field itself and (the history of) its relations to the larger dynamic fields within which it is embedded. In the case of the PSP, the Bourdieusian framework has provided valuable tools to analyse the link between the social past and the social present, and also a link between the 'micro' and 'macro' levels of analysis (Emirbayer and Johnson 2008: 34–7; Gorski 2013b). A Bourdieusian framework also makes the presumption that child welfare does not name an institution but rather a more complex entity (a *field*) that is both the result of various historical processes of differentiation and struggles as well as an arena of ongoing struggles (Bourdieu 1998 [1994]: 41). A Bourdieusian perspective therefore helps to direct sociological analysis towards structural properties of social space: to fields as distributions of capital and as configurations of dynamic relations of interdependence (Emirbayer and Williams 2005: 716).

By adopting Bourdieu's thinking tools to study the PSP and the child welfare field more broadly we feel we have been able to identify both continuities and discontinuities in its practical operation *in time*. Historical analysis of fields enables deeper understanding, in this case of the logic of the PSP operating in a given social field and in its intersectional location in several other fields. To conclude, Bourdieusian tools offer an instrument for breaking self-evident, commonsensical, and natural 'truths', such as revealing the 'naturalness' of the nuclear family model as the foundational belief in the PSP.

* * *

Sources of data [Abbreviation as used in this chapter]

Archival and other original sources

Jyväskylä City Archives (Jyväskylän kaupunginarkisto):

- Annual reports of the local social welfare board 1960–86 [SLKVK]
- Minutes of the local social welfare board 1969–80 [SLK]
- Minutes of the general division under the board 1960–76 [YOK]
- Minutes of the child welfare division under the board 1977–86 [LSJ]
- Child welfare case file records (Fa2: 23–56) [HA]

National Institute for Health and Welfare Archives (THL:n arkisto)

- Guidelines given by the National Board of Social Welfare 1969–80 [SHYK]

Group interview of social workers [GI]

Acts

Act on Welfare Administration 1950 /Laki sosiaalihuollon hallinnosta 34/1950. Suomen asetuskokoelma vuodelta 1950. Helsinki: Valtioneuvoston kirjapaino.

Child Welfare Act 1936 /Lastensuojelulaki 52/1936. Suomen asetuskokoelma vuodelta 1936. Helsinki: Valtioneuvoston kirjapaino.

Child Welfare Act 1983 /Lastensuojelulaki 683/1983, Accessed 13 April 2014. http://www.finlex.fi/fi/laki/alkup/1983/19830683.

Child Welfare Act 2007 /Lastensuojelulaki 417/2007, Accessed 13 April 2014. https://www.finlex.fi/fi/laki/ajantasa/2007/20070417.

Committee reports [KM]

KM 1971: A25. Sosiaalihuollon periaatekomitean mietintö. Helsinki: Sosiaali- ja terveysministeriö.

KM 1972: B135. Suojelukasvatustoimikunnan mietintö. Helsinki: Sosiaali- ja terveysministeriö.

KM 1973: 86. Sosiaalihuollon periaatekomitean mietintö II. Perheiden ja alaikäisten sosiaalihuollon järjestämistä koskevat ehdotukset. Helsinki: Sosiaali- ja terveysministeriö.

Other sources

Helasvuo, K. 1974. Tukihenkilöt – käynnistyvä työmuoto, *Lapset ja yhteiskunta*, 33 (4): 98–104.

Hiltunen, M. 1974. Käytännön kokemuksia tukihenkilötoiminnasta, *Lapset ja yhteiskunta*, 33 (11): 303–7.

Saloranta, A. 1974. Tukihenkilötoiminta, sen asema ja rooli lastensuojelutyössä, *Huoltaja*, 62 (8): 348–53.

Notes

1. The article is a joint effort stemming from the research project "Intergenerational Partnerships: Emerging forms for promoting children's well-being", funded by the Academy of Finland (grant no. 134922).
2. This may itself be taken to signal the child welfare field's fairly low level of autonomy. In fact, very little is known about the 'open care' measures used in Finland, as well as in other Nordic countries. (Pösö et al. 2014; 910.)

3. In this section we make use of different types of historical documents: first, policy texts such as committee reports, laws and national guidelines by the National Board of Social Welfare, and also some professional texts such as trade journal articles.

   Our analysis is of one local case (Jyväskylä, a Central Finland town). The empirical data includes annual reports and minutes of the local social welfare board and the child welfare division (or corresponding division) subordinated to the board, social work case file records and municipal guidelines. Also one group interview was conducted with three social workers who were operating the practice in the 1970s and 1980s. From among over 40 case file records 17 case files were eventually selected for a more detailed analysis. We will refer to the data by using running 'case numbers' (HA 1–17). The methods included text analytical methods in the case of documentary data combined with systematic thematic analysis of the transcription of the group interview.

   Both the minutes of the board and case file records produced in child welfare social work are confidential documents. They were collected in the local archives. The consent to deal with the data was gained from the local social welfare authority, and since the work in question is part of the PhD work of the first author, the consent was acquired by her. Only she processed the confidential documents. The consent obtained did not require disguising the location.

4. As municipalities did not have enough trained professionals to work in open care, there was also an economic incentive to recruit (non-professional) support persons to work in open care. (SHYK 1974–1979; KM 1973:86: 96; KM 1972:B135: 100.)

5. The members of the social welfare board are selected by the political parties represented in the municipal council and are, according to valid legislation, the final decision-makers in social welfare issues. The Act on Welfare Administration (1950, 6 §) stipulated that the members of the board should be both men and women and at least one member should be a health care professional and one a professional in education.

6. In many cases a recommendation for a support relationship came also from other professionals, for example the family counselling clinic, school welfare officers or school psychologists. Their proposals clearly had weight in social workers' assessments of a child's need for a support person. (e.g. HA 6, 8, 10–12, 14.)

7. Research literature on professionalism tends to underline the trust that lay people (i.e. non-professionals; here including volunteers) must place in the professional. The professionalisation of social work in the period studied in this chapter thus involved the struggle of social workers to win that trust, also in their (ambiguous) relations with other agents in the field. Note that Bourdieu was highly critical of the concept of profession (see Bourdieu and Wacquant 1992: 241–5), whereas Schinkel and Noordegraaf (2011) argue that professionalism can usefully be interpreted as symbolic capital.

8. Balancing between supporting (or caring) and controlling is obviously one major classical dilemma in social work (e.g. Satka 1995; Saurama 2002). The dilemma is elicited and 'managed' in the social work field as a relational and historical formation in both contextually and temporally varied ways.

References

Alanen, L. 2011. Capitalizing on family: habitus and belonging. In L. Alanen and M. Siisiäinen (eds), *Fields and capitals. Constructing local life*, Jyväskylä: Finnish Institute for Educational Research, pp. 91–123.

Atkinson, W. (2014). A sketch of 'family' as a field: From realised category to space of struggles. *Acta Sociologica*, 57 (3): 223–35.

Bourdieu, P. 1987. The Force of law: Towards a sociology of the juridical field. *Hastings Law Journal* 38: 805–53.

Bourdieu, P. 1988 [1984]. *Homo academicus.* Cambridge: Polity.

Bourdieu, P. 1996a [1989]. *The state nobility. Elite schools in the field of power.* Stanford: Stanford University Press.

Bourdieu, P. 1996b [1992]. *The rules of art: genesis and structure of the literary field.* Cambridge: Polity.

Bourdieu, P. 1998 [1994]. *Practical reason: On the theory of action.* Cambridge: Polity.

Bourdieu, P. 2005 [2000]. *The social structures of the economy.* Cambridge: Polity.

Bourdieu, P. and Wacquant, L.W.D. 1992. *An invitation to reflexive sociology.* Oxford: Polity Press.

Brännström, L. et al. 2013. Long-term outcomes of Sweden's Contact Family Program for children, *Child Abuse & Neglect* 37 (6): 404–14.

Calhoun, G. 2013. For the social history of the present: Bourdieu as historical sociologist. In P.S. Gorski (ed.), *Bourdieu and historical analysis.* Durham & London: Duke University Press, pp. 36–66.

Deer, C. 2008. Doxa. In M. Grenfell (ed.), *Pierre Bourdieu: Key concepts.* Stocksfield: Acumen, pp. 119–30.

Emirbayer, M. and Johnson, V. 2008. Bourdieu and organizational analysis, *Theory and Society*, 37 (1): 1–44.

Emirbayer, M. and Williams, E. 2005. Bourdieu and Social Work, *Social Service Review*, 79 (4): 689–724.

Gorski, P.S. 2013a. Bourdieu as a theorist of change. In P.S. Gorski (ed.), *Bourdieu and historical analysis.* Durham & London: Duke University Press, pp. 1–18.

Gorski, P.S. 2013b. Bourdieusian theory and historical analysis. In P.S. Gorski (ed.), *Bourdieu and historical analysis.* Durham & London: Duke University Press, pp. 327–66.

Halliday, S. et al. 2009. Street-level bureaucracy, interprofessional relations, and coping mechanisms: A study of criminal justice social workers in the sentencing process, *Law & Policy*, 31 (4): 405–28.

Harrikari, T. 2008. *Riskillä merkityt. Lapset ja nuoret huolen ja puuttumisen politii-kassa.* Helsinki: Nuorisotutkimusseura/Nuorisotutkimusverkosto.

Höjer, S. and Forkby, T. 2011. Care for sale: The influence of new public management in child protection in Sweden, *British Journal of Social Work,* 41 (1): 93–110.

Kendrick, A. 2013. Relations, relationships and relatedness: residential child care and the family metaphor, *Child & Family Social Work,* 18 (1): 77–86.

Kröger, T. 2011. Retuning the Nordic Welfare Municipality: Central regulation of social care under change in Finland, *International Journal of Sociology and Social Policy,* 31 (3/4): 148–59.

Lenoir, R. 2003. *Genealogie de la morale familiale.* Paris: Editions du Seuil.

Moilanen, J. 2011. Lasten ja nuorten tukihenkilötoiminta ja sukupolvisuht-eiden muuttuva hallinta. In Satka, M. et al. (eds), *Lapset, nuoret ja muuttuvat hallinnan käytännöt.* Tampere: Vastapaino: pp. 279–318.

Moilanen, J., Kiili, J. and Alanen, L. 2014. Support person practice in the Finnish child welfare field. A relational analysis. In T. Harrikari, P.-L. Rauhala and E. Virokangas (eds), *Social Change and Social Work. The Changing Societal Conditions of Social Work in Time and Place.* Aldershot: Ashgate, pp. 175–92.

Noordegraaf, M. and Schinkel, W. 2011. Professional capital contested: A Bourdieusian analysis of conflicts between professionals and managers, *Comparative Sociology,* 10 (1): 97–125.

Pösö, T., Skivenes, M. and Hestbæk, A.-D. 2014. Child protection systems within the Danish, Finnish and Norwegian welfare states – time for a child centric approach?, *European Journal of Social Work,* 17 (4): 475–90.

Pulma, P. 1987. Kerjuuluvasta perhekuntoutukseen. In P. Pulma and O. Turpeinen (eds), *Suomen lastensuojelun historia.* Helsinki: Lastensuojelu keskusliitto, pp. 11–266.

Rauhala, P.-L. 2001. Kunnallisen sosiaalitoimen ja valtion suhde Suomessa: Valtakamppailuja, jännitteitä ja vuorovaikutusta. *Yhteiskuntapolitiikka,* 66 (4): 301–17.

Regnér, M. and Johnsson, L. 2007. The 'ordinary' family as a resource for single parents – on the Swedish contact family service, *European Journal of Social Work,* 10 (3): 319–36.

Satka, M. 1994. Sosiaalinen työ peräänkatsojamiehestä hoivayrittäjäksi. In J. Jaakkola et al. (eds), *Armeliaisuus, yhteisöapu, sosiaaliturva. Suomalaisen sosiaalisen turvan historia.* Helsinki, Sosiaaliturvan keskusliitto, pp. 261–339.

Satka, M. 1995. Making social citizenship. Conceptual practices from the Finnish Poor Law to professional social work. Jyväskylä: University of Jyväskylä.

Satka, M., Moilanen, J, and Kiili, J. 2002. Suomalaisen lapsipolitiikan mutkainen tie, *Yhteiskuntapolitiikka,* 67 (3): 245–59.

Saurama, E. 2002. *Vastoin vanhempien tahtoa.* Helsinki: Helsingin kaupungin tietokeskus.

Schinkel, W. and Noordegraaf, M. 2011. Professionalism as symbolic capital: Materials for a Bourdieusian theory of professionalism, *Comparative Sociology,* 10 (1): 67–96.

Swartz, D.L. 2013. Metaprinciples for sociological research in a Bourdieusian perspective. In P.S. Gorski (ed.), *Bourdieu and historical analysis.* Durham & London: Duke University Press, pp. 19–35.

Uhlmann, A.J. 2006. *Family, gender and kinship in Australia. The social and cultural logic of practice and subjectivity.* Aldershot: Ashgate.

Urponen, K. 1994. Huoltoyhteiskunnasta hyvinvointivaltioon. In J. Jaakkola et al. (eds), *Armeliaisuus, yhteisöapu, sosiaaliturva. Suomalaisen sosiaalisen turvan historia.* Helsinki: Sosiaaliturvan keskusliitto, pp. 163–260.

Ward, A. 2004. Towards a theory of the everyday: The ordinary and the special in daily living in residential care, *Child & Youth Care Forum*, 33 (3): 209–25.

Webb, J., Schirato, T, and Danaher, G. 2002. *Understanding Bourdieu.* London: Sage.

Woolford, A. and Curran, A. 2013. Community positions, neoliberal dispositions: managing nonprofit social services within the bureaucratic field, *Critical Sociology*, 39 (1): 45–63.

10

Decision-making Processes in Review Meetings for Children in Care: A Bourdieusian Analysis

Karen Winter

Introduction

In the UK and elsewhere parental and child involvement in social services review processes for children in care is a legal requirement and is seen as an essential mechanism through which the needs of children are identified and longer term plans for their care drawn up. Existing research indicates that despite significant improvements in law, policy and practice to secure greater involvement, and some positive parental and child experiences, important significant barriers remain. The gap between these broader developments and the experiences of many children and their parents suggests the need to reconsider the micro-dynamics within review meetings through which decisions are arrived at. Using Bourdieu's concepts of capital, field and habitus I report on the analysis of a single case study from a larger research project on the participation rights of young children in care. Applying the concepts provides insight into the social and relational processes that occur within the structured space of the review meeting. The case-study analysis reveals practices by social workers that perpetuate the marginalisation of both parents and children during the review meeting. I argue that theoretically informed research regarding social and relational processes within review meetings is important to improve understanding regarding how and why decisions are arrived at and I suggest that this knowledge could contribute to the development of practice in this area.

Current research, policy and practice regarding review meetings for children in care

With some regional variations there are, across the UK, statutory regulations and guidance relating to children in care which state that all children must be the subject of a review process that comprises a meeting, occurring at prescribed intervals and involving the child, their parents/main carers and key professionals (HM Government 2010; Review of Children's Cases Regulations (NI) 1996; Review of Children's Cases (Wales) 2007; Guidance on Looked After Children (Scotland) Regulations 2009). The purpose of review meetings, often referred to as LAC (looked-after-child) meetings, is to consider the child's needs and to agree to a plan that addresses these needs contextualised in their future care and contact arrangements. Social workers' understanding of 'the child's needs' is shaped and informed by the prevailing, dominant professional discourse, which underpins the management of and planning for children in care. In the LAC system, definitions regarding children's needs are located within developmental psychology; they focus on the sequential and age-related dimensions of children's physical, intellectual, social, emotional and psychological development. For example, the assessment and review forms for children in care that social workers must complete require that information is collated and organised under the domains of: health; education; family and peer relationships; self-care and competence; identity; emotional and behavioural development; and social presentation (Parker et al. 1991: 34). The regulatory framework reinforces the organisational imperative for social work professionals to be familiar with child development theory and manifestations of unmet need. It also requires social worker ability to identify the causes of impaired parenting capacity (such as parental domestic violence and abuse, mental health issues and alcohol and/or drug addiction) and to quantify their impact on children's development, using the technical terms and language contained in the forms and guidance accompanying the regulations. Thus these elements of the statutory framework provide social workers with a focus on protecting children from risk and harm and on providing services to ameliorate the impact of harm.

The same statutory regulations and guidance also make clear that the involvement of children and parents in these meetings is a legal requirement and is of central importance. So emphasis on protection and provision is complemented by emphasis on participation. Furthermore, recent legal and policy developments have all significantly strengthened children's involvement in the LAC review decision-making processes. Adoption and Children Act (2002) in England and Wales, for example, led to the requirement that all local authorities have in place Independent Reviewing Officers to: chair children's review meetings; oversee the care plans; and ensure their compliance with human rights considerations. This role has been further bolstered in England and Wales through the Children and Young Persons Act (2008). In addition many children in care now have access to advocacy services (Oliver and Dalrymple 2008; Barnes 2011). Parental involvement in the review process is a theme running throughout all legal provisions (McCann 2006) and has been reiterated in the most recently published English regulations on care planning, placement and review (HM Government 2010).

Research regarding review meetings indicates: that there has been a positive attitudinal shift in favour of parental and child involvement in decision-making meetings (Thomas 2005); that practice has improved (Thomas 2005); and that there is an acknowledgement of the positive personal benefits to children and parents stemming from their involvement (Cashmore 2002). However, research also identifies ongoing barriers to involvement in review meetings both in the UK (Thomas 2005; McCann 2006; Leeson 2007) and internationally (Vis and Thomas 2009; Pölkki et al. 2012). Some parents have complained they lack information, preparation and support and are fearful about contributing to the discussions in meetings (McCann 2006; Ofsted 2008). Children have highlighted their concerns about the structure, location and processes of the review meetings and about negative impacts on their self-esteem and self-confidence, arising from continued experiences of marginalisation and exclusion (Leeson 2007; Thomas 2011; Ofsted 2011).

While this body of research focuses on the effectiveness of the procedures, little research seeks directly to examine, understand and conceptualise the micro-dynamics of the decision-making processes during review meetings (Thomas 2011). This gap means that, as a profession, social work has not fully reflected critically on the question 'where in the review meeting does power lie and how is it exercised?'; it also means that attempts to improve practice only partially succeed. The single case-study analysis in this chapter uses a conceptual framework that engages with questions of power and influence in statutory review meetings. In so doing, the case study, which is illustrative rather than definitive, takes forward Garrett's observations (2007: 239): he argued that 'Bourdieu's theorization – what has been described as the "conceptual arsenal" – might assist the social professions to evolve better forms of practice'.

Review meetings and the concepts of field, capital and habitus

A review meeting represents a legally mandated structured space where professionals (including representatives from health, education and social care), parents and the child are required to come together – with the same common interest, namely the statutory requirement to review and agree to a plan for a child who is in the care of social services (HM Government 2010; Thomas 2011). It is commonly thought that the Chair possesses and wields ultimate power in the decision-making process (Ofsted 2011). However this oversimplifies power relations and ignores their dynamic, diffuse and contingent nature within review meetings. Of particular interest are questions relating to the social positioning of participants in relation to each other and to the child; the types of knowledge shared about the child; the perceived legitimacy and value of that knowledge; and the strategies by which this is shared and with what effect in terms of gaining influence over the shape and content of the care plan.

By applying Bourdieu's concepts to statutory decision-making frameworks, we may conceptualise a review meeting as a field: 'structured spaces of positions' where 'all the agents [people] that are involved in a field share a certain number of fundamental interests, namely everything that is linked to the very existence of the field' and (where) they are 'engaged in (a) struggle to accrue, acquire or keep a certain form of capital' (Bourdieu 1993: 72–3). Bourdieu adds that 'the structure of the field is a state of the power relations among the agents or institutions engaged in the struggle, or, to put it another way, a state of the distribution of the specific capital which it has accumulated' (1993: 73). Hence the state of the relationships within the field, which are characterised by subordination and domination, are determined by the amount and type of capital possessed (Houston

2002: 157). We may note two further important things from this – a field exists only in relation to the capital that is being contested; and relations within the field are not on an equal footing. So what, within a LAC meeting, can be defined as capital?

In discussing and agreeing to a care plan for a child, under the auspices of a LAC review meeting, I argue here that the capital that participants trade in and compete over is not the child or the plan for the child per se but 'knowledge of the child' or 'who knows the child best'. Bourdieu (1986) conceives capital to be one of four types: economic capital (property and material possessions); cultural capital (what is understood to be the legitimate skills, knowledge, behaviour and competencies needed to gain and maintain power within a particular field); social capital (the quantity and quality of relationships and networks with others); and symbolic capital (positive recognition, prestige and/or honour associated with the acquisition of one or more of the other types of capital). Symbolic capital can refer to a wide range of 'species of capital'. In this chapter the species of capital around which the review meeting is organised and over which participants trade occurs via contested knowledge claims about the child (here defined as 'knowing the child' capital or 'who knows the child best').

With regard to relationships in the review meeting, the participants have unequal status – relationships are characterised by patterns of domination and subordination. Professionals occupy dominant social positioning compared to parents and children. However, according to Bourdieu (1993) it is not just one's subject positioning but one's habitus which is crucial to the processes of grading, obtaining and keeping 'capital', in this case 'knowing the child' capital. Bourdieu (1993: 88) states that 'those who dominate the field have the means to make it function to their advantage' that is they are 'endowed with the habitus that implies knowledge and recognition of the immanent laws of the field, the stakes and so on' (1993: 72).

Bourdieu defines habitus as 'systems of durable, transposable dispositions' (1992: 53) – taken-for-granted ways of understanding, thinking and doing which are internalised by people through their daily experience acquired through their social position within specific fields. As noted by Swartz (2002: 655) there are a number of examples of habitus: class habitus; status group habitus; gender habitus and more specialised types of professional habitus. Garrett (2007,

2009) argues for a social worker professional habitus, for he identifies practices, methods and attitudes adopted by social workers, largely unconsciously, though their daily work experience and position as qualified social workers (Garrett, 2009). This could be read to imply that all social workers act and operate in the same ways; however, as Bourdieu (1993: 86–7) points out,

> the *habitus* (original emphasis) as the word implies, is that which one has acquired, but which has become durably incorporated in the body in the form of permanent dispositions... But then why not say 'habit'? Habit is spontaneously regarded as repetitive, mechanical, automatic, reproductive rather than productive. I wanted to insist on the idea that the habitus is something powerfully generative... It's a kind of transforming machine that leads us to reproduce the social conditions of our own production, but in a relatively unpredictable way.

Hence as Swartz (2002: 645) points out, while no two individuals are the same and 'their respective biographies yield different habituses' there is also a collective nature to habitus resulting from one's collective position in social hierarchies and social structures. This is why, in this chapter, I use the term 'professional habitus' in a generic sense to highlight the strategies, tactics and methods that social workers use in the competing claims over knowledge of the child and through which their dominance in the field of review meetings is reinforced. This does not mean that social workers consciously set out with an array of techniques to 'gain the upper hand' in the decision-making processes but rather, that these operate 'at a practical, informal, and tacit level' (Swartz 2002: 635). Parents, by comparison, occupy a subordinate subject positioning within the field of the LAC meeting. The concept of the parental habitus, again generically applied here, allows for an exploration of those behaviours, attitudes and dispositions that reinforce their subordinate position within review meetings. While Bourdieu (1990a: 10; 1990b) acknowledges that the habitus is unique to individuals he also points out that there can be a collective habitus, a set of dispositions, borne out of the commonalities of experiences in relation to broader social structural factors. Hence it is possible for there to be a collective parental habitus where dispositions have been shaped by and emerge within the context of exposure to a constellation of multiple difficulties (as indicated later in the chapter).

The shared experience of the parents with whom social workers are likely to come into contact is explained by Bourdieu (1998: 2–5) when he describes them as in 'despair (because) the state has withdrawn, or is withdrawing from a number of sectors of social life for which it was previously responsible: social housing, public service broadcasting, schools, hospitals, etc.' Swartz (2002: 645) further explains the possibility of the development of a collective parental habitus, noting that 'people internalise basic life chances available to their social milieu – what is possible, impossible, and probable for people of their kind. Chances of success and failure are internalised and then transformed into individual aspirations or expectations'. Bourdieu (1990a: 116) applies the same idea to the children of these parents, suggesting a collective experience: 'It has often been noted that the children who are labelled "unstable" by academic specialists as well as by the evaluations of psychologists or physicians (who often do little more than give the former a sort of "scientific" seal of approval), bear inscribed in their habitus the instability of the living conditions of their family, that of the sub-proletariat doomed to insecurity in their conditions of employment, housing, and thereby of existence.'

This chapter, in applying Bourdieu's concepts, focuses on: identifying the contested knowledge claims in respect of the child and which of these is the most valued and why; what tactics and strategies professionals and parents seek to gain or maintain dominance; and lastly the impact of these on children's and parents' involvement in the review meetings. Before this, I briefly discuss the research.

The research and the case study

The research took place between 2005 and 2008; I explored the participation rights of the young children in care – specifically their involvement in LAC review meetings. Through ten detailed case studies, using innovative participatory methods and 39 interviews with children (aged 4–7 years), their parents and social workers, I explored the children's participatory potential, experiences and opportunities, and parents' and social workers' perspectives. Here I report on the analysis from one of the case studies (the 'A' family – each member of the 'A' family being given a pseudonym beginning with 'A'). I chose this case study because it fully illustrates the dynamics and social relational processes that are lived out within the field of the review meeting. Furthermore the themes raised by the parents are also, largely, shared in common with other parents involved in the research study. And finally the analysis described here is the forerunner to a detailed interview with one of the four children (Aine). The case study reveals how social workers and parents dominate and occupy the social space of the meeting, reducing the children's social positioning to that of 'silent onlookers'. In contrast, the detailed in-depth interview with Aine (aged 6 years) reveals that, given the opportunity, she is able to express deeply held views and opinions about her experiences at home and about coming into care (Winter 2011: Chapter 5).

Known here as Mr and Mrs Armstrong, the parents had four children, Angela (aged 4 years), Ann-Marie (5 years), Aine (6 years) and Andrew (11 years). The family had been known to social services for several years. Mrs Armstrong spent most of her childhood in residential care following experiences of sexual abuse and neglect. Mr Armstrong was also known to social services, having engaged in localised criminal activity and also having experienced abuse and neglect. Neither had any formal educational qualifications, they had never been in regular paid employment and lived in state-owned housing on an isolated estate in an area characterised by high levels of multiple deprivation. Their adult relationship was punctuated by incidents of alcohol misuse, mental health difficulties, domestic abuse and violence. Following a spate of anonymous referrals after the birth of the youngest two children, social workers removed all the children from their parents' care, having found them in appalling conditions in the family home. Court proceedings, initiated by social services, resulted in care orders being granted, with the children remaining in long-term foster care. The care plans for the children were regularly reviewed in line with statutory obligations. I discuss first the analysis of decision-making processes within the review meeting, beginning with an exploration of the capital that social workers and parents 'traded on'.

Knowledge claims about the child in the review meeting

Two main types of 'knowing the child' capital appeared to be traded on in the review meetings. The first I call the *'objective/assessed knowing the child'* capital, owned by the social work professionals. Obliged by a statutory duty to complete a form for review meetings, social workers are required to organise and categorise their knowledge of the child according to its predetermined requirements regarding children's developmental needs and these include education, health, identify, self-care skills, for example. The formal nature of the form, combined with its statutory basis and emphasis on reporting facts and recording measurements of change (as opposed to recording opinion and feeling), suggests that the knowledge contained therein is 'scientific', 'objective' and this, combined with the dominant social positioning of the social worker, results in this type of knowledge acquiring 'high value' status within the field of the meeting.

Within this context social workers' knowledge claims (in other words the capital they trade on within review meetings) are typified by an approach characterised by 'my-observation-and-assessment-of-this-child' rather than 'my-relationship-with-this-child'. As indicated above, this knowledge is framed by discourses associated with the whole *raison d'être* of the review process (Garrett 1999) – the care by the state of children where a combination of abuse and poor parenting by birth families has led to children having unmet needs; low self-esteem and poor outcomes. Knowledge claims are framed within these dominant discourses. The social worker's knowledge of Aine, the 6-year-old (then in foster care) is framed by the discourse of 'unmet needs' and 'poor parenting' (Garrett 1999). In discussion with me as the researcher, the social worker describes Aine as:

> very needy, she seems to have competed a lot for attention and affection... I mean there are still behavioural issues... Just trying to get ways of dealing with them that's not confrontational and not you know not repeating the cycle.

In another example, the social worker presents her knowledge of Andrew (11 years old and living in residential care) using the same organisational categories:

> ... he's been subjected to a horrible parenting and misdemeanours throughout his wee life. Em, he is quite damaged. Very confused

and very, very hurt and he's very keen to be loved. I think he's afraid of rejection.

I give these examples here to highlight that the knowledge claims over the child, traded on by the social worker in the review meeting, are congruent with organisational discourse regarding state intervention into the lives of this family – namely that impaired parenting capacity has had an adverse impact on the children's developmental needs.

A second type of 'knowing the child' capital is the *subjective/ relational knowing the child'* capital, claimed largely by the parents. This type of knowledge claim draws on the experience of a personal relationship with the child and within the private sphere of the birth family. It is historical, personal, subjective, anecdotal, from memory, by word (rather than written script), woven through and within the child's lived experience of family life, pre-dating social work involvement and therefore (largely) inaccessible to the social worker. Compared with the 'objective/assessed knowing the child' capital owned by professionals this 'subjective relational knowing the child' capital owned by parents with subordinate social positioning is perceived by social workers as of less value. In the 'A' family, Mrs Armstrong defines knowledge of her son Andrew through: the maternal relationship, similar shared childhood experiences with him and 'blood ties'. She states that:

> Yea…he's not a good mixer…well he mixes with younger kids than himself…you see he has…difficulties…I should know I'm his mother and I went through the same thing [referring to her own care history and childhood difficulties]…Me and Andrew is close and I know he is finding it hard what with us away an all.

The importance of Mrs Armstrong's knowledge claim lies in her assertion/belief that, the maternal relationship and similar shared childhood experiences cannot be reproduced or owned by the professionals. No one else can be Andrew's *birth* mother. No one else therefore can lay claim to the unique experience and knowledge that accompanies the birth mother-son relationship.

The 'subjective/relational' type of 'knowing the child' has other facets. For example, Mr and Mrs Armstrong describe their children's positive contributions to and participation within the private sphere of the family home. Mrs Armstrong described Aine as 'doing woman things' like cleaning and said Andrew 'helped look after the younger kids' and:

> helped fetch the nappies when one of the wains had done a stinky, did a bit of the housework, ran and got you things, played with the kids to stop them crying and helped his daddy.

> Mr Armstrong: Aye he helped me outside.

Again the significance of this type of 'knowing the child' rests on its inaccessibility to the social workers because it is historical, before their involvement commenced. In another example Mr and Mrs Armstrong strengthen their knowledge claim by confidently predicting their son's future choices:

Mr Armstrong:	In another five years [Andrew's] gonna be left school...he's gonna be going out into the world by his own
Mrs Armstrong:	He'll likely say 'I'm going to find mummy and daddy'
Mr Armstrong:	If he's not back with us by the time he's sixteen. What age is it that they put them out of care?
Mrs Armstrong:	Sixteen
Mr Armstrong:	Once they say there you're gone he's gonna make a beeline for something. And he's gonna get as much information as he can and once he finds out where we are. I'll tell you something...not anything in God's creation will stop him getting to us.

Both these types of knowledge claim – the 'objective/assessed' and the 'subjective/relational' –have strong foundations. But it is hard for each to concede any truth in each other's claims. These polarised positions are reinforced by the differing social positionings of the social worker and the parents within the review meeting. The struggle for dominance over 'knowing the child' capital reflects Bourdieu's analysis of the field of relations:

> ...in a field, agents and institutions are engaged in a struggle, with unequal strengths, and in accordance with the rules constituting that field of play, to appropriate the specific profits at stake in that

game. Those that dominate the field have the means to make it function to their advantage, but they have to reckon with the resistance of the dominated agents. A field becomes an apparatus when the dominant agents have the means to nullify the resistance and reactions of the dominated. (Bourdieu 1993: 88)

Two things reinforce these inequalities – the subject positioning of the professionals and parents and the tactics, processes and strategies by which they seek to conserve and/or accumulate the most valued knowledge claims over the child. I turn now to these issues.

Subject positioning of the parents and social workers within the field of the LAC review meeting

I have noted that social workers occupy dominant positions within the LAC review meeting. So it is not surprising to find that they adopt ways of thinking, doing and seeing that reflect these broader organisational discourses regarding 'looked after children' (LAC), centring on unmet need, poor parenting and alternative care arrangements for the child (Garrett 1999, 2009).

The parents, as previously argued, are positioned in a subordinate position within the field of relations. Mr and Mrs Armstrong, like so many other parents known to social services (Bebbington and Miles 1999; Winter and Connolly 2005), have experienced a constellation of difficulties. Their subordinate social positioning is further reinforced because their parenting has been defined by social workers as inadequate, dangerous and/or inappropriate and the mark of this has been the removal of all their children from their care and the provision of alternative state care for them.

Mr Armstrong understands and accepts this: 'It's like whenever they first took us to court. Right as soon as that went into court we'd admitted that we'd done wrong'. The basic inequality in the parent/social worker relationship is a fact recognised on both sides. The experience of the relationship by the parents is one in which their 'differences' within this hierarchy of social relationships is tangible:

Mr Armstrong: Yea…all the while you have to be careful what you say in case them uns [*social workers*] take it the wrong way. Like you have said something bad and they could cut your contact

> Mrs Armstrong: Yea. Like they have this over you that we've got your children and you might not get to see them.

According to Bourdieu, 'actors' within the 'field' (here meaning participants within the review meeting) operationalise strategies and tactics to both maintain and accrue capital or to subvert it. These are discussed below.

Habitus and strategies, tactics within the review meeting

Bourdieu (1993) argues that 'capital is effective *in relation* [original emphasis] to a particular field and therefore within the limits of that field. Subjects' strategies of action are determined by their positioning in the field. For those in dominant positions, conservation strategies are enacted with the aim of preserving the distribution and valuation of the different capitals and of safeguarding, preserving and even enhancing their position within this hierarchy. Dominated actors, on the other hand, operate subversion strategies in which their aim is to transform the fields' system of authority including its relative valuation of different capitals' (Bourdieu 1993: 73). In relation to the parental habitus of Mr and Mrs Armstrong, social workers have characterised their dispositions in two main ways: negative labelling and being set up to fail and written off. Mrs Armstrong, for example highlights the enduring influence of her own care history on her current relationship with social services and Mr Armstrong similarly draws attention to the fact that he cannot escape the poor reputation of his other family members:

> Interviewer: Why do you think that they haven't fully involved you in all of these meetings in the way you're talking about?
>
> Mrs Armstrong: I think it's mainly because Abigail [*ex social worker*] is now involved. (They) know my past...I think that's a lot to do with it
>
> Interviewer: And so what's the problem with her knowing your past? ...
>
> Mrs Armstrong: Because of the time I was raped and [they] took me into care
>
> Mr Armstrong: Again to me that's something that happened in the past...Now wait till you hear this

Mrs Armstrong: The first thing [*the social worker*] said was has he
[Mr Armstrong] ever raped you or hit you
Mrs Armstrong: Because his family has a bit of a reputation
Mr Armstrong: One bad Armstrong means the rest of them is
going to be bad too.

In light of the above, the parental habitus is developed by the parents around the belief that 'there is something wrong with us that goes back a long way and that we can never be cured of or free from'. The parents try to subvert this by adopting parenting techniques within contact sessions with their children that they know social workers think constitute 'good enough' parenting:

Mrs Armstrong: [*The social worker*] sits in to see how the contact
goes. Fine. I mean I went out of my way. I bought
paints, loads of paper, made cards...glue everywhere like, glitter but she doesn't even say that's a
good idea or anything
Interviewer: Really?
Mr Armstrong: ...There's a lack of positive feedback coming from
them. I like to see more. I'd like to see them, one
being more relaxed and us as parents being able
to say to our children what we want to say to
them without them turning round and saying
'You can't say that, you can't say that'.

The social workers do not praise their attempts at adopting the professionally accepted normative (middle class) parenting techniques. Instead they note the *lack* thereof. The effect of this is to perpetuate the images of inadequate, risky parenting rather than to accept the more complex, varied and ambiguous nature of the parents' skills and their positive (as well as their negative) interactions with their children. This adds to the parents' belief that they are always on the margins of involvement in review meetings – a finding of other related research – and that, within the context of being negatively labelled, there is little they can do to change this (Ofsted, 2008).

In relation to the professional habitus, I identified social workers as operating a number of strategies and tactics reflective of their dominant professional status and which maintain this dominance within the LAC meeting. These strategies include reliance on a body of written and verbal communication skills reflective of the review discourse – such as familiarity with certain forms, language and terminology. Successful engagement in a review meeting also depends on the ability to read, assimilate, organise and critically reflect on large amounts of information and to articulate specific queries/points at the required time, with the required language and in the required format as demanded by the procedural requirements of the review meeting.

Parents' and children's lack of access to these forms of capital reinforces their subordinate position. Below are some detailed examples of these processes in action. First the *structure* of the LAC review meeting has the effect of prioritising certain types of knowledge above other types. This suits the needs and interests of social workers but not those of the parents, as seen in Mrs A's comment below:

Interviewer:	So what kinds of things are discussed at the meetings?
Mrs Armstrong:	To me they're [the forms] are useless cos I mean they ask the questions on them and what are you supposed to say?
Interviewer:	[...] And what kind of questions do they ask you?
Mrs Armstrong:	Eh basically their health and their schooling
Mr Armstrong:	Their school's brought up. How are they doing in school, their health eh the health visitor's always there. She's been to every one of them eh their medical needs is all attended to blah, blah, blah...Just the usual load of bull
Interviewer:	[Later in interview] Do you not find those useful questions or?
Mr Armstrong:	How would we know about their care?
Mrs Armstrong:	We've asked the questions and they don't fire the answers

By its operating effects, the structure and requirements of the review meeting bolsters the dominant position of the social workers, who do not perceive the parents' questions about the details of the children's care as relevant and important but as subversion, as examples of non-compliance and as distraction. Another manifestation of the dominant professional habitus is through the *paperwork* or the LAC review forms:

> Mrs Armstrong: Whenever you go to them (the meetings) you're given pieces of paper that size and there's a lot of writing on it and you're maybe given sometimes ten to twelve sheets for each child and you're given maybe ten fifteen minutes to go through them ...
>
> Mr Armstrong: You're not actually getting proper time to go through them
>
> Mrs Armstrong: Before they (the professionals) went in they had read all this paperwork for each child [but] we were given five minutes to go through nearly half a telephone book.

Within this context, set by the needs of the review process and dominated by the social workers, Mr and Mrs Armstrong believe that their own written contributions are not treated seriously and that they have no impact on the decision-making process:

> Mr Armstrong: All we get is these green forms to fill in
>
> Interviewer: So they're like consultation forms?
>
> Mr Armstrong: There what you call your contribution. What you put down there they read that out to everybody concerned at that LAC review
>
> Mrs Armstrong: Well they're supposed to
>
> Mr Armstrong: We don't know if they're doing it or not
>
> Interviewer: Right so you fill those in but you don't know actually whether they are read?
>
> Mr Armstrong: Once we send them back there she could open them and just go like that there [*tossing form to one side*].

Mr and Mrs Armstrong make a number of observations about how their spoken contributions are treated: They feel that their own contributions are often cut short:

> Interviewer: Did you get a chance to put forward your views in that or any other meeting?
>
> Mr Armstrong: Well, it goes like this, love. They have a set time for these here meetings and everything has to fit

in that time, say two hours or whatever. So if you
want to say something sometimes you get the
look from the social worker which says 'don't be
saying that there' or they slap you down and shut
you up and cut you off

Further, they believe that their contributions are not properly recorded
in the minutes and lastly that the contributions of others are given
'more airspace'. Attempts by the parents to acquire these valued
forms of capital and to challenge the *status quo* are regarded with
suspicion and as a threat. Within this context the parents' actions
end up as more likely to reproduce their positioning rather than to
transform it. The tactic, for example, used by the parents of taking
their own notebook to meetings to record in writing what is being
said (in much the same way as other professionals do) is constructed
by the professionals not as the parents taking the meeting seriously
but as an attempt at undermining the proceedings. Professional suspicion and mistrust reinforces the parents' subordinate position. This
is illustrated below:

Interviewer: What about your relationship with social services?
Mr Armstrong: To me personally they're treating us as children.
                 They are not treating us as adults. They're not
                 giving us
Mrs Armstrong: The adults' way. They're not giving us our rights
Mr Armstrong: They're not giving us our rights as adults which
                 would be to sit down and discuss things in an
                 open and relaxed
Mrs Armstrong: Environment
Mr Armstrong: Environment
Interviewer: When you say 'Treated like children what does
                 that actually mean?
Mrs Armstrong: You get shoved away
Mr Armstrong: You're being shut up.

Hence one of the main effects of these tactics and strategies, within
the field of the review meeting, is that the subordinate position of the
parents is reinforced and the dominance of the social worker upheld.
Furthermore, from these subject positionings, both sets of adults try

to lay claim over the child and to occupy the subject position of the child. The effect of this, as explored below, is that the child becomes someone who cannot know him or herself and whose participation is compromised.

The social positioning of the child in the review meeting and impact on participation rights

To summarise so far, subject positionings within the field of relations are characterised by the social worker's dominance and the birth parent's subordination. It is hard for the social worker to concede that there has ever been anything positive in the birth parent-child relationship and it is hard for the parents to concede that their actions may have had a detrimental impact on their relationship with their children. The social worker relies on procedures and policies underpinned by developmental psychology to qualify, legitimate and validate their knowledge and ownership. The birth parent relies on subjective, personal and private memories and daily experience to qualify, legitimate and validate their knowledge and ownership. The child's social positioning in the field is a subordinate one. It occurs at a structural level, where the combined influence of adult discourses on risk, harm, age-related ability means they are reliant on the social worker and birth parent to be their voice. In the following analysis, it can be seen that parents and social worker both express knowledge claims about the child that, filtered through age-related discourses about childhood competence and capacity to understand, have the effect of denying the child the opportunity to express her or his own knowledge claims.

The social worker, working within the influence of a developmental and age-related discourse, positions the child in such a way as to query their competence and capacity to be involved in decision-making, essentially implying that children cannot know themselves and therefore should not be involved in decision-making. Firstly the four children from the 'A' family are perceived to be unreliable, for example:

> Social worker: Because if he says something today, tomorrow he'll change his mind. At the time you speak to him he seems clear but by the time he mulls it over in his mind a few times he goes back to it, it's totally an abstract ...You know he hasn't grasped (...) the point really that you wanted him to grasp.

Secondly these children are not the best judges of what's best for them:

> Social worker: But then I suppose it goes back to children don't always know what's best for them. They don't always know exactly what because maybe they don't understand why they're doing what they're doing and they kick against it, they fight against it.

Thirdly the children are being asked to discuss topics they have little idea about:

> Interviewer: And what about Angela and Ann-Marie?
> Social Worker: Well I don't think Angela takes it all on board really. Ann-Marie? You would say to Ann-Marie we're going to have a meeting you know to talk about, you know, you and Angela...And she looks at me as if and just shrugs her shoulders ...

On the other hand, where a child expressed a view congruent with the social worker's (that the children have experienced poor parenting, have been damaged and should never go home), the social worker supported the social positioning of the child as competent to express a view:

> Interviewer: You involve all of these children as far as you can?
> Social Worker: As far as I can because it's about them and I like them to be able to voice something you know. Even if it's only eh you know from Angela, that she loves (her new) mummy and daddy and this is her forever house and she's happy. It's only a sentence but I think because it came out of her mouth I think it's important.

The subordination of the child's social positioning is further reinforced through the parents, whose support of their child's right to participate in decision-making is conditional. Where the parents believe their children to be expressing a view supportive of a return home they challenge the decision-making processes, claiming it to be unfair and distorted:

Interviewer: In the meetings do you think they [the children] are given enough say about what happens to them?

MrArmstrong: No. Andrew and Aine is not being given any influence...No not anything about what they would want. Like if Andrew was to sit in them meetings and say 'I want to go home to my mummy and daddy' I guarantee you that wouldn't be referred in the minutes.

However on occasions where the children have expressed contrary views (such as the desire to live with a foster family) Mr and Mrs Armstrong query the validity of those views and claim that their children have been unduly influenced and coached by the social worker. This type of knowledge claim over Andrew is about who has access to the truth and therefore to 'rightful' claims over Andrew, as seen below:

Interviewer: How did [Andrew] get his views across?

MrArmstrong: He wrote them but it's not his handwriting and they're not his questions

Interviewer: They're not the child's questions?

MrArmstrong: You would know yourself love if you were at it

MrsArmstrong: You know your own child like

MrArmstrong: Like there was one particular one 'When am I going to get a foster family', now that's my child's question?

MrsArmstrong: No that's them talking to him about fostering

MrArmstrong: That's them putting words into his mouth

MrsArmstrong: Drumming it into him like.

In the following example Aine's parents say that it is the foster carer who described Aine in a meeting as happy and settled, but that this view does not equate with their experience of Aine and Mrs Armstrong makes sense of this by stating:

No...and a lot of Aine's stuff comes back through her foster carer rather than through Aine herself...In contact [with us] she is asking all sorts of questions like 'When are we coming home?' and we have to say that 'The house is not ready yet. Mummy and daddy are still getting the house ready but that is a lie like cos the welfare don't want us to have the kids back and so what do we really say? That's a hard one.

The parents' presentation of the children's social position is further supported by their belief that Aine is a disturbed and unreliable child:

MrsArmstrong: I think the [foster carers] are kinda mixed up with Aine cos she's a very hard child to get to know like…see the different things that run through that wee girl's head like…

MrArmstrong: She's hyper

MrsArmstrong: One minute she's into the Irish dancing. The next minute she's into horse riding and the next minute she is into this that and the other. What can you do like?

Aside from questioning her competence to express a view, the parents also query the validity of the methods professionals used to gain Aine's views.

Interviewer: And what do the drawings from Aine say?

Mr Armstrong: Well the drawings from Aine you'll see a house

Mrs Armstrong: […] You can read anything into them, that's our house, this is my [new] family

Interviewer: With the drawings is there a commentary?

Mr Armstrong: It's just the drawing

Mrs Armstrong: It's just the drawing

Mr Armstrong: You could read maybe half a dozen different things into it. Dr Ashley, the psychiatrist, he could pick out two dozen different things into it.

The analysis highlights that the children's subordinate subject positioning is further reinforced by both the parents and social worker who make knowledge claims over the children through the shared discourses of age-related competence and critique of the methods used to ascertain the children's wishes and feelings. The child's space is occupied and premised on the notion that children cannot know themselves. The result is that children in this review meeting are denied the possibility of: telling their story; discussing their knowledge of their circumstances and expressing any views they may have formed.

Concluding thoughts

Regulatory frameworks regarding children in care are geared to ensuring that there is full involvement of children, parents and professionals in decision-making and that there is a record of *what* decisions have been arrived at. They are much less well geared to accounting for *why and how* those decisions have been arrived at. The aim of this chapter is to provide a detailed theoretically informed analysis of one case study to draw out some of the social and relational processes through which decisions are arrived at. Given the centrality of the review meetings in determining major decisions regarding children's lives it is concerning that, at the very point where the professional, parent and child interface and interact within this structure, so little is known about the accompanying social processes and micro-dynamics.

Bourdieu (1999: ix) supports the use of a single case study when he states that 'the sociologist must learn how to discern the sociological relevance in conversations that are resolutely individual and personal'. The reason for this is that it is 'a specifically sociological transformation that "carries over" the everyday lives of ordinary people into an understanding of the social world in which they, and we, live'. However, in his own work, he draws multiple case studies together, stating that 'it is not enough to explain each point of view separately. All of them must be brought together as they are in reality... to bring out everything that results when different or antagonistic visions of the world confront each other' (Bourdieu 1999: 3). This is why, in the introduction, I described a detailed case study as illustrative rather than definitive. Another limit to this analysis is that the chapter is an exploration only of parental and social worker perspectives. It excludes other professionals who work with and on behalf of children in review meetings, including independent advocates, foster carers, health workers and teachers. So the analysis could be usefully built upon to consider the social positioning of other actors within the review meeting, their knowledge claims and their impact on decisions arrived at. This would be by way of taking up the challenge recently articulated by Thomas (2011: 390) who in his review of research regarding care planning concluded that further research in this area would be useful to explore 'how things are working and what is making a difference'.

As a final reflection, and in light of this analysis, consideration needs to be given to how review meetings could be improved. The chapter has revealed that there is a tendency for adults to underestimate the capacity of some young children to possess insight and expertise about their circumstances and to articulate their experiences and views. A central focus in improving review meetings has to be children's own knowledge claims (which is the capital they 'trade in'), the value adults attach to these knowledge claims and the mechanisms through and by which they are expressed and become influential. One way of challenging dominant discourses is by placing into the public domain of the review meetings the deeply held insights, experiences and views that young children in care have shared and that have been hitherto hidden, denied or minimised. Those who are familiar with Bourdieu's work may disagree that this strategy will achieve the effect of changing the habitus because the habitus comprises enduring and largely unconsciously held dispositions. However Bourdieu argues that the 'habitus, as the product of social conditionings and thus of a history is endlessly transformed, either in a direction that reinforces it ..., or in a direction that transforms it and, for instance, raises or lowers the level of expectations and aspirations'. Furthermore he observes that 'habitus...can also be *controlled* through awakening of consciousness and socioanalysis' (Bourdieu 1990a: 116).

Hence in the context of the review meeting, where some adults may define as exceptional the competence, expertise and capacity of young children in care and to interpret children's expressed views as unusual or belonging to the adults, something new is needed. I argue that it is the consistent practice of placing young children's own lived experiences into the public domain of the review meeting (through innovative methods and facilitated by a supportive carer/worker) that provides adults with new ways of seeing children, thinking about them and relating with them. This in turn can have a transformative effect on professional/parent practice within review meetings – reshaping adult values about, attitudes towards and relationships with young children in care.

References

Adoption and Children Act 2002, London: The Stationery Office Limited.

Barnes, V. 2011. Social work and advocacy with young people: rights and care in practice, *The British Journal of Social Work*, ISSN (print) 0045–3102 (Epub ahead of print).

Bebbinton, A. and Miles, J. 1989. The background of children who enter local authority care. *British Journal of Social Work*, 19(1): 349–68.

Bourdieu, P. 1986. The forms of capital. In J. Richardson (ed.), *Handbook of theory and research for the sociology of education.* New York: Greenwood, pp 241–58.

Bourdieu, P. 1990a. *The logic of practice.* Stanford, CA: Stanford University Press.

Bourdieu, P. 1990b. *In other words: Essays towards a reflexive sociology.* Cambridge: Polity Press.

Bourdieu, P. 1993. *Sociology in question.* London: Sage.

Bourdieu, P. et al. (eds). 1999. *The Weight of the world: Social suffering in contemporary society.* Cambridge: Polity Press.

British Association Adoption and Fostering 2010. *Conference on attachment and care planning in children's services*, Belfast: BAAF.

Cashmore, J. 2002. Promoting the participation of children and young people in care, *Child Abuse and Neglect*, 26 (8): 837–47.

Children and Young Persons Act 2008, London: The Stationery Office Limited.

Garrett, P. M. 1999. Mapping child-care social work in the final years of the twentieth century: A critical response to the looking after children system, *British Journal of Social Work*, 29: 27–47.

Garrett, P. M. 2007. The relevance of Bourdieu for social work: A reflection on obstacles and omissions, *Journal of Social Work*, 7 (3): 355–79.

Garrett, P. M. 2009. Pierre Bourdieu. In M. Gray and S. A. Webb (eds), *Thinking about social work: Social work theory and methods.* London: Sage, pp. 33–42.

Gray, M. and Webb, S.A. (eds). 2009. *Social work. theories and methods.* London: Sage.

Guidance on the Looked After Children (Scotland) Regulations 2009 and the Adoption and Children (Scotland) Act 2007, Edinburgh: The Scottish Government.

HM Government, 2010. *The care planning, placement and case review (England) regulations 2010.* London: The Stationery Office Limited.

Houston, S. 2002. Reflecting on habitus, field and capital, *Journal of Social Work*, 2 (2): 149–67.

Leeson, C. 2007. My life in care: experiences of non-participation in decision-making processes, *Child and Family Social Work*, 12: 268–77.

McCann, J. 2006. *Working with parents whose children are looked after.* London: National Children's Bureau.

Ofsted, 2008. *Parents on council care. A report on parents' views by the Children's Rights Director for England.* London: Ofsted.

Ofsted, 2011. *Children on Independent Reviewing Officers: A report on children's views by the Children's Rights Director for England.* Manchester: Ofsted.

Oliver, C. and Dalrymple, J. (eds). 2008. *Developing advocacy for children and young people: Current issues in research policy and practice*. London: Jessica Kingsley Publishers.

Parker, R., Ward, H., Jackson, S., Aldgate, J. and Wedge, P. (eds) 1991. *Looking after children*, London: HMSO.

Pölkki, P., Vornanen, R., Pursiainen, M. and Riikonen, M. 2012. Children's participation in child-protection processes as experienced by foster children and social workers, *Child Care in Practice*, 18 (2): 107–25.

Swartz, D.L. 2002. The sociology of habit: The perspective of Pierre Bourdieu, *The Occupational Therapy Journal of Research*, 22: 615–95.

The Review of Children's Cases Regulations (Northern Ireland) 1996, London: The Stationery Office Limited.

The Review of Children's Cases (Wales) Regulations 2007, London: The Stationery Office Limited.

Thomas, N. 2005. Has anything really changed? Managers' views of looked after children's participation in 1997 and 2004, *Adoption and Fostering* 29 (1): 67–77.

Thomas, N. 2011. Care planning and review for looked after children: Fifteen years of slow progress?, *British Journal of Social Work*, 41 (2): 387–98.

Vis, S.A. and Thomas, N. 2009. Beyond talking – children's participation in Norwegian child protection cases, *European Journal of Social Work*, 12 (2): 155–68.

Winter, K. 2011. *Building relationships and communicating with young children in care: A practical guide for social workers*. London: Routledge.

Winter, K. and Connolly, P. 2005. A small scale study of the relationship between measures of deprivation and child care referrals, *British Journal of Social Work*, 35: 1–16.

Index

Printed and bound by CPI Group (UK) Ltd, Croydon, CR0 4YY